MY TIME AT TIFFANY'S

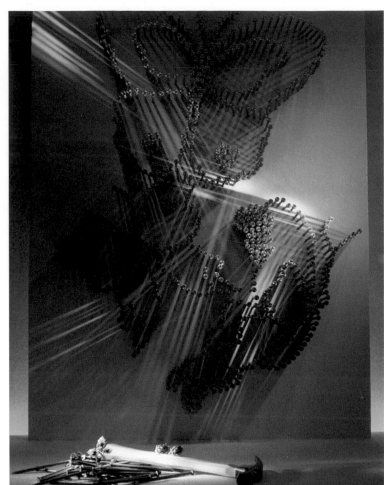

MY TIME AT

TIFFANY'S

BY GENE MOORE
AND JAY HYAMS

ST. MARTIN'S PRESS / NEW YORK

Frontispiece: *November 22, 1987. Swirling nails. Every window of this display had its hammer—to give the sense that the displays had been made just a moment earlier—along with a pile of nails to contrast with the jewelry.*

Created and produced by
Cynthia Parzych Publishing, Inc.

Project editor: Kate Kelly
Design by Jos. Trautwein
Jacket design by Michael Accordino
Typesetting by Pagesetters, Inc.
Color separations by Oceanic Graphic Printing, Inc.
Printing and binding by C&C Printing Co., Ltd.
Printed and bound in Hong Kong

Photo Credits

Cris Alexander: 14, 38 (right), 42 (right), 46, 224; Leland Cook: 159; Ken Duncan: 194; Fifth Avenue Display Photographers: 9, 10, 23, 24, 25, 26, 53, 60, 65, 71, 74, 79, 116, 132, 133, 163, 182, 193, 196, 197, 199, 202, 203, 211; Seth Joel: 150; Sam Kirkpatrick: 2, 6, 190, 221, 222, 223; Alen MacWeenie: 5; Nick Malan Studio International: 13, 19, 30, 32, 96, 97, 98, 99, 100, 104, 105, 112, 115, 118, 119, 120 (right), 121, 122, 124, 126, 127, 128, 136, 139, 140, 141, 143, 144 (top), 146, 148, 149, 151, 154, 156, 158, 169, 170, 171, 172, 173, 174, 175, 176, 177, 178, 180, 181, 184, 185, 186, 187; Ralf Manstein: 212, 213; Jerry P. Melmed: 106, 160; Gene Moore: 38 (left), 39, 40, 41, 42 (right), 43, 44, 45, 58, 95, 120 (left); Lee Prescott: 129; Virginia Roehl Studio: 8, 15, 31, 48, 56, 64, 66, 68, 69, 72, 73, 75, 76, 78, 81, 82, 83, 84, 85, 86, 87, 88, 89, 91, 93, 94, 103, 108, 111, 130, 131; Tiffany & Co.: 1, 20, 22, 62, 152, 153, 201, 208, 209, 214, 215; Susan Aimee Weinik: 4, 63, 232

Published by St. Martin's Press
175 Fifth Avenue
New York, NY 10010

Library of Congress Cataloging-in-Publication Data

Moore, Gene.
    My time at Tiffany's / Gene Moore and Jay Hyams.
        p.   cm.
    1. Show-windows—New York (N.Y.)—History—20th century.
    2. Advertising—Jewelry trade—New York (N.Y.)—History—20th century.   3. Commercial artists—United States—Biography.
    4. Moore, Gene.   5. Tiffany and Company.   I. Hyams, Jay, 1949–
II. Title.
HF5849.J6M66   1990
659.1'57—dc20
[B]

ISBN 0-312-03473-3

F O R   D A K I   A N D   C E C I

CONTENTS

THE DOWNTOWN LION

AN UPSIDE-DOWN LOVE LETTER: it's a simple trick, really, but it always works, so I've done it several times. You just write out a love letter, or if your handwriting is less than legible you get someone else to do it—we all know how to write love letters, even if we so rarely have the joy of receiving them—and, anyway, what the letter actually says isn't of much concern, for people will know it's a love letter by what you place around it, by the mood you create, lighting being more important than words. Then you put the letter in a window display so that it's upside down to the people looking in.

People will pause—if you've done your job, the window will stop them and make them look—and when they spot that letter they'll stay put to decipher it. Some will work it out in a straightforward way, just staring down at it; others will crane their necks to get the advantage of a slight angle; some will turn, put their backs almost right up against the window glass, and then twist their heads around—doing so seems to help them read upside-down writing. They'll all want to read the letter—someone else's letter, of course.

They're all reading someone else's mail, but it's nothing more than curiosity and certainly nothing wicked or punishable. The letter is from someone else's life, and we all want to know about other lives. Curiosity about other lives is just a way of dreaming about our own lives, about other possibilities. Like riding along in a car and looking out

Preceding pages: *The "Hard Heart" from Valentine's Day 1990 was a pure product of Tiffany's window display department, its bricks made of Styrofoam, gesso, paint, and cheesecloth.* Right: *Trips to Italy often make their way into Tiffany's windows. This photograph of Richard Giglio on stairs in Spoleto was used in displays that went in on January 18, 1960. I framed the photograph with real shutters painted black to give passersby the sense of being indoors looking out.*

the window at all the homes you're passing and wondering about the people who live in them. Or, even better, like riding in a train in Italy and looking out at the small villages on hills, all trees and shadows and such a sweet calmness. And you can dream of a life there, of living behind one of those dark windows with its geraniums and looking out of that window on a warm evening. There in that window you'd have another life, a beautiful life, maybe even a life with love.

Which brings us back to the letter in the window: dreams about the possibilities of other lives have a lot to do with why people buy things and with how merchandise should be displayed. You don't buy something beautiful ;ust to own it—that would be tawdry— you buy it to put beauty into your life, for it comes from another world, a beautiful world that you want to make your own. Store windows exist to show scenes from that other world.

There are many possibilities, and dreams can come true. That's a nice, simple fact. I, for instance, was born in the wrong place. I knew that right away, or at least soon enough, and didn't need anyone to tell me: in Birmingham, Alabama, on June 10, 1910. I was the youngest of three boys, but I never lived with them or with my parents. My parents divorced when I was three, and since nobody knew what to do with me, I got passed around a lot. I spent most of those years with strangers. I don't imagine I was too much trouble, for I was shy and spent my time reading and drawing and taking apart dolls and toy cars. No matter where you are, you can usually find something interesting to look at and think about. I loved the outdoors—and attics. But I wasn't happy, and the best thing to say about all that sad confusion is that I lost early on whatever fear I may have had, and without fear getting in your way, you have loads of possibilities.

I planned my escape. I knew where I wanted to go because dreams of other worlds managed to make their way even as far down south as Birmingham. There were the movies, for instance, and I spent every Saturday sitting in the theater absolutely awed by those tales of other lives. Silent films in black and white: I think we looked harder at those films, got more meaning out of every gesture, every facial expression or sidelong glance. I remember Pola Negri, Gloria Swanson, and Barbara La Marr: the word was glamor, and they had it. I was enthralled. The arrival of sound made it painfully clear the world of the movies wasn't located near Birmingham: my Alabama drawl rang grotesque compared with those elegant voices. I decided to copy them. I chose models for my new accent—Clive Brook and William Powell among them—and worked to erase the South from my voice.

There were shows, like the Ziegfeld Follies, there was ballet—and how I loved the ballet. Ruth St. Denis and Ted Shawn brought their version of modern dance to Birmingham; even the Ballets Russes made an appearance. I remember the night I went to see that show. An association known as the Music Study Club of Birmingham, Alabama, had arranged it, and I was then working for the club as an usher—for free, with no salary, just to see the shows. The night of the Ballets Russes poured rain, sheets of it, and to get to the theater I was going to have to make my way to a streetcar stop, take a long ride across town, and then walk again to the theater. I carefully pressed my clothes, particularly my pants, and then got dressed. I put on my shirt, tie, and jacket and my socks and shoes, folded the pants, put on a raincoat, and with the pants held inside the raincoat and the bare skin of my legs occasionally flashing from under the raincoat's edge, I made my way through the rain to the Ballets Russes. When I got to the theater I slipped on my pants, dry and still nicely pressed.

Movie screens and theater stages. The curtain comes up and another world begins: the lights and all those wonderful people with wonderful ideas. I kept a scrapbook with clippings of my favorite movie stars and performers and subscribed to magazines like *Photoplay.* I went to the movies and saw every theatrical and dance production that somehow found its way down to Birmingham. Becoming a performer was one sure way up

Robert McKinley's version of me sketching on a bench in Central Park, from Tiffany's windows of May 7, 1981. During my early years in New York I did indeed go to the park to make sketches. On the bench next to me is a miniature copy of my first book, Windows at Tiffany's.

April 2, 1987. Eggs in a basket defy gravity for Easter. Such a pile is begun by gluing one egg to another and moving on from there; the final structure is hollow and stands alone quite nicely.

and out of that old town, and when I was twelve I dreamed of being a concert pianist. I played the piano and was, in fact, very good. I had a ukulele, too, but its jovial twangs didn't offer the same possibilities.

People called me Charley then, my full name being Charles Gene Moore. I don't remember when it changed to Gene. I still call myself Charley when I talk to myself, and I do that often—it's a habit that comes of being alone. I also talk to what other people consider inanimate objects, but that comes from experience, not loneliness: everything has something to say, you just have to know how to look and listen.

Just when it was I decided to become a painter—I can't remember deciding, it was a desire that surely had always been there—is also lost deep in the past. I was sketching animals and houses when I was three, and by the time I was ten I was turning out recognizable portraits. Becoming a painter meant giving up that opening-night excitement, the crowds and the lights, but it was my true passion.

I had some good teachers in high school—most were amused by my evolving accent—and for some of them I managed to be a passably good student. My math teacher thought I was stupid, but that's only because math played no part in my thinking and my fantasies; knowing how many is never as important as recognizing enough. I was good at geometry—and physics. I didn't much like rules, I guess they rankle most kids, but I liked the laws of physics because they were presented as immutable but left plenty of room for play. Gravity, for instance: you can do away with it so easily, and once it's gone things stop falling and breaking and float up to where you can get a really good look at them.

After high school I got a job selling shoes at the College Slipper Shop. I had plans: I was saving my money to go to the Chicago Academy of Fine Arts. In 1929 I had enough and I went.

A bad year for my plans to become a painter, a bad year for everyone. I was there in Chicago, studying art, when the country tumbled into the Great Depression. I didn't want to return to the South, but I had to leave Chicago—I couldn't get a job there—and in the end I found myself back down in Birmingham.

I had a new plan: to go to New York and become a great painter in that wonderful city. All my favorite dreams fit into the shape of the distant skyline of New York, but getting there took five long years of a series of jobs. In the best of times, struggling young artists take odd jobs to earn money while waiting for their dreams; but these were the worst of times, and people were standing in line for jobs that no one had wanted just a year before. I worked in an ice-cream factory and as an usher at the Alabama Theatre. I painted constantly, mostly portraits, sometimes selling them, sometimes bartering them for meals. I also painted several murals and studied with Louise Cone, a well-known Birmingham artist.

In 1934 I got a job in Nashville, working in the display department of the General Shoe Corporation, a big shoe company and factory. I didn't have much to do with display, just covered panels and made silk-screen cards that were sent out to stores throughout the country. But I was earning $12 a week and had Saturdays off.

I spent those Saturdays window-shopping. One Saturday afternoon I stopped in front of the window of a ladies' ready-to-wear shop. And something wonderful happened: I recognized the mannequins in the window. Made of cloth, the mannequins had faces painted to resemble movie stars: Greta Garbo, Joan Crawford, Joan Bennett, and several others. Although they had strange, shapeless, stuffed-fabric arms and hands with long red fingernails glued to the fingertips, I thought they were exciting. They brought life to that window, and in that moment there in Nashville I became mannequin conscious. Sometime later I learned those mannequins were made by Cora Scovil.

I fell in love while I was in Nashville, and I got my heart broken. A sad story. Back in Birmingham I got a job on a WPA project, teaching people on relief. They'd set it up in an old abandoned cotton mill, a great big crazy building, all long rooms full of worktables and benches with people making toys, making quilts, making anything to sell. Most of those people were black women, and my job was to teach them how to paint the toys, the dolls and the animals. I'd sit there and work with them, and around four o'clock every afternoon one of them would suddenly start singing, slowly and sweetly, and the others would soon all join in: spirituals and church hymns that filled that big, empty building with a wonderful sound. As though they knew my own heart and my own secret longings, I was always moved, and sometimes to tears.

There was a woman there in Birmingham who had a music store—I'd done a portrait of her in exchange for meals—and she mentioned to me that she was moving to Virginia, her husband had landed a job up there. Did I want a ride north?

In Virginia I got on a bus for New York, and I stepped down out of that bus into a warm Manhattan afternoon. This was in August 1935. I was twenty-five years old and all alone; I had $14 and no one to call when that ran out. But I wasn't afraid. I felt then, and I know now, that my life had at that moment finally begun. I had a self-imposed ultimatum. "Charley," I told myself, "you have five years to make a go of it. Otherwise, you have to go back to the South." I walked all the rest of that day, up and down the streets, and I walked all that night. I read newspapers looking for a job. There were none.

I saw the sun come up over the city, and then later that morning, when the streets were again calm after the rush-hour crowds, I was in front of the New York Public Library, leaning against the pedestal of one of the lions—the lion on the left as you face the library, the downtown lion. I was reading through another newspaper: no jobs.

I asked the lion what I should do. My first conversation with a New Yorker.

"Follow my nose, and you'll find a job," said the lion.

"You're kidding," I said.

"Try me," he said.

The nose of that lion points down East Forty-first Street, and I hadn't wandered halfway down that block when I saw a sign in a window: Boy Wanted. Morehouse-Gorham, a religious bookstore. The man in charge, Mr. Barlow, was very kind. Like most of the people working in that shop, he was from Milwaukee, site of the company's headquarters. Perhaps that's why he didn't notice my accent, or perhaps I really had done away with it in those Birmingham movie theaters. He certainly didn't catch on that I'd just stepped off a bus. Since he was looking for a delivery man, he asked me if I knew my way around New York. Did I know the subway? Did I know the Bronx and Brooklyn? Of course I didn't, but that's not exactly what I told him. I got the job, went to a dime store, and bought myself a bundle of city maps.

I didn't last long as a delivery man. The problem had to do with service entrances. I'd take my packages of books to deliver to church officials throughout the city, and I'd go up to a front door, knock, and then ask for Father Whomever, and the housekeeper or doorman would direct me around to the service entrance, sometimes pointing the way with a righteous forefinger. I'd never heard of anything so ridiculous. I brought the books back undelivered. But they were nice people at the store and found other work for me, dusting books and sweeping floors.

New York was wonderful. I had escaped to the best of all worlds, where my life was just beginning. The subway was exciting. And up and down Fifth Avenue—traffic then moved in both directions along the city's avenues and streets—ran double-decker buses, open on the top. That's where I'd sit, even in the winter with the snow blowing down and the tops of the skyscrapers lost in a cloudy silver shine. The conductors would come around to collect the fare—they carried a little machine you shoved a dime into. How they hated me: to get my dime they had to climb up into freezing air. But before my first winter in New York I'd never seen snow, never known such cold. I was thrilled.

After about eight months at Morehouse-Gorham I had saved enough money to devote myself to painting. It was nearly summer again when my money started to run low, and I got a job in a bookstore in Great Barrington in the Berkshires. I'd work in the store in the mornings and go out and paint in the afternoons. Sometimes I painted what I was looking at, sometimes what was in my head. As always I did portraits. While I was there I held the first showing of my paintings and sold all I had, about fifteen to twenty oils and watercolors.

For a few days following the show I had money and the idle dreams that come with it. An attack of appendicitis changed all that—the money I'd made from the exhibition went to pay for an operation in a hospital in Pittsfield.

I didn't have any money when I returned to New York, and I had trouble finding another job, but I did have a girlfriend. I was having dinner one night with her and her father, and he turned to me all of a sudden and asked, "How'd you like to go to South America?"

Perhaps he was trying to get rid of me. I liked his daughter but said, "Sure." He told me to be at a certain pier the next morning at eight o'clock.

Thus I became a waiter aboard the cruise ship *Southern Cross*, bound for Trinidad, Rio, Montevideo, Buenos Aires, and other distant ports of call.

There were rules on that ship, one being that waiters were not permitted to speak to passengers. But a Columbia University professor and his wife wanted to speak to me and got permission from the purser. Nice people, they later bought a painting from me back in New York.

May 27, 1965: the first use in Tiffany's windows of my South American hummingbirds. I originally spotted them in a glass case in a Rio shop window.

In Rio—I think it was Rio—I bought twelve stuffed hummingbirds with beautiful feathers and long, pointy beaks. I had no plans for them, but they had something sweet to say. When I proudly showed them to the purser he claimed it might be against the law to bring such feathered souvenirs into the country. My birds, he thought, would have difficulty getting through customs. I got around that by stuffing the dozen birds, dangerous beaks and all, into my underpants before getting off the ship. They made it home with me and have since appeared in window displays.

Once off the ship I was again out of work, but I had enough money to paint for a while. When the money ran out it was time to hunt up a new source of income. From being a waiter I went to being a busboy in the employees' cafeteria of the Guaranty Trust Company: $10 a week.

Then, in 1936, I got a job with the Bois Smith Display Company, an outfit that made props for store window displays. My job was making papier-mâché flowers. One day a man came in with a dog made of chicken wire covered with colored leaves. He was a

freelance window dresser and wanted more of the dogs for a display he was doing at Bonwit Teller. The name of the display was "The Hounds of Spring." The man's name was Jim Buckley.

Perhaps I could have recognized my fate sooner—I believe in fate—perhaps I could have laid out my dreams, studied them, and reached the correct solution. But I hadn't. Until then, I still planned to be a painter, but I was becoming sadly aware that I was never going to be great. And I didn't want to be a painter if I couldn't be the best. Then Jim Buckley and "The Hounds of Spring" walked into Bois Smith.

I made the dogs, and Buckley was pleased with them. About a year later, in 1937, he was taken on by I. Miller as display director. He asked me to be his assistant.

I. Miller was a shoe company with four stores—450 Fifth Avenue, 565 Fifth, on Thirty-fourth Street between Sixth and Seventh avenues, and at Broadway and Forty-sixth Street—four stores with windows the two of us had to change every week. It was a lot of work, and sometimes we took on freelance help, but we had no staff, and Buckley made all the plans. He was a genius, open to everything and seeing everything, and that was the magic I learned: that display is one of those rare, wonderful crafts that encompass the

Right: *Tiffany's window of December 1, 1961. A city full of snow. It's New York, of course, and the snow is made of a mixture of kosher salt and the display tool called diamond dust (ground glass).*

Opposite: *Late on a Bonwit Teller window night. After raising the curtain, I'd go outside to check how the display was working. Bonwit's windows were six feet deep and twelve high.*

world. We put shoes in all those windows every week, but the displays were never the same, Buckley was always thinking, and he made me think. It was while working with Buckley that I began to be serious about display.

It was fun. It required all my imagination and then more—I had to look harder all around me, inside me, at everything. It required a kind of luck, the luck in colors and shapes and the way zany ideas suddenly make perfect sense. And I sensed what I thought I had lost: opening-night jitters, the excitement of a performance. Display, I found, is a lot more fun than painting and a lot less lonely.

A ballet window at Delman's celebrates Alicia Alonzo.

In 1938 Buckley moved over to Bergdorf Goodman. I stayed on at I. Miller for a while, but always dropped by on Bergdorf's window night, when they changed the display, to help out and learn. Then Buckley took off for Europe, and Bob Riley became display director at Bergdorf's. He asked me to come work with him and gave me the windows of Delman's, the shoe department of Bergdorf's, to do on my own. From 1938 to 1940 I did the windows of Bergdorf's and Delman's, and then from 1940 to 1945 I did only those of Delman's.

Bergdorf Goodman is on Fifth Avenue at the corner of West Fifty-eighth Street, right across the street from the Plaza Hotel. The store had moved there from its original location on West Thirty-seventh Street in 1928. They'd put up a new marble building on the site where Cornelius Vanderbilt had had a mansion.

Other stores were moving into that area, for the fashionable center of Manhattan was, as always, shifting uptown. The city's oldest stores began where the city began, down around Wall Street, and moved north as the city grew. For example, Lord & Taylor, founded in 1826 on Catherine Street, moved first to Grand and Chrystie streets (1853), then to Broadway and Grand Street (1860), then to Broadway and Twentieth Street (1869), and finally to Fifth Avenue and Thirty-eighth Street (1914), where it stayed put. The first

important store to make the daring leap past Thirty-fourth Street—once considered the absolute northern boundary—was Franklin Simon, which opened at Fifth Avenue and Thirty-eighth Street in 1902. Forty-second Street then became the dividing line, and the first store to cross it was Saks Fifth Avenue, which opened at Fifth Avenue and Fiftieth Street, just south of St. Patrick's Cathedral, in 1924. (Its first window displays at that location featured raccoon coats and chauffeurs' livery, and the story goes that they sold out their entire stock of silver pocket flasks the first day.) The wonderful toy store F. A. O. Schwarz, founded in 1870 on Broadway and Ninth Street, made its way to Fifth Avenue and Fifty-eighth Street in 1930. That same year, Bonwit Teller moved from Fifth Avenue

A prop matched to shoes. The figure is made of chicken wire covered with suede colored to match the colors of the shoes. The character is taken from the commedia dell'arte.

and Thirty-eighth Street to a building at 721 Fifth Avenue, on the corner of Fifty-sixth Street (site of today's Trump Tower). In 1938, when I started at Delman's, Bonwit's was in the process of adding two floors.

All those stores were on Fifth Avenue, then as now the center of the city, and they were all clustered around what was, to me, the city's true heart, the broad corner where Fifth Avenue crosses Fifty-seventh Street. On the southeast corner of that big crossroads were two stores I liked, right next to each other: a clothing store called the Tailored Woman and Park and Tilford, a drugstore with a famous soda fountain. New York was full of drugstores with soda fountains back then, but Park and Tilford was special. I can remember sitting on a stool at that counter and having an ice-cream soda. Right across the street was a marvelous Child's restaurant.

With all those stores and all those windows, there were lots of window dressers around, and I wasn't the only artist, the only would-be painter, doing window display. Many people got their start in window display. L. Frank Baum worked as a window dresser before writing *The Wonderful Wizard of Oz*, organized the National Association of Window Trimmers in 1898, and even edited the first magazine devoted to window display: *The Shop Window: A Journal of Window Trimming*. During the 1920s, Norman Bel Geddes was head of display over at Franklin Simon, and Maurice Sendak worked on the windows at F.A.O. Schwarz.

During the late 1930s, when I got my start in window display, the reigning style was surrealism. Few styles could have been better suited to windows, because surrealism has to do with dreams, with unconventional ways of looking at things. I think you can still see signs of Magritte in store windows. The leading window trimmers of those years— Tom Lee at Bonwit Teller, Henry F. Callahan at Lord & Taylor, Jim Buckley at I. Miller, Marcel Vertès at Saks Fifth Avenue, and, yes, Gene Moore, particularly for my later work at Bonwit's—are often cited in books on modern art for their manipulations and adaptations of surrealism. We used surrealism, and many of the leading surrealist artists—people like André Breton and Marcel Duchamp—designed window displays.

And Salvador Dali. He was here in New York in 1939 and designed a set of absolutely mad windows for Tom Lee at Bonwit Teller. In one of the windows he covered the walls with pink satin, with hand mirrors hung up everywhere. In the middle was a bathtub with water and narcissus—those who recognized the flowers may have understood the pun on narcissism—and coming out of the bathtub were disembodied hands holding mirrors in which was reflected a mannequin wrapped in feathers. She was a bloody mess, with all kinds of creepy crawling insects in her hair.

The story goes that somebody changed Dali's display, he heard about it, flew into a rage, and came over one night armed with a sledge hammer and smashed the window. He may have made up that story himself, for he managed to turn the incident into a major cause célèbre against artistic censorship. In truth, the store got complaints, the display people were going to make a few changes, and Dali himself was there in the window, but he slipped and knocked a leg off the bathtub, which took off on its own, right through the window—just an accident. It was quite a mess, but those windows put Dali on the map.

I don't remember seeing those windows. What I remember about 1939 is terrible news from Europe and a lot of construction in my neighborhood. Over at Bonwit's they were busy putting up a new twelve-story addition, and a hole suddenly appeared on my favorite corner. Gone were the Tailored Woman and Park and Tilford. We all wondered what they were going to put up in that great big hole in the ground.

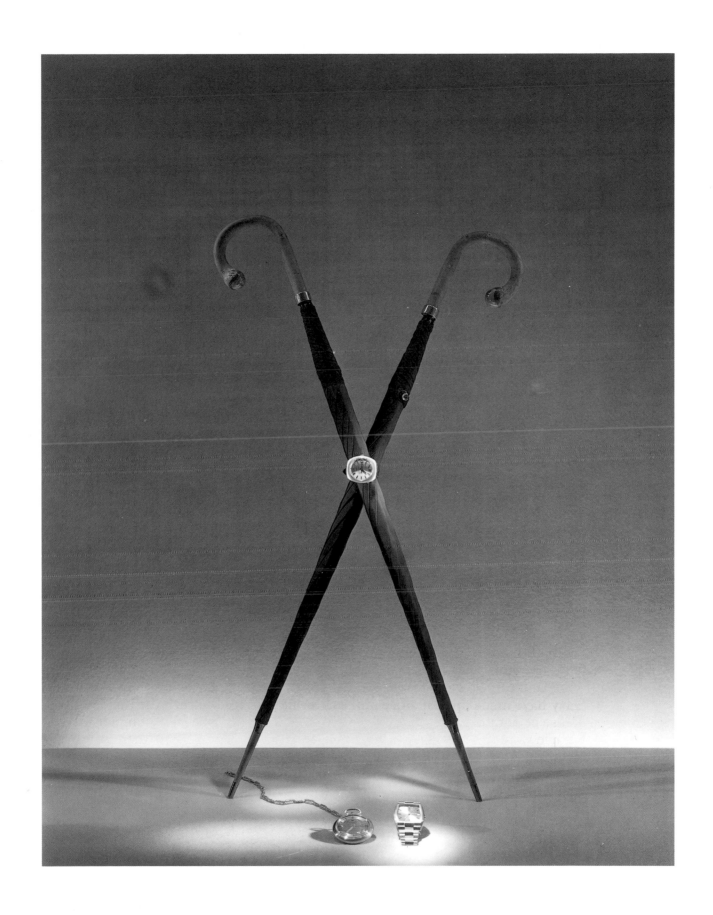

April 3, 1972. This window was inspired by hard April showers and by umbrellas I saw in the windows of Uncle Sam's Umbrella Shop. I wasn't thinking of Magritte, only of soggy New Yorkers passing along Fifth Avenue.

MANNEQUINS AND PERFUME

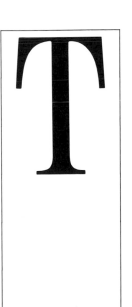

THE OLDEST TIFFANY WINDOW STORY I know dates back to the 1850s, about one hundred years before I became involved with the store. Like most tales from ancient history, this one features monstrous beasts and bloodshed, and while it lacks the kind of instructive moral we learn to dread at the end of most old tales, it does have something simple to say about window dressing.

The store was then more than a decade old, having been founded in 1837—under the name Tiffany & Young, for Charles Lewis Tiffany and his partner John B. Young—at 259 Broadway, way downtown across from City Hall Park. In 1847 the store had moved uptown the distance of one city block to 271 Broadway, north of Chambers Street, at that time quite a popular part of town. Just about the center of town, really, for the city's fashionable borderline was then Canal Street—proper ladies refused to be seen on the other side of it—and up at what is today Fifth Avenue and Fifty-seventh Street there was nothing but an old farmhouse amid open fields and a few stray pigs.

Six blocks farther along Broadway, at the corner of Ann Street, was P. T. Barnum's American Museum. This tale's monster was one of Barnum's elephants, a certain Mr. Forepaugh, and he was personally responsible for the bloodshed: he somehow killed eight men. I imagine he trampled them. For these crimes Mr. Forepaugh was sentenced to death by strangulation. (But who has the hands to strangle an elephant? And the will?)

On the best of terms with his neighbor Barnum, Charles Tiffany was able to buy the body of the executed—and wonderfully famous—elephant. He had the elephant skinned and the hide tanned. The reassembled beast was then put on display in the store's window along with a sign announcing that various articles made from the hide of the terrible mankiller would soon be on sale. (I once startled myself with the thought that they chose to strangle the poor thing to avoid unsightly gunshot holes in any of the future luggage and handbags, but I truly don't believe Mr. Tiffany and Mr. Barnum, shrewd businessmen though both surely were, can have been capable of such cruel foresight.)

An elephant in the window: must have been a big window, certainly far more spacious than those I've had the pleasure to work with. Some people may find it nasty, and others downright barbaric, but standing up a dead elephant in a store's front window is just an example—I'd call it graceless—of basic window-display theory: "Here's our fine elephant: would you care to purchase some?" In just that way, fruit vendors display their merchandise, colorful pyramids of tangerines and melons, maybe a few sliced in half to show off their juiciness. Put your merchandise in the window: what could be more basic than that? It certainly doesn't ask much imagination of the potential customer and hearkens back to the bygone days when a lot of the people walking along city streets were illiterate and needed the services of such totems as cigar-store Indians and carved trade signs swinging in the breeze over store entrances.

Such basic displays do work, however. So many New Yorkers crowded the store when the elephant-hide articles went on sale that the police had to be summoned to help keep things neat.

Aside from its lesson in window dressing, that story reveals an important and I would say traditional aspect of Tiffany's: the store has always been in close touch with the city, with New York and New Yorkers. Thanks to his bloody deeds—and, I'm sure, a heady dose of Barnum publicity—Forepaugh's name had become notorious among New Yorkers, and even in death he remained a popular local character. People couldn't help but recognize the elephant in Tiffany's window.

Another Barnum-related window display offers an even better example of this Tiffany civic-mindedness. This story dates to the Civil War—during which Tiffany's sold swords "for all loyal states"—by which time Charles Tiffany's partners had left, and the store was known simply as Tiffany & Co. A Paris branch of the store had been opened, and the New York store had again moved uptown, this time all the way to 550 Broadway, between Prince and Spring streets: today's SoHo. A bigger store with bigger windows.

Eighteen sixty-three, dead center in the Civil War, and yet the major concern of many New Yorkers was an upcoming marriage. The very small General Tom Thumb—fully adult he was thirty-three inches tall, and Queen Victoria gave him his rank—was one of Barnum's most celebrated attractions. Barnum later acquired other midget performers, Commodore Nutt and Mercy Lavinia Warren Bump, best known to her adoring public as Miss Lavinia. As all the world soon came to know—Barnum made the private lives of his performers public knowledge—both men were hopelessly enamored of the dark-haired Lavinia, but try as she might, she just couldn't decide which to marry. There were jealous outbursts between the two suitors, and on one delicious occasion the commodore floored the general with a punch. In the end Lavinia opted for Tom Thumb, and they were married in New York's Grace Episcopal Church, at Broadway and Tenth Street, on February 10, 1863. The reception was held at the Metropolitan Hotel. The newlyweds stood on a grand piano to receive their guests.

The city's streets were jammed: this wedding was an exciting public event. People wanted to get a look at the small spouses and also at the lavish gifts sent them from the world's notables. These gifts included a miniature horse and carriage of silver filigree made especially for the couple by Tiffany's. To make sure all New Yorkers could see this

September 3, 1987. For Tiffany's 150th anniversary Robert Heitmann created miniature recreations of Tiffany's stores. Shown here is the store ca. 1854 with Atlas over the doorway and a newsboy hawking his wares.

Further scenes from the 1987 anniversary windows. Above left: This is the store on Union Square, with Lillian Russell, Diamond Jim Brady, and the famous silver bicycle. Above right: The store at Fifth Avenue and Thirty-seventh Street. Louis Comfort Tiffany and friends, dressed for a costume party, pose for a picture. Opposite: The store today with next to it the farmhouse that occupied the spot in 1837.

creation, it had been set out on display in the store's window for several weeks before the wedding day.

All the chronicles agree that the carriage in the window was a sensation. The truth is, there were occasional crowds in front of Tiffany's windows long before I came on the scene. But then again, that wedding took place near Valentine's Day, so I think I'd have done something in the window to mend the commodore's broken heart. A love letter signed Lavinia? Mercy?

Atlas first appeared over the store's entrance at 550 Broadway. You can be cynical and choose to see him as a cigar-store Indian: a nine-foot-high statue of the Titan Atlas bearing on his shoulders not the world, which is the weight put on him in Greek mythology, but—as is suitable for a company famous for its timepieces in a city famous for its haste—an enormous clock. Because he's greenish, people think he's made of bronze or some other metal, but he was carved out of wood by a man named Henry Frederick Metzler. With its works made by Tiffany's, the clock kept good time, and businessmen and messengers rushing past the store would glance up at it to get the hour. That's important to keep in mind: no matter where they're off to, New Yorkers won't even consider the possibility of arriving late, so it's hard to get them to slow their paces. I like to think it takes a kind of art to make them stop and look hard at something, to make them actually *see* something.

Along with the city's other fashionable stores, Tiffany's continued to move uptown. In 1870 it moved onto the former site of a church on Union Square. By then there was a London branch as well as the one in Paris. And in 1878 an enormous diamond, the largest and finest yellow diamond ever found, was discovered in South Africa's Kimberly Mine. Tiffany's immediately purchased it, French jewelers spent a year carefully studying it, and it evenually became the Tiffany Diamond, 128.51 carats with 90 facets.

In 1905 the store moved into a building on Fifth Avenue at Thirty-seventh Street that had been modeled after Venice's sixteenth-century Grimani Palace. There was no name

ce stood at this location in 1863

on the outside of the store, only its palatial splendor and the tireless Atlas serving to give away its identity. Many people stood in nervous awe of Tiffany's and thought of it as a museum that occasionally agreed to part with its holdings.

Not that the store ever lacked customers. Indeed, its clientele has always included a host of New Yorkers and out-of-towners, as well as the nation's—and the world's—leading lights, from such locals as the Vanderbilts, Morgans, Astors, Belmonts, Rockefellers, and Havemeyers to England's Queen Victoria, the emperor of Austria, kings of Italy, Belgium, Denmark, Greece, Spain, Portugal, and Rumania, khedives of Egypt, shahs of Persia, and czars of Russia. Presidents of the United States have been patrons: Lincoln bought his wife a pearl necklace. Diamond Jim Brady dropped by from time to time with his penchant for ladies' garters and had Tiffany's make a solid gold chamber pot, with an eye in the center of the bottom looking up, for Lillian Russell. Some of Miss Russell's other fans had Tiffany's make her a solid silver bicycle. Famous performers have always been seen leaning over the jewelery cases: Geraldine Farrar, Enrico Caruso—who bought his wife a ruby bracelet—Mary Pickford, and Douglas Fairbanks. Another popular New York couple received a wedding gift from Tiffany's: a sterling silver chocolate set went to F. Scott and Zelda Fitzgerald. Perhaps when they came down to pick it up they rode on the roof of a taxicab, as was their habit back in those zany days. Miffed one afternoon when a store manager hesitated about approving his check, Al Jolson offered to prove his identity: "Tell the old buzzard to come down here, and I'll sing 'Mammy' for him."

Although filled only with jewelry, the windows of the Thirty-seventh Street store attracted the usual window-shopping crowd, and one evening around 1928 songwriter Jimmy McHugh and lyricist Dorothy Fields stood in front of those windows beside a young couple. The girl said something to the boy, and he answered, "I wish I could, too, baby, but I can't give you anything but love." Bill "Bojangles" Robinson took the resulting song and "Digga Digga Do" through 518 performances at the Liberty Theater.

After nearly thirty-four years at Thirty-seventh Street, Tiffany's prepared to move uptown again. There went the Tailored Woman and Park and Tilford's fabulous ice-cream sodas. Out of the hole rose a seven-story building of granite and limestone (the world's first fully air-conditioned store). Atlas was there on the new building, of course, mounted over the Fifth Avenue door, with his always accurate clock giving the time of day to new generations of ever busy New Yorkers.

In October 1940, when I'd been in New York for five years, the new Tiffany & Co. opened its doors to the public. I'd been watching the construction from my office on the fourth floor of Bergdorf's, right above Delman's, and I frequently walked by and looked in the windows—a lot of piled up merchandise—but I never gave even a moment's thought to going into that famous old store.

I was thinking of the ballet, of artists and their art, of broad sheets of seamless paper, and papier-mâché trees with sturdy branches, and, most of all, of ways to fit those together with twenty-eight ladies' shoes. "The best shoes you can buy are the best buy"— that was Delman's slogan. There were variations. For New Year's it became "Any year and every year the best shoes you can buy are the best buy." While working at Delman's, I had that slogan, three big windows and three small ones, one assistant, and the store manager giving me fourteen pairs of shoes to display every week in each window. Herman Delman, the owner, left me alone to do my work as I saw fit. He was a kind and generous man, but I still had to deal with all those shoes.

Most store display windows at that time were real windows. From within the store you could look out the windows at the people passing by, and people on the sidewalk could look through the windows into the store. At Delman's, I could close off that opening with sheets of paper or other backdrops, or I could construct forms, like the papier-mâché tree, to support shoes in the air across the opening. Sometimes I dangled shoes in the air from strings, sometimes I piled them on boxes, sometimes I had the shoes tearing through a paper backdrop. I used them as ornaments on Christmas trees, put flowers in them, put them into carts and baskets, stuck them onto all kinds of sculptural forms: almost always, twenty-eight shoes.

June 18, 1987. Tiffany's boxes have always been popular,
and during the store's 150th anniversary it seemed
right to use some in a celebration of the Fourth of July.

I designed and made most of the backdrops and props, but for others I hired artists. I found myself in a position to do a wonderful thing: I could help young artists, give them work and, even more important, give them exposure. Since 1938, when I began at Delman's, to today, I've commissioned works from more than 800 artists, more than any other window dresser in New York. I've never felt I had to understand or even like an artist's work to use it. And art works wonderfully in windows: with proper lighting it can be better displayed than when placed side by side with other art in a gallery. I've

Something can always happen, or nearly happen, even with boxes of shoes. This mannequin in a Delman's display is in no real danger, and you can sense she knows it.

always paid the artists, of course, and some of them really needed the money. Some of them, too, have gone on to become quite famous.

Beginning in 1941 we had another topic to put in the windows at Delman's: the war, with bond drives and Red Cross appeals. I can remember fitting blown-up photographs of marching soldiers across the windows, each photograph bearing in its center a big red cross. The war had other effects on my displays, including blackout curtains and lighting restrictions. During those years the stores along Fifth Avenue no longer touted the newest French fashions, the most enticing new French perfumes. No more European magazines, no more *haute* anything.

I was called up for my army physical but was rejected because of poor eyesight. I have an unusual eye defect that makes me see everything in extremely soft focus, gives me an impressionistic view of the world. I have eyeglasses that correct my vision, of course, particularly for seeing close up, and a doctor once considered operating on my eyes to correct my distance vision but determined that the operation would have failed. I wasn't convinced I wanted the operation, for I feared it might change my work in some way. The way I see in the distance is the way I prefer seeing. I've always loved impressionist painters.

DELMAN INC.

Window display at Delman's. To make an opening in no-seam paper you don't cut a dainty hole: you stand behind the paper and punch through with your fist. Of course, you've got to control the tear and use only a little temper.

Another aspect of my person, my shyness, I did hope to change. Being shy was interfering with my life, with my work. Being in business involves acting, and I couldn't act. I was so shy I was scared of talking on the phone to strangers. Late one night in 1941, another night when I couldn't sleep, I decided the only way to overcome my shyness was to put myself in the most embarrassing situation in the world and live through it. The most embarrassing situation was obvious: a beginners' ballet class. The next morning I enrolled at the School of American Ballet and found myself at thirty-one wearing tights in a chilly room beside the sleek bodies of arrogant preteens.

I survived and learned to dance. My instructor, Muriel Stuart, had studied with Pavlova, Cecchetti, and Graham and was as fine a teacher as she was a dancer. When I'd

May 20, 1970. A Tiffany's display using rope, a simple color in a simple form. The silver candlesticks, with their swirling pattern that matches the rope, are merchandise.

been studying for three years—and I really was good—she said to me one day, "Gene, I think you should now get in the corps de ballet of one of the companies, and I can get you in." I said, "Muriel, it's time I quit. I don't want to be a ballerina." I quit, but that training has helped me position otherwise well-bred porcelain dolls in windows—even the French ones get lazy and slouch—and I've often been thankful for it when stepping in and out of awkward corners. But it hasn't kept me from falling.

I made other changes and decisions during the war years. I burned my paintings. That was hard, part of me still yearned for that, but I knew I'd never be a great painter. And I gave away my piano. I had bought a small grand piano on time; every week I went down to make the payment. But I decided I would never really play well enough, there wasn't time in my life to practice, and it was just too late. I felt I had to give it up and concentrate on something new.

Then Sarah Pennoyer called me. She was the head of advertising at Bonwit Teller and had more than a little say-so over publicity, display, and the business of the store's buyers. She said she wanted to have a little chat with me, so one morning I walked across the street from Bergdorf Goodman to Bonwit Teller and found myself offered a new job. I was to replace Ed Ballinger, who had himself replaced Tom Lee when Lee had gone off to serve in the military.

Fashion and burlap bags in a Valentine's Day window at Bonwit Teller. The bags, marked "sugar," are from a wholesale sugar company.

The idea of being display director for a big store like Bonwit's thrilled me. So did the idea of $10,000 a year—a lot of money in 1945—and all those beautiful big windows. The only unhappy person was Mr. Delman, who offered to match anything Bonwit's offered, just to make me stay. But I had to go. It was a step up in the direction I had chosen for myself. (I was replaced at Delman's by my assistant, Sonny Hawkins.)

At I. Miller, Buckley and I had done all the windows for all those stores alone, and at Delman's I'd had a single assistant. My world was far more crowded at Bonwit's. There were strangers to meet, to work with and get along with and, perhaps, even become friends with. Aside from the ever-present and all-powerful Mrs. Pennoyer—I took to calling her the queen of all the Russias—there were buyers and advertising executives and a display staff of thirteen people. It was fun. My ballet training paid off.

At Bonwit's, I was in charge of both the interior display for all seven floors and the window displays, two different departments with two different staffs. The store had sixteen main windows, eight on Fifth Avenue and eight along Fifty-sixth Street. Doors on the main floor led into the windows: you opened the door and stepped up a single step into a narrow void space, behind the back wall of the window, and then stepped around into the window. Those windows had wooden floors and were twelve feet high.

I could do as I wished in those windows, and when I first came to Bonwit's I wanted

Bonwit Teller pre-Christmas perfume windows.

to simplify the displays to make them more effective. Instead of cramming windows with a variety of merchandise and mannequins, I banished any distracting clutter and tried to get at the meaning of the merchandise, to take an idea, a simple idea—a striking pose, a humorous situation—and use it to make a suggestion, locate a point of view, but leave plenty of room for the customer's imagination. With some exceptions, I rarely used more than one or two mannequins in a window, and instead of doing an all-out "head-to-toe" job with accessories I tried to use only the most essential. I had glamorous merchandise to work with, and I wanted people to see it just the way they dreamed of it. I was excited by what I had to work with, and I sought to share that excitement.

I wanted to create a world in those windows—the world of Bonwit's merchandise, the world of the dreams implied by stunning gowns or by simple sweaters knit for schoolgirls.

To do so meant showing situations, with clear and understandable relationships among the props and mannequins. I wanted there to be an obvious reason for the mannequins to be there. I wanted them involved in doing something, not just showing good posture to best show off what they were wearing. If I had a room, I wanted the feeling that someone had just come in or just left—a handkerchief on a dresser, some item dropped or left behind. Out of such relationships I could bring that make-believe world to life. And without those possibilities I would have been bored to death.

I've been lucky—or perhaps I've been demanding—but I've always been allowed to do what I believed best. The buyers at Bonwit's realized I was on their side, I was building an image for the store. I was very strict and fussy about what went into those windows. I selected the garments that would be used together with the buyers and built windows around the merchandise, always trying to play up the designer's mood. I went to runway shows with buyers and sometimes picked out dresses simply because I knew they'd look good in the windows.

To show fashion properly, I had to understand it, and during my years at Bonwit's— 1945 to 1961—I immersed myself in it. I read all the magazines, followed the Paris collections when they finally reappeared with the end of the war, and became involved in what was happening on Seventh Avenue, the center of New York's garment industry. I worked with designers, and to understand better how clothes are made I spent hours turning clothes inside out.

My first windows at Bonwit's involved suits, dressy suits. I made enormous cords, like rope but made out of cotton dyed a marvelous deep red, and had those cords with tassels everywhere. The whole window was hanging with enormous cords and tassels, like a stage curtain.

The war had not yet ended, and there were still lighting restrictions, no spotlights permitted, and blackout curtains. So I turned to Vermeer for another set of windows. In a Vermeer painting the light comes through a single window, and I built interiors based on Vermeer paintings and used a navy flashlight to provide the right light: it came through a window, of course. The mannequins were dressed in Pauline Trigere's at-home clothes based on paintings by Vermeer that I had shown her.

Mrs. Pennoyer herself inspired a set of windows, though she didn't mean to. During my first year at Bonwit's she had a phone installed in my office, a direct line to her office, so she could just push a button, my phone would buzz, and I'd jump to the ceiling. It drove me crazy. She drove me crazy. I decided to do some telephone windows.

The display was for furs, the motif was pure black and white, and the unifying device in each window was a black phone, for each presented a female mannequin in a phone conversation, with snatches of what she was saying written out on a display card. Some of those well-dressed women were in desperate straits ("But hurry—I'm running out of nickels!"), others were in a normal rush ("I don't know where your white tie is—but hurry!"), or were being catty ("She just walked in, drenched in ermine"), or simply wishful ("Hope Bill gives it to me for Christmas!"). There was a switchboard-operator mannequin, a phonebooth, and telephones. Real ones, of course.

I'd needed eight phones for the displays in the eight Fifth Avenue windows, but had been able to turn up only seven. This was right after the war, and telephones were still hard to come by, but I knew just where to get the eighth. The next time Pennoyer pushed her button, nothing happened.

She called me on another line. "You're some smart fellow, aren't you?"

"Mrs. Pennoyer," I explained, "I really needed eight telephones." She laughed and had another phone installed.

Among the most popular mannequin windows of my early years at Bonwit's were the "Fireman Red" windows. With red the apparel color being sold, I had mannequins dressed in red involved in various situations with firemen. The most popular of the scenes had a fireman shielding his eyes from the heat while roasting a hot dog against the bathing suit worn by a mannequin: that red was hot.

Also popular was the "Great White Robbery," a display for white merchandise that starred a masked mannequin who, gun in hand, stole articles of white clothing from other mannequins. Each window presented a different crime scene—a fire escape, beach cabana, pullman coach. A wanted poster, "Wanted White," appeared on the side panel of each window, complete with a sketch of the bandit, her alias ("Swim White, alias the Seal," for example), height and weight, identifying features, and "last seen in the vicinity of" whichever department sold the merchandise in question.

Putting mannequins in real poses, having them talk on the phone or tote pistols, made passersby stop and look, for people weren't used to seeing mannequins do anything but stand stock-still. Mannequins had always been motionless. The generations of mannequins date back to the inevitable prehistoric monsters, and their evolution runs from sluggish brutes—we know them today as dummies—to clear-eyed, reasonably sapient beings. In the beginning were wicker silhouettes, but these soon gave way to wirework dummies; then came an age of sawdust-filled torsos with papier-mâché heads; next were wax figures, but these melted under the hot lights and were replaced by heavy plaster figures, and these begat composition, which begat plastic, which stood on steady legs of fiberglass.

Cora Scovil, the manufacturer responsible for the cloth mannequins with painted faces of movie stars I'd seen that afternoon in Nashville, was a leader in the movement toward more realistic mannequins. During the early 1930s, her lifelike figures changed the public conception of mannequins in general.

Left: *A publicity shot taken in the couture salon of Bonwit Teller. To get the chandelier in the picture, the mannequin and I had to dance on a table.* Opposite: *Sometime before 10 o'clock on a window night at Bonwit Teller. Each mannequin does something different, each calls for a certain mood, a certain fashion. Before being dressed, they just stand around in the big, dark store and wait their turn.*

Mannequins have always had a certain glamor attached to them, at least here in New York. Perhaps it's because of their association with the fashion industry, perhaps because they're stand-ins for live models, for the women each generation holds up as its most beautiful. Mannequins are so much a part of New York that some have had bit parts (not walk-on, please) in Broadway shows: *All American, No Strings*, and *Do Re Mi* featured mannequins. So did Moss Hart's *Lady in the Dark*, which opened at the Alvin Theater in 1941 and starred Gertrude Lawrence and Danny Kaye. That story includes a publicity-stunt romance between a Bonwit's mannequin and a Saks mannequin.

The show's props included a mannequin, and the propman dutifully supplied them with a standard—for those days—plaster mannequin, which weighed the standard eighty-five to one hundred pounds. Those plaster or composition mannequins were so heavy you could hardly lift them, and when one of those big girls stepped on your toe you knew it. Moving that monster across the stage proved impossible, and one of the show's producers mentioned the problem to his wife, who just happened to be a sculptress and had once worked with Cora Scovil. She designed and built a better, much lighter mannequin. The woman was Lillian Greneker, and she eventually went into business making mannequins of papier-mâché, fiberglass, and light plastic that weighed fifteen to twenty-five pounds.

When I began working at Bonwit's I fell heir to a mannequin population composed of Grenekers and Brosnans, mannequins made by Mary Brosnan, another manufacturer who'd originally worked with Scovil. To me, Brosnan was the best. Her mannequins were more realistic in their faces, their poses, than other mannequins. When I was told I could get a new set of mannequins, I had them made by Mary Brosnan. I liked Mary, enjoyed working with her—she had a factory downtown, then moved over to Long Island City— and all told must have made five sets of mannequins with her.

The first set of mannequins I did with Brosnan were made in crazy poses so that if I hung them in the air they looked like they were flying, and yet if I stood them on the floor they looked like they were standing up. They were fun, and I had a lot of fun working with them.

I had an apartment then at 15 East Fifty-seventh Street, on the fourth floor. I used to blow bubbles out the window and watch them float down to the street. It was amusing to see how people walking by responded to meeting a bubble, and it gave me an idea for my flying Brosnans.

Together with the electrician at Bonwit's, I built a bubble machine, the first one I ever saw. We filled a big tank with soapy bubble-making liquid and constructed a wheel with rings that entered the liquid and then passed in front of a fan that blew to make the bubbles. Constant bubbles. We set this apparatus on a shelf at the top of the window. The bubbles floated down amid the Brosnan mannequins, and I had those girls, dressed in nightgowns, flying through the air.

There were problems. Liquid from the bursting bubbles ruined the merchandise, so I had to change the nightgowns several times, and we had to refill the liquid in the bubble-making machine every day. One of us would hold the ladder while the other poured the liquid. One morning, while I was holding the ladder, the whole shelf collapsed, and the falling bubble machine hit me on the head. I was knocked silly and also soaked in bubble juice. My staff picked me up and carried me along Fifth Avenue and around the corner to my apartment, a chilling experience, for this was in wintertime. Once home, I got in the tub—it seemed the right thing to do with all that bubble liquid on me—and then I started laughing and couldn't stop. They called for a doctor, who informed me I'd had a slight concussion, but I couldn't stop laughing.

For a short time after that the people at Bonwit's called me Double-Bubble Moore. While the display was still in, someone came by and bought the bubble machine out of the window.

Those who visited Bonwit's on window night sensed a chaos that really wasn't always there. This newspaper article's illustrations show me putting together windows. The stuffed tiger is for the perfume Tigress. The woman carefully sewing at upper left is the dancer and actress Maria Karnilova. She needed extra money, could sew, so I took her on.

Don Freeman's NEWSSTAND watches a Fifth Avenue WINDOW DRESSER AT WORK

"I MUST HAVE MORE STARS AND SNOW FLAKES!"

ONE MIGHT SUPPOSE that all the window designers in town were knocking themselves out these days stuffing reindeer for Christmas displays, but Gene Moore, chief window designer for Bonwit Teller, is not being so obvious. In his display department, on the fifth floor of the Fifth Avenue store, he was tearing himself apart last week getting his eight new windows ready.

I found myself up there in a maze of manikins, all being weirdly draped. Mr. Moore began telling me ecstatically how his latest designs had given him greater satisfaction than any he had yet concocted. Each of the eight windows symbolizes a famous brand of perfume—he showed me the list: Stradivari, Tapestry, Bright Star, Breathless and Fabulous, Saint and Sinner, Shocking, Tigress, Perhaps. Mr. Moore was especially breathless about the Perhaps window, "but I have no favorites," he hastened to add when he saw me taking notes.

He took me around the shop, referring to this dummy or that, "his girls," as we went. We stopped in front of one blank-faced figure. "She doesn't look like much now," he remarked, "but wait till we give her the gook! She'll make a gorgeous saint." The shop resounded to such words as *sparkle, flex* and *gook. Gook* was the word I heard most frequently. It is used to describe everything. All the way from seaweed and fungi to fancy jewelry.

Pointing to an animal rug on the floor, Mr. Moore said, "We wracked our brains trying to find a stuffed tigress, but there isn't such an animal to be found in this city—excepting, of course, the Natural History Museum. But they wouldn't let us have her, naturally." The old gooks!

FIXING UP THE "BREATHLESS AND FABULOUS" WINDOW—

While using mannequins by Mary Brosnan I brought back glass eyes. Mannequins hadn't had glass eyes since the 1920s, the days of all-wax mannequins. A man in Paris named Pierre Immans had produced them. Once in a while you still run across one stranded in an old beauty parlor. When I started at Bonwit's, mannequins had painted eyes that gave them blank, lifeless expressions. So I added glass eyes, even eyelashes.

By this time, Lillian Greneker had retired from the Greneker Corporation, and it was being run by Edgar Rosenthal. Rosenthal gave me a call one day and said he wanted to make mannequins for Bonwit's, said if I'd design the mannequins, he'd give a set to Bonwit's—free. That's how I became involved in the actual designing of mannequins. I worked with Greneker for several years, and the mannequins I designed were sold all over the country. Once I started working with Greneker I had to stop using mannequins by Brosnan: it would have been unfair for me to use another company, particularly since Greneker was giving me the mannequins free. A new set twice each year.

I longed for nipples, but I'm not responsible for them. Someone else came up with nipples on the breasts of mannequins. The belly button is mine, though. I was up in the Bronx at the Greneker factory one day and just poked my index finger into one of the clay figures to show where I wanted it. This was nothing lascivious—the addition of a properly placed navel helped me center garments on mannequins.

The faces of mannequins interested me most of all. I've always loved faces, and painting portraits was a special pleasure. In 1947 I began photographing people. A friend of mine, Cris Alexander, an actor and artist, was very much involved in photography, and since I enjoyed watching him work I started to play around with cameras, too. It was great fun, and until 1957 I worked at it as a sort of part-time career. I took pictures of the performers—actors and actresses, opera stars and ballerinas—under contract to Sol

Hurok's agency. I developed a system with theatrical people. Rather than photograph them during the daytime, I'd take them at night after a performance, when they were exhausted and couldn't offer a lot of resistance. Around eleven they'd come offstage all keyed up, and I'd point my camera at them and snap away without any film. When they were finally relaxed I'd load the camera and go to work. I saw a lot of dawns come up with those people.

One of the most interesting models I used for a set of mannequins was Vivien Leigh. I had worked on a series of photographs of her with Cris Alexander while she was in New York with Laurence Olivier and the Old Vic Theatre, and she agreed to let me make her into a mannequin.

I love Colette. It's an old love and one of my strongest. In 1951, somewhere along the French Riviera, Colette met an actress named Audrey Hepburn and immediately insisted that Hepburn be given the lead in the forthcoming Broadway adaptation of her *Gigi*. Thus Audrey Hepburn came to New York, Richard Avedon photographed her for *Harper's Bazaar*, and I saw the photograph. I called Avedon, found out where Hepburn was staying, asked her if she'd agree to become a mannequin, and eventually photographed her at Alexander's studio. She was so very beautiful, radiant and feminine, an ideal Colette heroine. And tall, taller than I am. We became friends, and she later used the photographs I'd taken as her first publicity pictures with Paramount for her first movie, *Roman Holiday*.

I also photographed top fashion models and used some of them for mannequins. Among the models I photographed were Phyllis Cook, Sunny Harnett, Suzy Parker, and Dorian Lee. Harnett was famous for her smile. In an age of haughty models, she alone smiled, dared to show her teeth, even when posing for fashion magazines. She was a lanky

Above left: *One of the photographs of Audrey Hepburn I took in order to make her into a mannequin.* Above center: *Suzy Parker.* Above right: *Gloria Vanderbilt asked me to take some publicity photographs of her and showed up at the studio wearing a knit dress. I didn't like the dress, and she seemed nervous, so I asked her to put on one of my shirts. The shirt worked, her mood changed, and that's when I took this picture.*

Left: *The beautiful and absolutely unknown model who posed for this Bonwit Teller perfume window was, in fact, my friend Cris Alexander.* Opposite: *Alexander without the makeup in the doorway of a Pennsylvania farmhouse.*

girl, not cold and fancy pretty, but with a distinction that was beautiful. And she was always laughing. I turned her into the first smiling mannequin and then went further by turning her, in another set of mannequins, into the first reclining mannequin. No one had ever seen a mannequin lie down, much less smile. She was lying down in various poses—in one set she was resting her chin in her hands—and always smiling. I had one of her hips up to better show off the clothes—and those long legs.

Suzy Parker was from Texas. Tall, with wonderful cheekbones, she inspired a mannequin for Bonwit's windows. She became very famous and then got into movies, with roles opposite Cary Grant and Gary Cooper. Dorian Lee, Parker's sister, became one of my most popular mannequins.

People recognized the mannequins in my windows. Some of the mannequins even acquired fans. In November 1947, feeling a tad bored with mannequins, I dressed a few windows with headless dummies, the way windows had been done twenty years earlier. People noticed. They missed their mannequins. Lester Gaba, a columnist for *Women's Wear Daily*, found his own way to chat about the mannequins. Although he often made flattering comments on my windows, he and I didn't get along. He wrote an article in which he claimed to have climbed into one of my windows to speak with Dorian. He said she was his favorite; but she was almost everyone's favorite—she was beautiful—and I don't think she'd have given him the time of day.

I admit I once kissed one of my mannequins, but I won't tell which. I just wanted to see what it would be like. It was like kissing a desk. The experience did not affect our relationship.

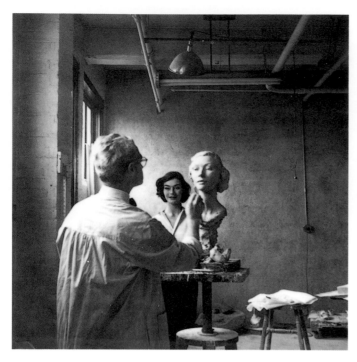

Above: *The sculptor Benjamin Hawkins in his studio at Greneker working on a bust of Anne Gunning, an Irish girl who was a model with the Ford Agency.* Right: *Rosalind Russell mirroring the pose of one of the mannequins I made of her.*

Even with their new faces and poses, mannequins still had drawbacks that dated to their earliest days. Their bases, for instance, were a constant problem. Back then, mannequins were mounted on a rod attached to a circular metal base (today's stand on their own with inner wires or have clear glass bases). I did just about everything to hide those bases, covering them with cork, grass, fabric, and most of all confetti.

For one particular back-to-school display I decided to use open textbooks to cover the bases. I spread the entire floor of the window with open books. As always, I finished the display late at night. I didn't bother to examine the open books. A few days later, a man stormed into Bonwit's and demanded to speak at once to the manager. Our windows, he announced, were obscene. I got a polite call from the manager, who asked me to make a small change in the display. One of the books, evidently an anatomy textbook, was open to an illustration of female reproductive organs. I'd had no idea those books were so interesting and went down at once to take a look. The book in question was nowhere near the front of the display and was, instead, in the middle of the window. That man had studied those books carefully. I flipped through the book—it had wonderfully explicit medical drawings—and left it open to an illustration of male genitalia. I waited. No one complained.

Male mannequins were rare in store windows until 1949. In November of that year, I decided to use some—forty, to be exact—in a display I was doing of Norman Norell gowns, the first time I'd displayed his fashions. I used a female mannequin as a star, with the male mannequins standing in line to form a background, just like the chorus line of a musical comedy. They were dressed in evening clothes, white tie, tails, and top hat; she was wearing a beautiful Norell gown, white satin with a big pink sash and a pink artificial rose. The rose spoiled the whole thing, so I snipped it off.

The next day I got a call from Mr. Norell. "Who cut the rose off my gown?" "I did," I said. "It ruined an otherwise brilliant design." "Okay," he said and hung up.

We later became close friends. He was the only designer I'd ever ask to stop by on window night. I usually don't want designers or artists around, but I'd invite him over to help me choose the accessories, and he'd say no, no, there was no reason for him to come, he'd say I knew as much as he did; and I'd say no, no, please come, I need your help. And in the end he'd stand there and plead with me, "Would you please just do what you want? You know as much as I do." And I'd thank him. He was a terrific designer and a wonderful man.

After the Norell display, male mannequins suddenly became essential. Saks soon went me one better by using 150 males in a display, but they used only wing collars and white bowties to suggest the men, not real mannequins. Understandable: finding forty male mannequins hadn't been easy.

Using male mannequins could present problems. Bonwit's then had something called the 721 Club—the store's address was 721 Fifth—a group of salesgirls who helped men select gifts. Quite famous, this club did a lot of business for the store: all those bewildered men not knowing which way to turn or what to buy appreciated the feminine assistance. I did a set of windows on the club, and in each was a male shopper mannequin and a 721 Club girl mannequin. In one window the girl had just sprayed the man with some potent perfume, and he'd fainted—he was out cold on the floor with xs in his eyes.

A woman called the manager to complain. It seems she had just lost her husband,

Leon Danielian as I photographed him in Cris Alexander's studio.

I took the model Phyllis Cook and a heap of props into the woods around Mount Kisco, New York, to take a series of photographs for Vogue *magazine. The settings were real, and poor Phyllis got a terrible dose of poison ivy.* Opposite: *A pose for Lanvin's Arpege.* Right: *Sleeping by Schiaparelli. There were problems: the trees were in the wrong places, so I had to dig a few up and move them, and the wind kept blowing the smoke bomb's mist the wrong way. I shot her only when the mist came her way.*

and the supine mannequin so closely resembled him that looking in the window caused her great anguish. I pulled him out feetfirst.

In 1951 Bergdorf Goodman celebrated its fiftieth anniversary, an event I thought important enough for Bonwit's windows. In one window I had two mannequins wearing boxing gloves, one mannequin labeled Bonwit's, the other Bergdorf's, along with the message, "Happy birthday. You don't look a day over fifty, dear."

The boxing mannequins attracted much attention. One afternoon I ran into Andrew Goodman, Bergdorf's president. He wasn't pleased. "You're some smart fellow. It's our anniversary, and Bonwit's is getting all the publicity because of your windows." All I could do was wish him a happy birthday.

In most cases, I used only one or two mannequins in each of Bonwit's windows, but I relaxed this rule when working with junior wear. Standing alone under a bright light in the middle of staring eyes would scare the daylights out of a teenager. They travel in groups and tend to dress alike, so when I did junior-apparel windows I'd put in lots of merchandise and lots of mannequins: the crowds in the windows mirrored the squads of schoolgirls that invaded the store. In one summertime junior display I combined both the teenage crowds and my usual simplicity. In the two windows on each side of the Fifth Avenue entrance I had lots of mannequins holding autograph books out to a movie star, while the other windows were empty of mannequins and showed only deserted rocking chairs on summerhouse porches.

I had about six sets of mannequins at any given time, and I talked to them—along with my staff, they were part of my world at Bonwit's. I talked to them and put makeup

Adjusting lights while preparing a Bonwit Teller window. The curtain is up so I can see the display's reflection.

on their faces. I experimented with the makeup and went to the store's powder bar to make the colors I wanted. After several years I found that hard lines on an immobile face aren't good and that softer and more vague makeup is always best. Putting makeup on those faces was like theater, and my mannequins were my stars.

Believing that these stars of window displays had gone unnoticed for too long, I decided to do a set of windows at Bonwit's to show the public exactly how mannequins are made. The name of this display was "At Bonwit's a Star Is Born—Bonwit's Stars Pink." The model I chose for the display was Mary Sinclair, a popular television actress. Working together with the Greneker Corporation, I selected the eight most important steps—for the eight windows—in the making of a mannequin. The first window showed photographs of Sinclair in various poses along with the finished clay head on a model stand; the second had the wire armature twisted into shape and ready for the sculptor to start with the clay; the third showed the roughed-in figure in clay; the fourth the finished clay figure; the fifth the clay figure in the mold, with part of the mold cut away; the sixth the plaster cast from the mold; the seventh the various steps in making wigs; and the eighth the application of makeup to the mannequin's face. All these steps showed merchandise, of course: lots of pink apparel. The pink went well with the clay color of the figures, but it's also true that pink is my favorite color for women.

In 1953 the musical *Wonderful Town,* starring Rosalind Russell, opened at the Winter Garden Theatre. My friend Cris Alexander was in the cast. I wanted to meet Russell because, of course, I wanted to make a mannequin of her. I managed to meet her, photograph her, and make the mannequin. Then I decided to hold an opening night, like a Hollywood opening, with klieg lights and a curtain-raising ceremony to reveal her standing beside her mannequins. It would take place just after her performance at the Winter Garden.

She agreed, but only on condition I appear in the windows with her. "I can't," I said, "I just can't."

"Well, then I won't do it."

I finally agreed because I'd found a way to appear in those windows without looking foolish. The opening night came, mobs of people showed up, the street was blocked off, and police were called out to control things. The big lights sent their arcs into the sky over the store, and at the stroke of midnight the curtains went up on Miss Russell and her mannequin twins. When not matching the pose of a mannequin, she waved out the windows at the crowd of fans, and I stood off to one side, my Roliflex around my neck—when not in front of my face—pretending to be a photographer.

There were other opening nights at Bonwit's, and one of the nicest was also one of the first. It involved perfume.

I don't like perfume, but I love doing perfume windows because you can play on fantasies. Perfume itself is composed of fantasy. Each bears an exotic or suggestive name and comes in a special package, in a beautiful little bottle. Long before actually sniffing the scent, the customer has been drawn in by a subtle but alluring seduction.

No one had ever dedicated all of a store's windows to perfume. In fact, before I came to Bonwit's, the store had never done perfume windows. But I loved the idea, as did the cosmetic department's staff and the perfume manufacturers. My first perfume windows at Bonwit's had the added attraction of showing the first important collection of fine French perfumes since the war.

That first year, in December 1946, I used eight costumed mannequins to interpret eight French perfumes. One mannequin, wearing an 1830 ankle-length ball gown of ivory satin with loads of old rose-point lace, rhinestones, and sequins, acted out Revillon's Carnet de Bal. Another window had a setting of bare branches from which hung crystal chandeliers, with a mannequin wearing a bare-shouldered dress of accordion-pleated amber chiffon fashioned on Empire lines. She was seated at a harp. The perfume was Lanvin's Arpege.

People from the newspapers, theater, and radio were invited to attend the opening. They sipped champagne inside the store until midnight, when a gong was sounded, and then all filed out onto Fifth Avenue. As the curtains went up, I heard suitable and gratifying gasps.

Thus began my tradition of doing pre-Christmas perfume windows, a popular annual event that attracted much attention. Perfume became one of my specialties, particularly when I combined it with photography. I composed pictures that visually simulated the names of the perfumes, such as a woman asleep in a misty forest for Schiaparelli's Sleeping. Some of these photos appeared in magazines, like *Vogue.* I enlarged others for the windows at Bonwit's.

One year I took photographs reproducing famous works of art to show how various famous painters—Da Vinci, Monet, Picasso, and others—would have done photography had they been twentieth-century photographers. The model I used was Phyllis Cook. In another set of perfume windows, I presented rather suggestive interpretations of perfumes. In the window for Femme by Rochas the photograph of the model was placed behind a large spiderweb, and in the foreground were a rose and a stuffed cat toying with a mouse. The same model appeared in photos for other perfumes; that for Lanvin's My Sin showed her climbing out a window and down a ladder, leaving behind her wedding ring and a farewell note. Beautiful and absolutely unknown, the model attracted attention, and I received calls from fashion editors and photographers asking me where I'd

*"People who live in glass houses," from the 1949 Bonwit
Teller Christmas windows. Jac Venza did the painting, the
gloved hands belong to mannequin arms, and the glass is an
old bell jar.*

found her. I said she'd gone back home to Sweden. I didn't want to say she was a he—my friend Cris Alexander. Good makeup changes everything.

Another friend, the actor Farley Granger, posed for a series of perfume windows. In one of the photos I had him tied to a chair with rope. He'd acted in Alfred Hitchcock's film *Rope*, but the photo in the window was a play on the name of the perfume, Piguet's Brigand.

I learned a great deal from my experiences with photography. In particular, I learned the importance of proper lighting. Lighting is essential to display, a primary tool in creating illusions, in helping passersby see what you wish them to see. It can be used to promote color, to make a color the star in a window, or to improve subtly the appearance of merchandise.

Before the illumination of window displays became the minor science it is today, window dressers ran the constant danger of losing their displays in darkness. With more footcandles of natural light outside than artificial light inside the windows, passing citizens were as likely to admire their own reflections in the glass as they were to admire the carefully arranged merchandise. Then, during the 1930s, Irving Eldredge, display director at Macy's, had the bright idea of enlisting the aid of the theatrical arts—he commissioned a theatrical-lighting expert named Stanley McCandless to redo Macy's windows. McCandless had the windows rewired to take greatly increased candlepower, set up adjustable spotlights, and introduced the use of filters.

The new installation worked well until the heat of the lights set off the store's automatic sprinkler system. The addition of air-conditioning solved that.

Display windows have more in common with theater stages than wooden floors and the fact that both close with curtains. The shape of the space is similar, and so are the basic endeavors—creation of an environment and direction of the viewer's attention. Both are worlds of props and costumes and makeup faces. That Eldredge chose someone with theatrical-lighting experience stands to reason, and for that same reason I've been involved in several theatrical productions. The first was in 1948, when I designed the sets and costumes for the Equity Library Theatre production of *Pal Joey*.

I've always paid attention to developments in theatrical lighting in the same way that I've always found wandering the aisles of hardware stores time well spent. Although I'm often given credit for the innovation, I don't believe I was the first display director to install baby spotlights in windows. I certainly used them, along with track lighting, but my contribution was trough lighting, running fluorescent lighting along the back of the window. I knew that sending light up the back wall would create the illusion of depth, so I put fluorescent lights along the back of the window and hid them behind a long stand-up structure.

Antique stores are good locations for attentive wandering. In the store owned by Frederick P. Victoria I saw some old parquet de Versailles floors he'd just come by. I knew precisely where those floors belonged, and when they were being installed in the windows I left a space at the back for a lighting trough to be built into the floor, thus doing away with the stand-up structure. I later set up a similar lighting system in the windows at Tiffany's.

The lighting in my windows was a source of constant concern for me. It never seemed right, and I was always complaining about it. I was having lunch with Jean Rosenthal one day, and I told her how unhappy I was with my lighting, how I wished I knew more about it. No one knew more about lighting than Rosenthal. She had done all the lighting for years and years of New York plays as well as for Martha Graham. A kindhearted soul, she said, "I think you're lighting is very good."

"Well, I don't."

"All right," she said, "I'll tell you what. You take one side of Bonwit's, and I'll take the other. You light your side, I'll light mine, and then we'll see which is better."

That sounded fine to me, but it soon grew more complicated. "I want to bring in a lot of equipment for what I've got planned," she said. "Let's make a wager. If you win, I'll pay for the equipment, but if I win, you'll pay for it."

The window of Lenthéric. I'd been pressing flowers in books for two years, and for this display I put them between sheets of glass with a mirror in the background to repeat them.

I agreed to that, too, and on the next window night, after I'd set up the displays, she took four of the Fifth Avenue windows, I took the other four, and we both worked into the night, setting up our lighting. Each of us had no idea of what the other was up to, and in the end we walked outside and stood together on Fifth Avenue. I looked and she looked and then she said, "Oh, my God, you win. The equipment is on me."

"I hate to admit it," I said, "but you're right." She had lighted those windows the way she would a theater stage, lighting so strong that everything was lighted out of existence.

From then on I felt more satisfied with my lighting.

Lighting, props, and art came together wonderfully in the Christmas windows for 1949. As always, I had begun worrying about those windows in July, roaming the Metropolitan Museum of Art for inspiration. I ultimately decided to illustrate some of those silly old sayings we all rely on too often.

The windows presented miniature stages created by Jac Venza viewed through snowflake openings (then a struggling artist, Venza is today an executive with New York's Channel 13). Each little tableau represented a saying. The most popular had two small figures in a glass bell ("People who live in glass houses") in the center of a town square.

Giant accusing hands—mannequin glove hands—pointed at them from the surrounding doors and windows. Among the other sayings were "Don't count your chickens," "The grass is always greener," and "Fools rush in."

We changed the eight Fifth Avenue windows every week on Tuesday night, when the store was closed, and the eight side windows every week on Thursday morning, when the store was open. The two operations were very different. When changing the front windows, we'd line up the mannequins on the main floor outside the windows and play with them, dress them, calmly prepare them for their performance. While doing those windows we usually worked with the curtains closed. Then, at some crazy hour in the early morning, we'd open the curtains to see the reflection on the glass of how the display was coming along. It was easier and more comfortable than running outside. All display people know that if you go outside to take a look in, you'll find that outside it's pouring rain. (Or you'll get some earnest but unneeded suggestions from passersby.)

Working on late into the night in the cathedral hush of a big store is engrossing and entertaining. We chatted and sometimes sent out for food. But it was hard work and no party. Some of the kids would come in to work late the next day, but no matter how late we finally finished the windows, I always got in early the next morning to make sure everything was all right and to see what kind of response the new displays were getting.

It usually took all day Thursday to finish the side windows: it's hard to work on displays when a store is open. We had to assemble all the mannequins and props before the store opened and then dress the mannequins in the window, with people outside looking in, trying for our attention and offering suggestions. They always think it's cute; what they don't know is that if they're dressed in something light they kill the reflection. It can be trying.

Display work was primarily a nocturnal and thus all-male activity. Not by choice. It was then a common belief that window trimming was too physically demanding for women, and according to a New York State law of that period, females were not permitted to work past ten o'clock at night. I had only three women on my staff, and they had to depart long before the window-dressing hours arrived. Had my thirteen kids voted to join a union, I'd have had to face even more regulations, but I went to the store's management and convinced them that if they did what the union claimed it would do, the kids would have no need for the union. They listened and treated my staff well.

The purpose of the windows was to sell merchandise, and sometimes they worked all too well; I was forever being called down from my eleventh-floor office to open a window and pluck out a dress, coat, or handbag for a customer who simply had to have it that very instant. It sometimes happened that the customer wanted to buy the entire ensemble, everything the mannequin was wearing and carrying, the purse, the hat, the scarf—a nice tribute to my display work, but it left an empty window. Such customers often claimed they needed the merchandise in question as they were leaving the next morning for South America. That always amused me. I never told them I'd once left "the next morning" for South America and had done just fine without new clothes. I eventually persuaded management to institute a policy according to which no item would be removed from a window unless it was either as a favor to a treasured, long-time customer or was for a sale of over $1,000.

In addition to photography and work in the theater I also did freelance design. One of my clients during the early 1940s was Lenthéric, a cosmetics store in the Old Savoy Plaza Hotel on East Fifty-eighth Street. In 1944, before going to Bonwit's, I had bought a house in New Jersey. Flowers and grass, ferns and weeds—I regularly hauled hunks of my backyard across the river for my Manhattan window displays. With flowers and grass and mirrors I transformed the Lenthéric window into a garden. That window got afternoon sun, the lights added heat, and between the daytime sun and the nighttime artificial light those plants flourished. I had to trim the grass with scissors. Together with the flowers and grass, I once brought over a spider, and it very graciously spun a web right against a frame of the glass. People thought it was a prop.

Like perfume, lingerie offered room for fantasy in windows, so I always enjoyed working with it. Unfortunately, lingerie and sleepwear were not then considered fashion.

Perhaps that's why I decided to design a few lines for Bonwit's. I was good friends with the lingerie buyer, and she thought it was a fine idea, too.

The main idea with lingerie then was for it to be feminine and soft and always either pale pink or white. I thought it should also be sexy. It seemed to me that the private bedrooms in America's homes were potentially ideal places for sex. My first line of lingerie was made of a printed fabric that was transparent. Surely someone made see-through lingerie before I did, but theirs was probably sold mail order. The buyer and manufactuer claimed to be shocked, but no one complained, and the lingerie sold like crazy. I also designed pieces that were anything but risqué, full negligees and pajamas. Some could be worn out at night if used with a slip underneath—a form of very simple evening wear.

Swimsuits also interested me, and around 1954 I wondered why I'd never seen a swimsuit made of angora. Seemed like a good idea, so I borrowed an angora sweater from the sportswear buyer and went for a swim in it. It and I held up just fine. A manufacturer became interested, and in the end I had the entire bank of Fifth Avenue windows filled with angora swimsuits. As was fitting, I made fish of angora in all shapes and sizes and used them to create an underwater scene. They didn't look like any fish that had been displayed before.

That pleased me, for fish had been done to death in window displays—fish, seashells, sunbursts, and fishnets had all been used far too often. Although I had few dealings with other people in the display industry—I didn't "talk shop" with anyone—I was constantly aware that we fell into prop jags. Some of this was inevitable because the displays were tied to merchandise, which was tied to changing fashions and moods.

Sports cars and sports-car clothes had their day, too. Hoping to use blueprints of cars in the windows, I called eight car dealers, but they had none, Detroit had none, and for all my efforts I received only useless wash drawings of cars. I abandoned the cars and called the Goodyear Tire & Rubber Company and asked for 900 tires. They sent them right over. Such is the power of display.

The tires weighed tons but were beautiful. I had a construction department at Bonwit's, and we made wooden cores to put in the tires—they were without tubes—and built stands to hold them up. Towers of tires ten feet high, the perfect backdrop for a display of "proper attire." But the hot lights made the tires droop, the towers leaned, and we were kept busy saving the mannequins from disaster. There was also the unpleasant odor of hot rubber distracting first-floor shoppers.

My love for movies found an outlet in the windows, sometimes as a result of a promotional tie-in with advertisers and sometimes as a result of personal whim. I adored *The African Queen* and created a window related to the film with a card that read, "*The African Queen*, starring Katharine Hepburn and Humphrey Bogart." Bogart was in the city, saw the sign in the window, and charged into the store to complain: his name was supposed to go first.

I had better luck with a 1954 film called *The Egyptian*, which had beautiful scenery, if not much else, and was directed by Michael Curtiz. The display used fashions, evening clothes, based on scenes from the film. Pleased with my work, the Egyptian government gave a luncheon for me at the Waldorf-Astoria. They even gave me a commemorative tray.

I didn't go to that luncheon alone. Walter Hoving came with me. Hoving arrived at Bonwit Teller about one year after I did. He was a strong-willed man, and when I first met him I thought him the coldest I'd ever met, but during the nearly thirty-five years we worked together, I often saw another side of him, a warm and caring person he would never let show on the surface.

By the time he arrived at Bonwit's Hoving had already had a long, successful career. Born in Sweden of Finnish parents, he'd come as a child to New York with his family. His life in merchandising began with ten years at Macy's, during which time he rose from the research department to a vice presidency. He had strong beliefs concerning taste and style and at Macy's had had a table in his office spread with one hundred small objects, all

October 12, 1971. Kent Bedient showed me a paper flower he'd made, and it was sweet, but I wanted more in many more shapes. We made them together to create this garden for Tiffany's windows.

covered by a cloth. When interviewing people for the job of buyer or assistant buyer, he'd pull off the cloth and ask the applicant, "Why don't you put the objects that are well designed on the right side of the table, and the ones that are badly designed on the left side of the table." He'd leave the room, take a fifteen-minute walk through the store, and come back to evaluate the prospective employee's sense of style.

From Macy's he'd gone to Montgomery Ward in Chicago as a vice president of sales and advertising. He'd applied his concern for style and good design to every Montgomery Ward product. Once, while visiting a farm in the Midwest, he spotted a Montgomery Ward manure spreader. In response to his questions, the farmer reported that the spreader worked well, but it was the wife's comment that truly pleased Hoving. "It's pretty, too," she exclaimed, leading Hoving to note, "Good design is always appreciated."

Interior displays at Tiffany's during the late 1950s. Walter Hoving didn't like these Christmas decorations, or perhaps one of his friends didn't, but his secretary called me and told me I had to take them down by the next day. I didn't touch them, a week went by, and Hoving called. "You were right," he said. "The displays are beautiful."

From Montgomery Ward, Hoving went to the Associated Dry Goods Company, which owned Lord & Taylor. He had then become president of Lord & Taylor.

He made his presence known. At Lord & Taylor he became annoyed that Christmas appeared in store windows earlier and earlier each year and decreed that it would not arrive at Lord & Taylor any sooner than December 4. By mid-November, as all the other stores up and down Fifth Avenue put in their Christmas finery, he had second thoughts. "Rush in a temporary window," he ordered. "I don't care what it is, just so long as it's Christmas." The display staff had nothing seasonal to work with, but a simple truth about display is that no matter how little you have at hand, you can always come up with a good design. It was probably Dana O'Clare who got the idea, and he had Al Bliss, who ran a display house that made things for Lord & Taylor, make a set of big Christmas bells. Those bells were put out in the window even before the paint on them was dry. They became a Christmas symbol for Lord & Taylor and began a trend in New York stores of religious windows at Christmas with less emphasis on merchandise.

Because of his outspoken, stubborn opinions, Hoving was often in the news, and during his many years as head of the Fifth Avenue Association, an organization of avenue merchants, he frequently battled with city mayors and administrations concerning issues affecting business on Fifth Avenue. Once, he locked horns with Mayor Fiorello—the name means "little flower" in Italian—La Guardia. Hoving so angered the mayor that he snapped, "I'm not going to turn this city over to a floorwalker." Hoving replied, "May I remind His Honor that every floorwalker wears a little flower in his buttonhole?"

Hoving formed the Hoving Corporation, which bought Bonwit Teller in 1946. When he first arrived at Bonwit's, he called me into his office and said he wanted to go through the store with me. He wanted to go over my work as interior display director. The next morning we stopped on every floor and walked along all the aisles together. As we passed certain displays, he'd point and ask, "Why did you do that?"

I did away with my accent, but I'm still something of a Southern gentleman, and I

didn't appreciate Hoving's brusque approach. " 'Cause I wanted to" was my unvarying response.

One morning after I'd just changed the displays, he strolled into my office and announced, "I don't like your new windows." This was very early in the morning, and I didn't care to discuss the issue at length. "Listen, Mr. Hoving," I said. "Firstly, I must please me; secondly, the public; and thirdly, I hope you like them. If you don't, too bad." He left my office, and I began another day at Bonwit's.

Bonwit's, I learned, needed a symbol. Other stores had them—Lord & Taylor had its famous rose—and the sales people were casting about for something for Bonwit's. I was thinking about that one afternoon while looking around the gift department. I spotted a set of china cups and saucers decorated with bunches of violets. "That would be wonderful," I said to myself, and I took a cup and saucer to the next meeting of the advertising department. They liked it, and Bonwit's had its violets.

I love mice. For 1954's Christmas windows I chose Clement C. Moore's poem "A Visit from St. Nicholas," which begins, " 'Twas the night before Christmas, and all through the house, not a creature was stirring." I had those mice everywhere, and not little mice, but good-sized ones. They were stirring plum puddings, trimming a Swiss-cheese tree with tiny Christmas balls, taking a bubble bath, getting ready for the Christmas play (with a trio costumed as the Three Wise Men), and dressed up in Salvation Army uniforms. One bonneted mouse was holding out her tambourine to receive a wad of bills from a life-sized mannequin. A real-life Salvation Army band set up on the sidewalk beside the windows.

There was merchandise in those windows. Only later, just before leaving Bonwit's, was I finally able to do Christmas displays without it.

That year, Bonwit Teller was doing very well financially, and Walter Hoving was thinking about expanding. He would have liked to buy his old store, Lord & Taylor, but it wasn't for sale. Just next door, however, was Tiffany's, and that store had fallen on hard times.

DIAMONDS IN DIRT

THE MUSES ARE DAUGHTERS OF MEMORY, children of the Titaness Memory and the god Zeus. Straightforward enough: with a little bit of divine help, memory produces the arts and crafts. Of course, memory can also provide sleepless nights.

Ideas are everywhere, everywhere you walk, everyplace you travel, in every book you read, in every play you see. Everything in life is filled with ideas, but to see those ideas clearly you sometimes have to turn out the lights. Most of my ideas come to me at night when I'm half in and half out of sleep—a good time for memory to toss up a notion, for a gentle visit from the Muses. I've never blamed those nine wise virgins for the ideas I've put in store windows, and if I've offered them the occasional sacrifice, that was purely by accident. But I do curse them—and with the meanest words I've got—when they desert me, which they almost always do, and usually just a few days before a window night. Sometimes it seems the only way to keep ideas flowing is to be crazy. Once I was full of piss and vinegar; I now rely on sweeter sources of inspiration.

I have visions when I listen to music. I see pictures in my head—water and gardens, clouds opening for rays of the sun or parting at night for the moon. One of my favorite pieces is Franck's D-minor Symphony. It makes me think of woods, of deep forests,

perhaps because I first heard it in the woods. I listen to music constantly—Mozart, Debussy, Stravinsky—and also to other sounds. There was a brook on the property I had in New Jersey. It ran along just a few feet from my balcony. When I tired of the way it babbled, I'd step out into the water and move the rocks around to change the sound. Doing so changed the pictures.

Kismet: perhaps it's only humdrum fate decked out in a fancy costume, but *kismet* sounds prettier and holds more promise. Kismet is something you encounter on a busy city's street corner, like a long-lost friend, or the stranger whose love will change your world, or an idea. Street corners are wonderful. Everyone slows down at a street corner, becomes a bit more alert. You never know what to expect.

There's also serendipity, another pretty word that shows up best in happy accidents. Things can go wrong beautifully, and sometimes objects are more meaningful when broken. A crystal wineglass standing on a shelf is merely pretty. A broken wineglass on a table is an assembly of exciting reminders: glass, fragility, sharp, bright, clear, precious, diamonds.

I believe in kismet and serendipity, but I put my faith in breakfast. Starting each day with a good breakfast is vital to a satisfactory fate. I myself prefer tea. It goes well with my feelings for my cat—he'd be offended by coffee—and the roundness of the pot gives shape to whatever ideas came to me in the previous night's darkness.

On the morning of April 15, 1865, at precisely 7:22, the clock on Atlas's shoulders stopped. This was later found to be the exact moment of Abraham Lincoln's death. A schoolboy's tale, but it affirms yet again both Tiffany's venerable age and its place in American history. Perhaps there was a Tiffany clock on the mantel at Appomattox. Ulysses S. Grant had a Tiffany sword, the head of Mars in low relief on its grip and its sculpted guard graced with a wrathful Medusa.

Greek mythology on Union swords, famous Americans through years of history: Tiffany's name is inserted in our nation's past so tightly one sometimes forgets it's a store. There's that odd coincidence about Queen Victoria: Charles L. Tiffany founded the store in 1837, the year she ascended the throne; he died, at 90, in 1902, just months after her death. The years of Victoria's reign were rich and wonderful for Tiffany's, but when they were over, and Charles L. Tiffany was dead, the store declined fast. Or perhaps it just stayed the same.

From the death of Charles L. Tiffany to the mid-1950s, the store stood as an icon of the conservative, a form of "good taste" relied on by its clientele as agelessly "safe." Designs remained unchanged for decades and, to a certain extent, lost touch with contemporary ideas. But a certain group of people continued to rely on Tiffany's as the only place to buy an engagement ring, the only place for first sets of chinaware and silver. Unfortunately, that group was shrinking.

Many of the store's stockholders were Tiffany family members or friends of the Tiffany family, and they don't seem to have fretted all that much about their declining dividends. The chairman of the board, John C. Moore (no relation whatsoever to me), bought up the stock of those holders who grew restless. Although in poor shape financially, the store might have struggled on indefinitely had it not occupied space, prime Manhattan real estate. It was located on a busy city's street corner.

In 1954, news of Tiffany's plight reached Irving Maidman, a real estate man. Planning to replace Tiffany's seven floors with a soaring skyscraper, he began a campaign to buy up Tiffany's stock. Then the news reached Arde Bulova, president of the Bulova watch company. He, too, wanted Tiffany's—he wanted to put its famous name on his watches. These two men—Maidman after the land, Bulova after the name—represented the dark realities of the business world.

This tale's hero is Walter Hoving. When he learned his next-door neighbor was up for sale he, too, set about trying to acquire Tiffany's, but he wanted something more than the

Preceding pages: *May 15, 1957. Inspired by the building boom, these are diamonds in dirt from Tiffany's windows.*
Opposite: *A face from a fountain in the gardens of Tivoli, Italy.*

*September 10, 1984. "Did you know you have a broken glass
in the window?" asks the kindhearted New Yorker. Or
perhaps he's only delighted to have discovered a possible
error. So I ask, "Did you notice the hammer?" I broke the
glass with the hammer, and had to: otherwise the display
would have been just a row of glasses. The broken glass
proves the fragility of crystal, and the hammer shows how
the damage was done.*

land and the name: he wanted the old dream of the "Tiffany touch," the tradition of style and good taste.

The struggle for control of the stock was dramatic, with various agents—representatives of Bulova or Hoving or Tiffany's—racing around the country to locate stockholders and convince them to sell. In the end, Hoving and Tiffany's management had wrested 51 percent of the family-owned stock away from their competitors. In 1955, the Hoving Corporation took control of Tiffany's, ending the reign over the store by the heirs of its founders.

Hoving finally had what he had always wanted. At Macy's, Montgomery Ward, and even at Bonwit's, he had followed the standard policy of giving the customer what the customer wanted. Now he could give the customer what he, Walter Hoving, wanted the customer to have. Simply, Hoving believed Tiffany's had a mission to perform—nothing short of teaching the American public good taste.

He needed assistance, of course, and immediately set about hiring people who had what he considered proper qualifications. First to come was Van Day Truex, who was about to retire from his job as head of New York's Parsons School of Design. While at Parsons, Truex had popularized the so-called Parsons table, a design he had borrowed from the furniture designer Jean Michel Frank, whom he had known in Paris during the 1930s. The Kansas-born Truex was planning a quiet retirement, painting in the south of France. Instead, he found himself design director for Tiffany's, and he gave Hoving what he sought—provocative new styles and original designs. Among his many creations were his Bamboo flatware, silver berry basket, and cut rock crystal candlesticks; he also designed beautiful porcelain, including the private stock pattern called Framboises Roses, which he said was inspired by the fretwork design on a Japanese vase, and a color known as Madame de Pompadour pink.

With Truex's help, Hoving set about ridding Tiffany's of merchandise that didn't meet the store's new standards. In what became known as the Great White Elephant Sale, Tiffany's reduced the prices—in some cases drastically—of unwanted merchandise. A nineteenth-century sterling-silver tea set originally priced at $32,000 went for $12,000; a diamond-and-emerald brooch (the emerald said to come from a sultan's belt buckle) went from $52,000 to $29,700. The prices were slashed even on many lower-priced items. Hoving was cleaning off his shelves, making room for the new, reborn Tiffany's.

Hoving then hired the famous jewelry designer Jean Schlumberger and his partner, Nicolas Bongard. Schlumberger had begun his career in Paris during the 1930s, designing costume jewelry for such couturiers as Elsa Schiaparelli. His wonderful bijoux were popular with international tastemakers. Hoving set up Schlumberger in a private boutique on the mezzanine, and there Schlumberger, already known as the Cellini of the twentieth century, worked away on his innovative designs while listening attentively to daily soap operas on the radio. His work soon became famous for its inspiration—often taken from plants, animals, and the sea—and its originality—often combining precious and semiprecious stones in mounts made of both gold and platinum. He also made much use of enamel. He generally enjoyed breaking rules and attracted an enormous following.

Hoving didn't have to look far for his next recruit. He simply turned to me and asked if I'd like to do the windows at Tiffany's along with those at Bonwit's. Hoving had directed each of his new designers to create what he or she felt was best without any concern for whether an item would sell, and his instructions to me were similar. "I want three things," he said. "In the first place, don't ever tell me what you're going to do. Just surprise me. Secondly, don't ever try to sell anything. That's my job. And lastly, make the windows beautiful from your point of view, because I know your point of view is going to be, generally speaking, my point of view." He was true to his word and always gave me complete freedom with my windows at Tiffany's. Unlike at Delman's or Bonwit's, where I had buyers or department heads thrusting merchandise at me, no one at Tiffany's has ever even suggested that a particular item of merchandise be put on display in the windows. Not using windows to promote merchandise is rare in a store—perhaps unique—but then I've always done something else with the windows at Tiffany's. Years later, when an

Below: *An example of what Tiffany's window displays looked like before my arrival. At closing time, the merchandise was removed and the curtains drawn.*
Right: *The building on the corner of Fifth Avenue and Fifty-seventh Street.*

executive complained during a meeting that he never knew what I was going to do in the windows, Hoving leapt to my defense. "Don't ask Gene what he's going to do," he said. "He'll show you." I couldn't have asked for more.

Under Hoving's direction, Tiffany's was redecorated, and while the workmen tore out the old display cases—the so-called glass coffins—on the second floor and prepared the store for its renaissance, I made the acquaintance of my new windows.

Tiffany's has five windows, two flanking the front door on Fifth Avenue, three running down Fifty-seventh Street. Thus, together with the windows at Bonwit's, I had an entire block of windows on Fifth Avenue plus the Bonwit's windows running down Fifty-sixth Street and the Tiffany's windows on Fifty-seventh. Hoving eventually bought the building adjoining Tiffany's on Fifty-seventh Street, and its two windows served as displays of cosmetics for Bonwit's. (Employing my best balletic grace, I once leapt out of one of those cosmetics windows, landed on a sequin, skidded across the floor, and cracked an ankle. One pink sequin.)

The windows of Tiffany's are small: the display cases of a jewelry store. Only merchandise had been shown in those windows, in neat rows, with no design and no embellishment save, perhaps, a square of velvet used to set off the jewelry's sparkle. The jewelry was always taken out at night and the curtains closed. All the windows, in fact, were surrounded by heavy, pleated curtains. Before my arrival, the chore of setting up the window displays had been performed by Mary Terhune, her husband, Doc Terhune, and an assistant named Ron Prybycien.

My first act was to do away with that Victorian mustiness: I had the pleats removed from the curtains. By pushing my case long and hard with Hoving, I also got a few inches of depth added to the windows. The windows are thirty-six inches high and twenty-two inches deep; the width is five and one-half feet, but I had an adjustable frame installed in each, so the width can be reduced, the windows can be "closed down."

Early on, well before planning my first display, I made certain decisions about those windows, some any window trimmer would have made, others that were more personal. I

One of Tiffany's windows from the inside, showing the spotlights and the adjustable frame. Normally, the curtain would be closed at this stage of preparing a display, but the photographer who took the picture wanted to see the street.

saw immediately the windows had to "read" right to left; that is, window one is the window to the right of the front door on Fifth Avenue, two is next, and so on. Any running story or theme shared by all the windows would begin in window one and continue around the corner to end in window five. The two windows on Fifth Avenue and the three on Fifty-seventh Street form two groups. A story might run through all five windows, but the two major windows would always be windows one and two on Fifth Avenue, with the most important window being number two, the one on the corner. Turning the corner provided a nice intermission, a brief stroll between acts: in my form of street theater, the audience must move to make the scenes change. The three Fifty-seventh Street windows could bring a story to its conclusion, provide an explanation, or do something more—make an ironic twist, reveal an unexpected meaning. Each of the five window views has its meaning; all five together form yet another meaning, so that passersby are drawn around the building by curiosity and anticipation. From the beginning, the fifth window has required special thought, partly because it stands alone, separated from the other two windows on Fifty-seventh Street by Tiffany's side entrance. That window has always served particular purposes. To reach it, one must walk just a little bit farther, and I've always tried to make those extra steps worth the effort.

We began remodeling Tiffany's in August 1955, and the work went on until December. The work on the windows—adding those precious inches of additional depth,

December 2, 1955. A miniature room setting, including an archway and a staircase that leads to other rooms that can only be imagined. The chandelier is one of four that I bought in an antiques shop in 1956. The furniture, from Frederick Victoria, once belonged to the Cooper Union collection.

rewiring and installing new lighting, putting in the adjustable frames—had to be done early in the morning or at night to avoid interfering with the other operations in progress on the ground floor. Those five months were a lot of work, work for which I was never paid. "You make enough at Bonwit's," declared Hoving. "Well," I said, "if you feel that way." Walter Hoving was a canny businessman.

Since I was working for both Bonwit Teller and Tiffany & Co., I had two offices. At Bonwit's, my office was on the eleventh floor; at Tiffany's, it was eventually located on the seventh floor, but getting there took many years during which my office space was moved from floor to floor. At Bonwit's, I had my staff of thirteen; at Tiffany's I made do with one assistant, Ron Prybycien. Mary Terhune had taken another job in the store, Doc Terhune had become head of security, but Prybycien, twenty-one when I arrived at Tiffany's, stayed on in window display. While he was working with the Terhunes, his involvement in display had been restricted to covering wooden blocks in velvet and, around five o'clock each afternoon, removing the jewelry from the windows and then pulling the curtains closed. He soon discovered my approach to display is more active.

Since work on the store was completed in December 1955, my first Tiffany's windows were for Christmas. I'd been thinking about them since August. I had no further displays planned, just those Christmas windows. And I was scared to death. I knew what I wanted to do, but it was so different from what I'd done before, from what other people were then doing in store windows, that it frightened me. Looking back now, those windows don't seem so drastic, but the store was then being reborn, and it had fallen to me to create its new face, its new image.

I hoped for angels for windows one and two. I'd decided those windows should be religious, and I wanted to frame the main door with angels. For window one, I wanted an angel with a Christmas tree. These were to be of glass, so I went to Marianna Von Alesch, a glassblower I knew.

For the main window, window two, I wanted an angel of gold wire—a flying angel— and for that I turned to Mary Terhune, who had taken courses in jewelry and goldworking. I found a picture of the kind of angel I wanted in a book and showed it to her. She made it out of 18 carat gold wire.

July 9, 1984. Another of the four chandeliers in another imaginary setting. The reason for the display was my pleasure in finding the Parian porcelain statuettes visible through the arches.

To make window two particularly special, I wanted that flying gold angel to be carrying the Tiffany Diamond. It seemed right to show that beautiful stone in the first window displays of the reborn store. I'd been thinking of using the Tiffany Diamond since early in October. Nearly every day I'd pause by the case where it was displayed to look at it. The beauty of that single stone, its wondrous fire and glowing colors—red and green, orange and blue—fascinated me but also frightened me. I'd never handled a diamond, and that stone's beauty and value—at that time just over $500,000—unnerved me. Having agreed to let me use the diamond in the window—the store had to take out extra insurance, of course—but I knew I somehow had to overcome my fear. You can't be creative if you're afraid of your subject. That's something I learned early on as a painter.

The store had a glass replica of the diamond, and I decided that if I became familiar with the replica I'd lose my fear of the real stone. I lived with that glass replica for two months, carrying it around in my pocket everywhere I went and occasionally studying the real stone beside it. I grew accustomed to the weight and shape of the replica and eventually felt at ease with the real stone.

Trafficking in jewelry involves guards, safes with combinations, and steel boxes that lock with keys; all those soon became familiar parts of my life at Tiffany's. For jewelry destined for use in displays I had a big combination safe on the ground floor under window number two. For moving the jewelry from place to place, I had a small metal box.

When the day came to prepare the Christmas displays, I was given the Tiffany Diamond and put it and the other jewelry in the safe. That night, when I set about actually working in the windows, I took all the jewelry out of the safe and put it in the small box. As I moved from window to window I opened the box and took out that window's merchandise. When I arrived at window two, I opened the box, reached in, and, perhaps inevitably, found the Tiffany Diamond was missing. I searched the box: no diamond. I retraced my steps, looked in the other windows: no diamond. Panic. I sat down and tried to calm myself. That didn't work. I walked around again, racked my brain, tried to remember what I'd done with it. I knew I'd taken it out, had held it in my hand—and then I knew where it was. In my pocket. I'd grown so used to carrying the replica around with me that I hadn't noticed its weight.

So the diamond was there, in the hands of the angel. That gem attracted a lot of attention. Even longtime employees of Tiffany's were amazed to find they could see it clearly from way across Fifth Avenue.

The Fifth Avenue windows had their angels. The window displays around the corner on Fifty-seventh Street began with a room setting in window three—Tiffany's windows are just the right size for creating such miniature views. For window four I wanted a real sense of celebration. I took silver beads, attached them to silver chicken wire, and placed that over aluminum foil; on that silver over silver over silver I displayed a silver coffee service. The shine was wonderful.

Having made my point about Christmas, I wanted to dedicate window five to celebrating New Year's: it had to be champagne. I just happened to own a deer's head (in the same way I just happened to own twelve hummingbirds), and I stuck it through a sheet of paper—bursting in for the celebration—attached wineglasses to its horns, and set a bottle of champagne in a nearby bucket. Doing so, I unwittingly created my first tradition: since that first year, window five at Christmas has always been the "champagne window."

There was merchandise in those Christmas windows. That was my fault. I didn't want to use merchandise but thought I should, I'd been involved in merchandising so long

The first champagne window, from Christmas 1955. Once again I had to punch my fist through a sheet of paper, this time to make way for a celebratory deer's head.

at Bonwit's that I felt it was right for the store, even on Christmas. And, anyway, that "merchandise" included the Tiffany Diamond. The story goes that an eager salesman once asked Hoving what he'd get if he sold the Tiffany Diamond. Hoving's quick response was "Fired," so perhaps there was nothing on sale in at least one of those first Christmas windows.

With Tiffany's five windows added to Bonwit's sixteen, I needed ideas for displays, I needed imagination, and I needed artists. For most of my work I depended on my scribbled notes from sleepless nights, but I never had to go looking for artists. They came to me, just as they still come to me, in droves.

Yet one at a time. With few exceptions, the painters and sculptors who've made their way into my life have arrived singly, all by themselves, accompanied only by their art. Painting and sculpture are lonely pursuits, much different from the performing arts. Because of my work for the Sol Hurok agency and my passion for ballet, I've met a great many singers, actors, and dancers. They come in crowds, usually noisy and happy. You meet one dancer, and the next thing you know you've met the entire company and are immersed in their ongoing discussions of food. Even those dancers who seem to eat nothing love to talk about food. They help one another choose the right foods, for nothing goes into those bodies without study.

I don't know what painters and sculptors eat. Back when I was trying to make it as a painter I ate whatever came my way, whatever I could afford. I can remember buying rolls at Horn & Hardart's, the cheapest solid food available, and standing at the condiment table heaping on as much ketchup as those little rolls could bear. That was my dinner. Remembering those days, having lived that life—which was wonderful, even with all its real hardships—I enjoy meeting other artists, people burning with a desire to show me what they can do.

I've always paid a rental fee for any art used in my windows, and when a piece is sold out of a window, as has often happened, I don't ask for a commission. But money isn't the reason artists come to see me. From my first windows at Delman's through the sixteen years at Bonwit Teller and now thirty-five at Tiffany's I've always given artists credit. I was the first display director to do so regularly, and the knowledge that their name would appear on a credit card—a slip of paper—in the window next to their art has drawn the artists to me. I'm constantly commissioning artists to make me specific objects for use in windows I've planned, but I also ask artists to bring me their "serious" art. At Bonwit's, particularly during the late 1950s, I turned the windows into a modern art gallery, with works by as many as ten artists displayed in the windows alongside mannequins dressed in merchandise. Everyone benefited from my use of those credit cards: the artists got a free showing of their work, I got free decorations for my windows, and the store achieved a reputation for being avant-garde, for having truly modern taste.

Knowing and working with artists is always great fun, and I believe showing the public what's being done is important. Not everyone has the time or desire to visit the city's galleries and museums, but just about everyone—sometimes I think everyone in the world—eventually turns the corner at Fifth Avenue and Fifty-seventh Street.

The flow of artists to my door has been steady, and although I eventually use only one or two out of five hundred, I don't turn anyone away and agree to meet with every artist who calls. At least, every artist who doesn't have a gallery; those who do don't need me. From the beginning at Tiffany's, I've used paintings, tapestries, and fabrics as backgrounds for displays, but I usually prefer three-dimensional objects—sculpture, bas-relief, découpage, and found objects—since they lend themselves better to lighting, and lighting is always more than 50 percent of the total effect.

Oil paint and brushes, marble and chisels only begin the gamut of painting and sculpture. Painters paint on any and all surfaces and do so with anything whose passing will leave color; sculptors shape forms using fruit and paper, plastic and Duco cement. I never know what to expect when yet another unknown artist comes in my door. Some smell of chemicals, of their cramped workshops set up in garages out on Long Island or way over in some Pennsylvania woodland. Some have smudged and stained fingers. Clean fingernails are hard in the arts. There were years, particularly when I first began at Tiffany's, when the artists who stepped off the elevator to visit me really did wear hiking boots and goose-down jackets and lived in airy lofts down in SoHo. That was as close as we've come to having a uniform for artists. Some, of course, show up poorly dressed, but others are so well put together I want to ask the name of their tailor. Male and female, teenagers and old enough to be grandparents, they arrive toting cardboard boxes or black portfolios. Some are aggressively sure of themselves, others are like fidgety schoolchildren, staring down at their shoes or past me at some book on the shelf, or out the window at Fifth Avenue, where they'd much rather be, lost again in the crowd, not facing possible rejection. They come in, we say hello, I ask them what they do, and they reach for their boxes, zip open their black portfolios. Almost all of them say, "I'm an artist," and by now I understand what they hope me to know by those words.

They don't always claim to be artists. When James Rosenquist first came to see me, and I asked him what he did, he said, "I'm a billboard painter." "Great," I said, "let's see what you've got." He'd brought along photographs of his work, signs and billboards he'd done on Broadway. Great stuff. I wanted him for Bonwit's—nothing he did would ever have fit the windows at Tiffany's. We decided on big heads of silent movie stars, those ancient "queens," on no-seam paper eight feet wide and ten feet high. He did them in black, white, and gray, and they were sensational. Some of his later work still shows signs of those early billboards, paintings so vast they become somehow abstract. (I later learned he was from Grand Forks, North Dakota—someone else born in the wrong place.)

Judith Brown came to see me in my office at Bonwit's sometime in 1956. "What do you do?" I asked her. "I'm a welder," she said. I loved that. "Great," I said, "let's see what you've got." She showed me. She really is a welder, and a wonderful one, capable of bending metal—often pieces of scrapped automobiles—into squiggly sculptures of city skylines, families, faces, even the Three Wise Men. I first used works by Judith Brown at Bonwit's; she made her first appearance in Tiffany's windows—two angels and a reindeer head—for Christmas 1956. In May 1957 I gave her a one-woman show in the eight Fifth Avenue windows of Bonwit's.

November 9, 1956. Still lifes recreated with the help of Robert Rauschenberg and Jasper Johns. There is merchandise in each window, calmly inserted into those scenes of absolute silence.

Andy Warhol was reasonably well known by the time he came to see me, although he was still being called Raggedy Andy, not because his work was sloppy, but because of his appearance. He'd had success with book-jacket designs for such publishers as New Directions and with his drawings and paintings for I. Miller shoe ads—and I knew I. Miller—but stories about his mishaps were making the rounds. When he'd zipped open his portfolio to show his work to the art director at *Harper's Bazaar*, a cockroach had crawled out. Poor boy, that Raggedy Andy. But *Harper's* had given him assignments. He won awards for his work, for his "commercial" art, and he never pretended a difference between what he did to survive and what he called his art. To his credit, I think it was all the same to him. He was a very busy young man.

I used Warhol's art in several of my perfume windows at Bonwit's. In July 1955, just before my work began at Tiffany's, I made some wooden fences, and he covered them with graffiti for a series of windows. They were fun, full of a childish playfulness.

Robert Rauschenberg and Jasper Johns called themselves artists but were unknown when they first came to see me. Rauschenberg came first. He'd been down to Black Mountain College in South Carolina, had heard about me, and came up to my office at Bonwit's. He'd been doing work with enormous sheets of blueprint paper. He'd take these sheets and lay all sorts of things on them, flowers and ferns, sometimes a body. I used them in the windows at Bonwit's.

I liked Rauschenberg. He was very boyish and open and seemed crazy, like me, maybe even a bit more. During the period Rauschenberg was contributing to the displays at Bonwit's, he met Jasper Johns. They became friends and shared a loft downtown. Johns was less outgoing than Rauschenberg, but I recognized fragments of my own past in his story. He was from the South, born in Augusta, Georgia, and raised in Allendale, South Carolina. His parents had divorced, and he'd been raised by relatives. In the warm monotony of that quiet southern town, he'd decided to become an artist. There were no artists or art near there, so he'd left, come north to New York. When he met Rauschenberg he was working in a bookstore, but Rauschenberg taught him how to live

the way I'd lived back in the days of the *Southern Cross* and the Guaranty Trust—paint until the money runs out and then find temporary work.

During the same period of the 1950s Rosenquist and Warhol, Rauschenberg and Johns—the artists who shortly gave birth to the Pop movement—worked with me, most of all at Bonwit's. The first showings of Johns's paintings were in exhibitions I organized at Bonwit's. I'd ask him for a painting, he'd bring one up to the store, and I'd put it in one of the windows. He was then doing lots of flags and targets; in 1957 I showed *Flag on Orange Field* in a Bonwit's window. Sometimes Rauschenberg and Johns helped put together displays. They worked on a popular set of Bonwit's windows that had house painters up on ladders spilling paint down onto mannequins wearing coats, the colors of the paints matching those of the coats.

For Tiffany's, Rauschenberg and Johns served as a kind of display house. I'd tell them what I wanted, and they'd go off and make it. I never knew which of them did what, they worked so closely together, even sharing the same joint pseudonym, Matson Jones, which I think they made up from their mothers' maiden names. They started using that name when they began to get recognition as artists—they didn't want their commercial work confused with what they considered their real art.

Commercial art: the problem, of course, is the merchandise in the windows. At Bonwit's, the weekly selection of the merchandise to be displayed involved the fashion market, visits to showrooms with designers, discussions with buyers, the merchandising manager, and department heads, lots of talk, lots of planning. All this was necessary because at Bonwit's I was actually selling something; at Tiffany's, I'm not selling anything, at least not consciously. The selection of the merchandise to display at Tiffany's takes place in relative silence. On the day before the displays are to be installed, I walk alone through the store, up and down the aisles, looking for items that might fit with what I have planned. It's a well-stocked store, and I've never had problems selecting merchandise to work with my windows.

During my first years at Tiffany's I used more merchandise in the windows than I do today, reflecting, I imagine, my years at I. Miller, Delman's, and Bonwit's, and those early windows displayed some of the changes Hoving and his new designers were effecting in the store. There were ladies' handbags in some of the first windows, but they disappeared when Hoving decided to stop selling them (they have recently returned). When the store introduced its new vermeil, I used several pieces in the windows, and when the stationery department came up with a new type font, called The Hamilton, I designed a window around it. The experience of teaching manners to his children, Tom and Petra, led Hoving to write a book on etiquette, *Tiffany's Table Manners for Teen-Agers* (with such pointers as "You don't have to wait for your hostess to start eating, but don't leap at your food like an Irish wolfhound"). Out of my own politeness, I placed a copy of the book in a few windows.

I never planned the windows far in advance during my first years. Because of my work at Bonwit's—I was still changing those sixteen windows every week—I didn't have time to plan and prepare, but I also didn't really need to. I was full of ideas, there were so many things I had longed to do in windows, and each year in New York City offers an endless variety of subjects for window displays, some predictable, some absolutely unforeseeable.

There are the seasons, seasonal chores and seasonal woes. Spring-planting windows have long been one of my favorites, and when winter snow is blowing up and down the avenue I like to do windows with beach sand and seashells or other warming views just to remind shivering pedestrians with their collars turned up that this, too, will pass. Summer heat waves call for windows full of snow, or at least pitchers full of cool lemonade. Using the weather is an old trick. One November back in the early 1930s, when Lord & Taylor found itself facing sluggish coat sales, Dana O'Clare piled bleached cornflakes in a window to suggest snow—no merchandise, just the warning of the cold to come. It worked—coat sales went up 50 percent. At Tiffany's, my aim is different. I'm trying to bring relief to New Yorkers, and some years they've really needed it.

July 8, 1976. I knew this would work, had even done it before: the curved surfaces of the glasses and the water magnify the shells. Simple and clear, but people still came in to ask how I'd managed to squeeze those big shells into those little glasses.

Then there are the holidays. Christmas, Easter, and Valentine's Day are my favorites. Thanksgiving has received less attention, perhaps because I'm from the South, but I've done Thanksgiving windows and Halloween windows, too. A New York year also includes such planned events as the opening of Philharmonic Hall, Opera Week, and Broadway plays. Displays related to such events can be thought out ahead, but the city has thrown me topics that have called for quick thinking: you never know what news the morning paper will bring—or even if there'll be a morning paper. Even without newspapers, the windows at Tiffany's are always open with their special form of journalism. I consider myself a kind of reporter, for in my windows I report on events of the city.

Since I usually change the windows at Tiffany's every two weeks—only the Christmas windows and occasional late summer windows stay in longer—my office soon became, and has since remained, full of art brought in by artists, items picked up during travels (I took my first trip to Italy in 1951) or bought in five-and-dime stores (among the best places to shop for ideas), and props being made for future windows. Such "things" have always arrived before the idea or design. They sit in my office, and I play with them, look at them, think about them. Each time, of course, I have to come up with five variations on a theme. Four are usually easy to come by once the ideas start flowing. The quintessential takes a bit longer.

That my first Christmas windows were well received—six policemen had been called over to handle the crowds lining up in front of them—did nothing to calm my nerves. In addition to my work at Bonwit's, I found myself running a kind of show over at Tiffany's, and although I'd been doing display work for years, I suffered opening-night jitters with each new set of windows. I got—and still get—butterflies regularly, every other week. I believe that in this business, as in show business, you're only as good as your last performance. And people began to expect things of me: those six policemen became a Christmas tradition.

I followed the Christmas displays with a set of windows using architectural

December 30, 1955. Although modeled on a French engraving, this beaverboard staircase doesn't exist anywhere. In Tiffany's window it competes with the jewelry in a contest of dimensions.

April 20, 1956. The displays based on Palladio. I bought the five kinds of capital in different antiques shops over the years and made the columns myself.

structures, a miniature staircase, a gazebo, the quiet corner of a tiny garden. I laid a jeweled necklace along the staircase. I love to play such tricks with scale, to manipulate the viewer's perception of reality. Placing rare gems and metals in a disjointed context somehow underlines their exceptional quality. Lying helpless in a jewelry case, such a necklace is only a costly decoration, but located where it should never appear—on a flight of elegant stairs in some other world—it comes alive, seems almost impossibly complicated and beautiful, seems, in fact, to be something else entirely.

I was using merchandise, of course, but it wasn't always easy to find it. In one of that set's windows I used a pair of candlesticks as columns for a building, and not everyone spotted the merchandise. Spotting the merchandise in Tiffany's windows soon became a window-shopper's sport. Jewelry is particularly well suited to this game, but other kinds of merchandise, such as watches, bowls, glassware, and plates, work just as well. Placed in a carefree or unexpected way, merchandise can fit in so well it disappears, making the viewer, who knows the merchandise has to be there somewhere, look for it and happily discover it, rather than see it immediately.

For the next set of windows I borrowed stuffed animals from the American Museum of Natural History. I went up to the museum myself and chose them: a parrot, black panther, birds, even a monkey. There were real orchids planted and growing in those windows, and for each animal I created a world that filled the window. The monkey's leafy forest—he was happily hanging from a branch—was quite believable, at least for him. The presence of Tiffany's merchandise in that far-off land was far less congruous and thus delightfully provocative.

The plants in those windows needed daily watering, a chore that usually fell to Ron Prybycien. Just before ten o'clock each morning, with the usual crowd of people waiting

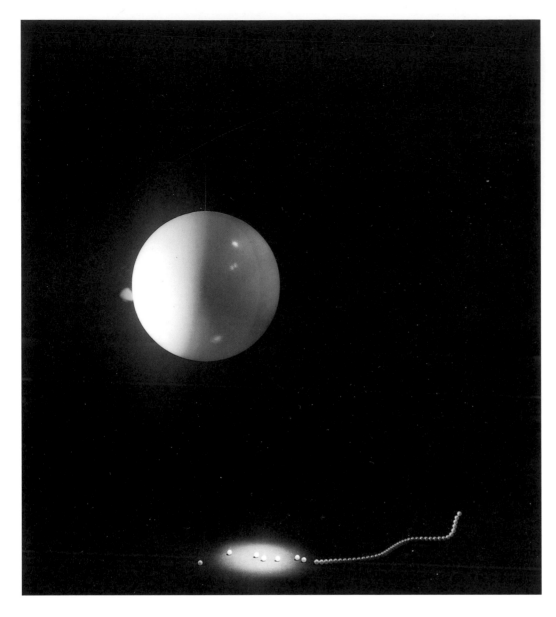

February 13, 1956. An instance of necessary destruction. The wooden ball, circle of light created by a single spotlight, and string of pearls had no feeling together. Breaking the string and slightly suspending the end brought in movement, and with it life.

outside for the store to open, he'd pull away the back wall of each window and go to work with his watering can. His activities would attract attention—you can't do anything in a store window without drawing onlookers—and when he got to the window with the panther he'd water the plants and then pat the big cat's head. Children loved it.

Then came Valentine's Day. For that first Valentine's Day I found some old Victorian valentines and copied them—frilly carriages. I had large geometric forms planned for my next displays, an idea from Euclid, from my old days loving geometry. I had those big shapes floating in the air. One was a white sphere, and I knew it called for pearls—real pearls, not cultured—but I saw something was wrong as soon as I'd laid the pearls out beneath the sphere. There was no life in all those white orbs. So I broke the string and let seven of those little pearls roll off. I also suspended the far end of the pearls in the air a bit. People commented on the broken strand of pearls. I suppose I was treating valuable merchandise like a prop, but breaking that strand was the only way to bring life to the display.

I've always liked the paintings of William Harnett, famous for his trompe l'oeil still lifes, and I turned to him for my next windows, attaching a mixture of merchandise and found objects to wooden planks. I stained the planks and rubbed them to dull them, and when I'd set up the lighting I got in the windows, crouched in front of those planks, and painted the shadows darker. You had to study those windows closely to determine which of the items were merchandise and which just old things I had lying around. I managed to get in some cowbells. I love cowbells.

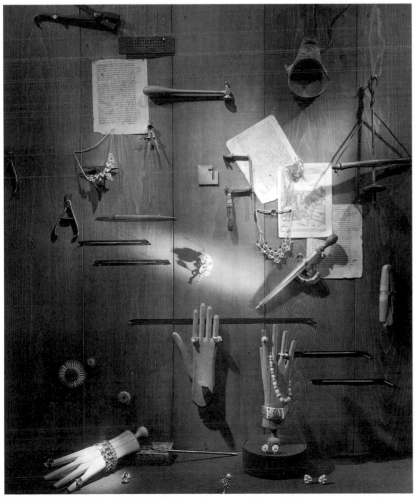

March 1, 1956. William Harnett in Tiffany's windows. Mixed in with the various objects are items of merchandise. The passerby can probably identify the merchandise, but has to look hard to do so—and getting someone to look hard at a window is what every window trimmer wants.

And then it was Easter. Easter is eggs, and I love eggs, each one perfect, each one a symbol of a new beginning. I also love butterflies and had a mobile of moving butterflies in one of those first Easter windows. Colored eggs are popular with children at Easter, and I had some in one of those displays, but I later banished colored eggs from my Easter windows. No true egg needs paint.

I managed to defy gravity in one of those first Easter windows by creating a basket with eggs piled one upon the next far beyond the usual bounds of physical laws. I did it by blowing out the insides of eggs and gluing the empty shells to a form. Such baskets have appeared in many other Easter windows, and blowing eggs has become such an Easter necessity that I sometimes dread that holiday's approach.

The next windows seemed simple enough: I covered all of each window with a plaster wall etched with floral designs; there were small holes in the walls, with a magnifying or reducing glass attached over each hole. When you looked through the glasses you saw something enlarged or reduced: a tea set was made tiny; an opal pendant glowed fantastically enormous. Perhaps because people had to line up to see through the magnifying glasses, the windows attracted crowds. One radio commentator—I think it was Dorothy Killgallen—reported on her daily show that 10,000 people were lining up each day, but I didn't see anyone out there counting.

The next set of five windows was based on the Italian Renaissance architect Andrea Palladio. I'd come across two old books of engravings of his works, and took some of those engravings and had them blown up, then cut out the front and back sections and set them up in the windows slightly apart to create depth. Since Palladio put statues on top of his buildings I hunted through junk stores and antique shops to find little figures. One of the

June 8, 1956. Since the windows have no real depth—only 22 inches—the creation of depth is a constant struggle. The distance between each of these sheets of torn paper is very slight, but the overall effect seems otherwise.

books showed different kinds of capitals—Corinthian, Doric, Ionic—so I made them out of wood and placed merchandise on top of them.

By then it was spring, so I filled a set of windows with flowers. The end of May called for wedding windows, and for those I had suspended hands performing suitable movements. From windows one to five the hands were slipping on an engagement ring, slipping on a wedding ring (the merchandise being the rings), cutting a cake (a real cake—its thick icing survived the lights—being cut with a Tiffany's cake knife), giving a toast (stemware), and writing thank-you letters (stationery). During my first year of windows, using stationery in window five became a kind of tradition, although it's one with which I often break.

For my next set of windows I created depth by using several layers of paper with an opening torn through each. You looked at the merchandise through the layers of torn paper. I used four sheets of paper, each mounted on a frame. I'd set a frame in the window and then tear it, put in another frame and tear it, and so on.

The weather was warm that June, and I knew the people looking in the windows were as uncomfortable as I was: a good time for ice. I did a set with candelabras standing amid icicles made of pointy shards of mirrors—I loved smashing those mirrors—jewels on ragged blocks of ice, deer in a cool forest covered with cobwebs. I rented a special cobweb-making machine for that one—it blew something like rubber cement to make cobwebs.

For the next windows I used painted cardboard sculptures of fish by Jonah Kinigstein, an artist who was a particularly good painter. Among the pieces for this series were two large lobsters, which I hung in a window in front of two suspended silver platters. But something was missing, the window felt cold, lifeless. So I ran out to a store, bought a lemon, and put it on the floor of the window. That did it—it added the necessary balance to bring the display to life. The lone lemon also marked my first use of fresh fruit in Tiffany's windows. (Other works by Kinigstein have appeared over the years in Tiffany's windows as well as in those of Bonwit's, where I gave him a one-man show in May 1957.)

Following Kinigstein's fish sculptures, I did a set using some old rope I'd found. This was special rope, with wire inside it, made to attach a glider to a tow plane. I had no idea of what to do with it when I bought it, but then I found an old book on knots. Ron Prybycien did the real work, struggling with that tough rope to make wonderful big coils and knots.

Rauschenberg and Johns made their Tiffany's debut in my next set of windows. I'd asked them to make caves. Caves are fantastic: you can feel more solitude in a cave than almost anywhere else. I was remembering a movie I'd seen years ago in Birmingham, a 1916 film called *A Daughter of the Gods*. It starred Annette Kellerman—she was known as "the Diving Venus"—and it was set in Bermuda caves. I fell in love with those caves, the shadows and glimmering water, and thought of them often. Since I believe in looking up old loves I went down to Bermuda in 1938 to visit the caves where the film was made.

Rauschenberg and Johns made me five caves of plaster with embedded cast leaves: a cave of ice, of solid stone, of black coal, wonderfully dark caves in which I placed pieces of jewelry—imagine finding a jewel in a cave—that shone with all their might against those eerie backgrounds.

Ron Prybycien made me a peacock out of wire for the next set of windows, and we used peacock feathers as background. I'd bought some clear plastic tubing, a good pile of it, not because it was inexpensive (it hardly cost anything), but because I thought I might someday find a use for it. I used it to create five windows right after the peacock set. After playing around with those tubes, cutting them up in various ways, I managed to create sculpture with them, forms full of reflected light.

The next windows featured Tiffany's vermeil, but I got tired of them after only a week and replaced them with a display of handbags set up in front of geometric shapes. By then it was November, and I turned to Rauschenberg and Johns again. I'd found an old book on seventeenth-century still lifes and decided to recreate those paintings in what I called dimensional paintings: accurately recreate them in three dimensions. I asked them to cast a pomegranate, a cantaloupe, a lemon, a cabbage and then paint them to look as

Opposite: *July 19, 1956. Jonah Kinigstein made these lobsters
to order. I measured the trays—they're merchandise—and
told him how big I wanted the lobsters. The lemon came
last. It was the right color and shape, and, anyway, the
lobsters needed it.* Above: *November 18, 1987. Still life with
a bowl of real lemons from a series of windows celebrating
Thanksgiving.*

real as possible. I wanted those objects to have a true painterly quality. For the cabbage they made each leaf separately and then put them together. With autumnal light and an ageless stillness, those windows worked wonderfully.

The end of November 1956, time for Christmas windows and for the welder Judith Brown. Her angels appeared in one window, the reindeer head in another. In the third window I used a balsa-wood reproduction of Notre Dame by Jordan Steckel, a sculptor who did work for me at both Bonwit's and Tiffany's, and called on Rauschenberg and Johns to make me a forest for the fourth. The forest was full of icy trees, dark and menacing. They made the ice using Duco cement, which looks like ice when it dries. There in that forest I set up an orchestra of gold and enameled monkeys standing on stumps playing their instruments. I painted the backdrop sky myself—dark and kind of spooky.

In the last window I had an articulated wooden artist's model riding a suitable mount—an articulated wooden artist's model of a horse—through a wreath. Tiffany's windows are simply too small for mannequins, and over the years I've turned again and again to those little wooden models, the only human forms, along with dolls and disembodied hands, capable of surviving in those confined spaces.

Those were Tiffany's windows for 1956: twenty-two sets, five windows each, 110 window displays. Hoving hadn't given me a budget; I imagine he feared that if he gave me one I might actually spend money. I had, in fact, spent very little. I'd spent no money and made no sketches beforehand. I've always felt that if you work from sketches, you're inclined to follow the sketch rather than allow things to happen as you work—which is much more important. I never know a window's final form until I'm right there, putting it together. Usually, after working hard on a display idea up in my office, when I go down to the window the whole thing becomes something else. It just doesn't work as planned. Somehow the space is different, and space is one of the primary things I work with—objects in space, the shape of objects in space, and the shape objects make out of the space around them. I planned all the windows only in my head, and those windows were mixed up with my plans for the windows at Bonwit's.

During this time, months—sometimes two or three—would go by in which I wouldn't see Hoving. When I did run into him he usually complimented me on my current windows, chatted a bit about Tiffany's, and then almost invariably said, "Gene, I don't see why you have to do Bonwit's windows as well as Tiffany's." He wanted me away from Bonwit's, wanted me over at Tiffany's exclusively.

I'd say, "Because I'm not through yet."

"What do you mean?"

"I just haven't done all that I want to do over there yet. When I have, I'll quit and be here completely." I still had too many plans for Bonwit's windows to consider leaving. It was a lot of work, I was forever charging up or down the short stretch of Fifth Avenue between the two stores, but I was content, and each idea touched off another.

Those who know me might have guessed my first windows for 1957. As soon as Christmas is over, as soon as January begins, I'm already weary of the cold and looking forward to summertime warmth. My first windows for 1957 were of seashells in beach sand and cool lemonade in tall glasses.

For a Bonwit's display that year, Jordan Steckel created large, op art backdrops of swirling geometric designs. For a set of Tiffany's windows that March I asked him for some geometric forms made of thin strips of balsa wood, thinner even than matchsticks. For one of them I wanted to show a pitcher pouring water. I told him the length of the stream of water, and the water he made of those wooden strips looked like joined crystals tumbling into the glass. The larger forms were extremely awkward and fragile, and while hanging one in a window I dropped it. One edge broke. Ron Prybycien reached over toward the broken pieces, but I told him, "No, leave it alone," for it was even more beautiful broken, nothing could have made it look more delicate. When he saw it, Steckel agreed: "It looks better than it did before."

March 1, 1957. Jordan Steckel made the pouring water for me out of thin strips of balsa wood. I told him the length I wanted and showed him the glass and pitcher so he could match the design.

May 8, 1957. The original thought was just of a diamond necklace inside an egg. Thoughts of eggs led me to the frying pan, but an ordinary frying pan didn't seem right for cooking up diamonds, and that led me straight to the hibachi. Pure logic.

The next month I used musical instruments suspended in the air with jewels around them to indicate their sounds, spreading out conelike into the air from the mouth of a saxophone, bouncing in the air over a drum. I painted the instruments white, for doing so moved them into fantasy, made them symbolic forms instead of everyday instruments.

In 1957 Ron Prybycien was drafted into the army. During the two years he was gone, Ron McNamer, who had been working in my display department at Bonwit's, took his place, so Tiffany's display department still had its Ron.

For Easter that year I had suspended hands breaking an egg into a frying pan (painted white, of course) standing in grass (real, of course). The shiny liquid pouring down from the broken egg into the pan was a diamond necklace. That necklace made a nice, viscous stream of liquid; people had to look twice to recognize it. I joked that this was the "Cook yourself an omelet, honey, or fry yourself an egg, so long as you get a diamond out of it" window. For another window I had a rabbit pulling a bracelet out of a hat. The rabbit was made by Jeanne Owens, a beautiful woman who also did work for me at Bonwit's. She'd been an Olympic swimmer together with Esther Williams and could do anything. Far more somber was a window in which I gave in to a personal request from Hoving: a white porcelain statue of Christ being taken down from the cross. Always religious, Hoving seemed to become only more so with each passing year.

The city itself suggested my next set of windows. Manhattan was then experiencing a construction boom. It had begun in 1955 when the Third Avenue Elevated Train—the famous "El"—was torn down, leading to a flurry of activity along Third Avenue and the Upper East Side. In 1957, sixteen new office buildings went up, including the thirty-eight-story Tishman Building at 666 Fifth Avenue, between Fifty-second and Fifty-third streets. Later, when work was finished on the Seagram Building, people ridiculed the Tishman as the crate in which the Seagram Building had been delivered. Such buildings were going up throughout my neighborhood. It seemed that every corner I turned led me past another construction site, deep holes in the ground stuck with steel girders.

I went over to F.A.O. Schwarz and bought myself a toy dump truck and steam shovel. And I got some dirt. I've heard people say diamonds are forever, but I think it's dirt. Dirt is forever. In one window I had the dump truck in the middle of piles of dirt about to add another pile; it was dumping a load of dirt, and—as I pointed out with a baby spotlight—resting on top of that dirt was a diamond necklace. In the matching Fifth Avenue window I had the steam shovel in the midst of its own dirt, lifting another piece of precious jewelry out of the ground. The remaining three windows continued the building theme: one had children's wooden blocks forming a walled villa decorated with more jewelry, another had cinderblocks supporting glassware, and the last had bricks with silverware. Once again my ballet training paid off: stepping out of that window I managed to kick over all the bricks and had to set them up again.

Those windows were popular. People were surprised and delighted to see expensive jewels treated without the usual respect. During this period Dorothy Killgallen complimented me in her column in the *Journal-American*, stating that "The best show in town is *My Fair Lady*, the best drama Eugene O'Neill's *Long Day's Journey into Night*. The best movie is *Funny Face* at the Music Hall. The best baked beans are at the

May 15, 1957. When they put up another skyscraper they first dig a big hole in the ground, and perhaps it really isn't so farfetched to imagine digging up diamonds in Manhattan dirt.

Left: *July 20, 1957. For this window I asked Robert Rauschenberg and Jasper Johns to make me a country road with telephone poles. I painted the sky to create the atmosphere. A car's just about to come by and run right over those jewels: you can almost hear it in the distance.* Opposite: *July 26, 1957. "Ice on Ice." The tongs are real: I got them from an ice house and then painted them white. It's an emerald-cut diamond, and the block of ice is plastic.*

Automat, the best roast beef is at El Morocco on Sunday night, and the best shop windows are Bonwit Teller's and Tiffany's."

But someone always complains. A representative of the De Beers Syndicate, the group that controls the diamond market, called to register a complaint about my treatment of those precious stones. Diamonds, he told me, were not made to be put in dirt. "Where do you think they come from?" I asked him. And, anyway, they're washable.

June came with sunny skies, and for some people such weather means sports. The five I chose were baseball, golf, fishing—I love fishing—badminton, and archery. The merchandise was particularly difficult to spot in the archery window. In a display with a bow and arrow, the only thing for sale was the tip of the arrow, an arrowhead that was in reality a jewelry pin. Following those first sports windows I got back to the business of putting diamonds in dirt.

I'd asked Johns and Rauschenberg to make me some outdoor scenes. I said, "Make me a swamp, a ravine, a wishing well, a rock, and a highway." I had some somber scenes in mind and painted dark skies as backgrounds. One window had trees growing out of a swamp. Another had a broken bridge jutting over a ravine. I used real water in these windows, with a circulating pump to keep it moving slightly. The well was by a tree, one of Matson Jones's famous bare trees. They made the rock out of painted papier-mâché, and I set it on real dirt. The highway, divided by a white line, was bordered by telephone poles—a lonely stretch of road in the middle of nowhere.

There was jewelry in all five windows, casually tossed in the swamp, dangling precariously in the air off the bridge over the ravine, dangerously near the well, atop the rock, and laid across the highway. Not the safest of places for expensive trinkets, not the kind of scenes associated with Tiffany's jewels. But diamonds look beautiful in dirt.

One of the windows of my next set was, I sometimes think, my best ever. I'd been reading a mystery novel, something about crime, and it reminded me of the underworld slang for diamonds: ice. All the windows were cold, for this was in the middle of July. In one of the windows, a fan blew over jewelry spread out so that the strings of stones formed the outlines of a cool breeze. Another had ice trays, and in one were lemons and ice and glasses with a pitcher under a beach awning. But the best was window two: an enormous block of ice (made of plastic) with ice tongs painted white resting against it and holding a diamond. Ice on ice: a simple, clear idea.

I used Rauschenberg and Johns for the next windows. They made forms like webs, and the jewelry placed on them almost took on the shape of insects. In one window the web became a trampoline, with the jewelry bouncing in the air over it.

Backdrops of old pictures of the constellations served in my next windows. I had nothing particular in mind, just wanted to use those pretty pictures of the stars and planets. I put a telescope in one, pointing up to outer space. I soon found myself accused of being prophetic: a few days after the windows went in, the Soviets sent up Sputnik I.

For the next windows, autumn windows, Rauschenberg and Johns made me plaster casts of leaves. I had them falling gently through the windows, each falling leaf carrying a jewel, or swept into piles, with jewelry swept in, too. In one, the falling leaves had

Left: *October 25, 1957. Coals glow in ashes and so do Schlumberger rubies. It's a real country stove, just the right size for the window.* Opposite: *September 18, 1957. I curved these photographs of old astrological prints to add dimension and give a better sense of sky. I had no intention of making Sputnik's roadmap.*

knocked over a glass, or at least that's what I'd intended. People wanted to know why the glass was on its side. I told them people fall over, why not a glass?

Late that October the city was hit with a cold spell, and I wanted something hot to warm everyone up. That called for a stove, a nice old-fashioned potbellied stove. The stove's door was open, a suspended hand was shoveling out some ashes, and bursting out of the open stove were nice hot rubies. Other jewels were mixed in the ashes. In window five on Fifty-seventh Street—the traditional stationery window—I had a roaring fireplace. There were letters in the flames, the typed words getting lost in the ashes. People stood still and looked hard in that window: any letter worth burning is sure to be interesting.

There was heat of another sort in my Christmas windows that year. I'd been to Italy again in the summer, had visited and loved Venice, and so I asked Jordan Steckel to create

Above left: From *Valentine's Day 1964, "Love and the Doctor."* Above right: *The sense of smell from March 3, 1958.*

a model of St. Mark's in balsa wood. I made it a winter scene, with snow made of salt mixed with ground glass to make it sparkle, and suspended the Tiffany Diamond in the air in front of that beautiful building. In another window I had a scene with a Madonna and a candle. That was the heat: the flame on that candle was real. I placed it between two sheets of plate glass, and the floor was covered with the salt-glass snow, so nothing could have happened even had it fallen over. No one noticed how realistically that flame flickered. Everyone assumed it was fake. In spite of cold rain and a brief subway strike, those windows drew the usual Christmas crowds. Perhaps it was just the chance to see that diamond. Handling that big bright stone still made me a little nervous—I was afraid I'd drop it, but I suppose it really wouldn't have shattered the way I feared.

I celebrated New Year's that year with Rosalind Russell and her husband, the producer Freddie Brisson. They were in New York because she was performing onstage in *Auntie Mame*, and Freddie, being a Dane, was cooking a goose. I was in the kitchen, helping him tend to his goose, and he asked, "Gene, how'd you like to work in the movies? Rosalind wants you to do the set decorations for the film of *Auntie Mame*."

I thought he was kidding and was overjoyed to find he wasn't. Rosalind was delighted when I said yes and told me someone from Warner Brothers would be getting in touch with me. Someone did, and I soon found myself involved in genuine Hollywood haggling. Following meetings with lawyers, long-distance phone calls, and terse telegrams, the deal was made. I was going to Hollywood to design a film. All I needed was Hoving's permission for a leave of absence.

"Sorry, you can't go," he said. "You're too important to Bonwit's and Tiffany's." I

asked him again, used more than once the word *please*. "Please let me go design this film. It's something I've always wanted to do."

"You don't want to design for the movies, Gene," he said. "That's no good for you."

Regardless of Hoving, I could have gone. Everyone, with Ron Prybycien first in line, told me I should just leave Tiffany's and go. But I stayed. Loyalty to the store, to the artists, to this city and my oldest dreams—I can't name one reason, but I said no to Rosalind and *Auntie Mame*. (For several years she refused to speak to me. Then I ran into Rosalind and Freddie in a restaurant. They were seated together, and perhaps she hoped I hadn't spotted them, but Freddie turned to her and said, "Don't you think it's about time you forgave Gene? It wasn't his fault." And she said, "Well, all right," and smiled at me. And then she kissed me and asked, "How are you?")

Above left: *The cat's cradle of May 15, 1958.* Above right: *Writing thank-you cards for a June wedding, from May 25, 1956.*

For Valentine's Day 1958 I played with puzzles. I blew up old engravings, scored them like jigsaw puzzles, and then removed sections. I laid out the missing sections in front of each puzzle and filled the hole in the puzzle with jewelry. Such displays involve passersby in a kind of active looking. They recognize the game, see a piece of the puzzle is missing, and look for it. Then, checking to see how the piece will fit into the puzzle, they discover the merchandise.

In March I did a series of windows using sculptural forms dedicated to the five senses: a nose in the air sniffing a floral pin for smell, an eye with a diamond ring for sight, an ear with earrings for hearing, a mouth with a wineglass for taste, and hands with flatware for touch.

The idea of using real grass in window displays dates back to the cosmetics windows for I did for Lenthéric, and by 1958 using real grass in Tiffany's windows, especially at Easter, had become a tradition. Every year, around the end of February, I have fresh grass seed planted in trays for Easter. Grass and clover. As soon as the trays are placed in the windows the heat, moisture, and lights make the grass flourish, and I have to lean into the windows each day and use scissors to trim it back.

In the 1958 Easter windows hands were pulling long necklaces up out of dishes full of colored egg dye: diamonds drawn from clear water, rubies from red, sapphires from blue. The three dishes were set out on the grass. Another window had an Easter bunny, made by Jeanne Owens, painting an egg resting on an easel. By then, the appearance in one of my Easter windows of a Bible (every year New York's Bible Society loans me the book) open to the end of Matthew had become traditional. It pleased Hoving.

Hoving pleased me by saving the life of a mouse that appeared in one of those Easter windows. Some people claimed he was a field mouse, but I thought him normal, just British—it seemed to me he squeaked with a British accent. I thought perhaps he'd come over from England in a barrel of china. Regardless of how he arrived at Tiffany's, he set up home in window one and began to make regular appearances, more like performances, four times a day. Dorothy Killgallen wrote about him in her column, and people crowded in front of that window to catch sight of the little mouse—they'd wait patiently for him to appear. He'd come out, stand on his hind legs, and eat clover. He wouldn't touch common grass. A very pretty mouse and obviously well bred, he delighted his every audience.

"You know you have a mouse in the window," nearly screamed the store manager, a man capable of amazing rage. "I'm going to set a trap." When the manager ignored my entreaties, I took this life-and-death matter upstairs to Hoving.

"He'll set no trap," pronounced Hoving without hesitation. Window one's mouse made his performances for the remainder of that display's two-week run and then disappeared.

I was very fond of suspended hands during that period, and in May I busied hands in all five windows with knitting, crocheting, embroidering. I needed help with those windows—I don't know how to crochet, knit, or embroider—and had to ask Sonny Hawkins (he'd left Delman's to become one of my assistants at Bonwit's) to stop by the store. He crocheted a form similar to the necklace I wanted to show in the window. The most difficult window had hands working a cat's cradle, so wonderfully complicated and, for me at least, so impossible to remember how to do. Hawkins knew how to make a cat's cradle, and for the duration of the display I actually knew how to do it, too. A few weeks later, of course, I'd forgotten.

Those windows were followed by a set with more sculptures by Judith Brown. Then it was June again, time for more sports—horseshoes, bowling, croquet, baseball, scuba. These were followed in July by some paper images of personified weather elements—the faces of wind, clouds, lightning, fog. After I set up those displays I took off for my summer vacation.

I came back in August. Early one Sunday morning, the last day of my vacation, I was fast asleep in bed when the phone rang. It was one of the guards at Tiffany's. "You better get over here right away!" he yelled into my ear. "A burglar broke in!" Perhaps I was just too sleepy—this was about 6:30—or perhaps I was just revealing my true concerns, but all I could think to ask was "Did they wreck my display?"

They had, or at least they'd wrecked the windows and removed the merchandise. Two men had driven up, climbed out of their car carrying sledge hammers, walked over to windows one and two, and swung away with those hammers at the thick, reputedly shatterproof glass. They shattered enough to make two wide holes, reached in, and grabbed about $163,000 worth of jewelry. The guards inside the store heard not a sound, and since the windows were supposedly indestructible, wiring them into the central alarm system had not seemed necessary.

The two thieves were never caught, the jewelry was never recovered. I was afraid Hoving might decide to change the store's policy and have the jewelry replaced at night with inexpensive merchandise or artificial stones. But that would never do. New York is an all-night city, and nighttime window-shoppers strolling along Fifth Avenue expect to see the real thing in the windows of Tiffany's. He did set limits on the total value of the merchandise I could display in any one window and in all the combined windows, and, not too surprisingly, he elected to change the glass used in the windows.

The glass company worked hard to develop stronger glass, and two top executives proudly brought over a pane of it to demonstrate its absolute indestructibility. Hoving gathered us all down in the basement and, being a strong man, decided to test personally the new glass. He swung at it with a pickax. His first stroke smashed right through, and the two executives went off to try again. They succeeded. The new glass proved its strength a few months later when a second robbery attempt was made. This time the burglars blasted away at the windows with guns, but they made only small holes in a corner. Throughout the next decade attempts were made to break that glass—a heaved

June 11, 1959. Not all of the holes are filled with cones, and those that are without have jewelry: once the passerby spots the trick, he or she looks longer to discover more.

brick once left its clear impression—and bullet holes were common sights, but that first was the only successful robbery.

I love birds, and the windows I've done with them always seem to please people. Near the end of September 1958 I used birds—real stuffed ones—together with fallen autumn leaves. The leaves were being raked, and the birds were discovering pieces of jewelry amid the leaves and happily pulling them out. There's something wonderful about how birds look at things, perhaps it's the way they tilt their heads, but they seem at once surprised and delighted with whatever they see, and their joy of discovery—how often does a worm reveal itself a diamond necklace?—seems to increase the viewer's pleasure.

Notwithstanding lingering nerves after the robbery and attempted robberies, I was given permission to use the Tiffany Diamond in the 1958 Christmas windows. It provided the Star of Bethlehem for a manger scene in one window, with the Three Wise Men, made by Judith Brown, in another. Those would have been the windows to break.

I began 1959 at the bottom of the sea with a summery theme for yet another cold January. The windows displayed an anchor hooking a necklace, block and tackles hooking glasses—the glasses looked very fragile together with that thick and mighty rope—and sea-bottom scenes with shells.

Ron Prybycien returned from his stint in the army in 1959. I was delighted to have him back but didn't want to see Ron McNamer leave Tiffany's—he was too valuable a person. I spoke to Hoving, explained how talented McNamer was, how he could design anything. "What do you think he could design?" Hoving asked me. The answer was jewelry.

"You're going to be a jewelry designer," I told Ron McNamer.

"But I don't know anything about jewelry," he complained.

"You will," I said. He was sent to Italy to study, became a successful designer for Tiffany's, and is now an independent jewelry designer.

For Valentine's Day I again used the hands: hands knitting hearts, needlepointing hearts, crocheting hearts, making hearts with cookie cutters. The knitted heart, done in heavy red yarn, was the work of Sonny Hawkins. I told him I wanted a knitted heart, told him the size, and, most importantly, told him to leave the needles in at the top for the suspended hands to hold.

For the Easter windows—with their real grass—I went further with the motif I'd used in my first Easter windows: impossible baskets of eggs, baskets in which the stacked eggs defiantly break the laws of gravity by remaining perfectly intact at great heights.

Easter and blowing eggs: each year my assistant and I must commence the tiresome blowing of dozens of eggs two months before the display. We don't throw out the insides of the eggs, but collect the stuff in a motley confusion of jars, and other Tiffany's employees cart them home and bring us back cookies and cakes. That almost makes the work worthwhile.

Instead of sports, I depicted industrious activities in my 1959 spring windows: hammers and nails and saws. The most popular of that series had five crystal glasses set out along a wooden board supported on a sawhorse, with a saw that had already cut halfway through the board. Just a few more saw strokes would see the board break and the glasses crash. Everything—the sawhorse, saw, board, and background—was painted white. It was just a matter of waiting for those glasses to fall.

In June I used artificial ice cream and ice-cream cones. The first window had three ice-cream cones with ice cream topped with jewels. The second had fifty-three ice cream cones in five rows inserted in holes in boards. Two cones were missing, their places taken by jewelry. People like to study such structures, counting the objects and searching out changes in the pattern.

There was a fly in window three, a normal fly, not even very big, but a loud buzzer. He'd set himself up in that window, and each time I leaned in I enjoyed a few moments of peace, thought perhaps he'd finally flown away, but then he'd appear again, buzzing everywhere, but most of all around my head. For three months he drove me crazy, and in September I decided to do battle.

The weapon I chose was hay: harvest windows for September. In window three I had a stack of hay with gold thimbles and needles—haystacks want needles. No sooner had I set up the display than the fly appeared, or was heard to appear, buzzed around and around, and then, just as I'd planned, buzzed right into that pile of hay. He was never heard from again.

Later that same September, in place of falling leaves I used falling jewelry, such as earrings tumbling down against a dark background. The jewelry proved good stand-ins for autumn leaves; I think we all recognize the special way a leaf falls to the ground. One month later I had shoes floating in the air against drawings by Richard Giglio. Giglio was a very funny man, very resourceful. He worked at Bonwit's and traveled a lot; we met up once in Italy. I later got him a job doing fashion drawings.

In addition to my Christmas windows at Tiffany's and Bonwit's, I came by a new seasonal responsibility in 1959. The Seagram's Building, a forty-story tower with a bronze sheath and curtain-wall construction, had been completed. Located where the Montana Apartments had once stood, on Park Avenue between Fifty-second and Fifty-third streets, it had been designed by Ludwig Mies van der Rohe and Philip Johnson. Emile de Antonio,

 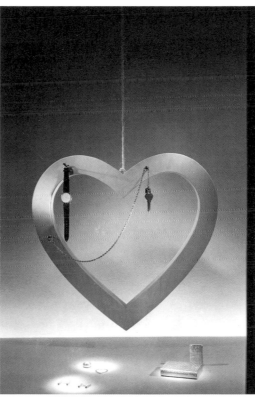 

February 4, 1960. A sugar-cube, wooden, and floral heart. A watch makes sense next to a heart, since both go tick-tock, and love and time, sadly enough, are related. The little key is important, too: locating the key to a wooden heart is rarely a minor task.

an agent for artists, a friend of Rauschenberg and Johns's and just about everybody else in the New York art world, called me to ask if I'd like to do the Christmas decorations around the Seagram Building. I went over and met Philip Johnson and started thinking about how to make that big building properly festive.

A few years earlier I'd helped open a new Bonwit Teller in Boston. It was set up in an old building, formerly the museum of natural history, and all around it were wonderful old oak trees. I fell in love with those big old trees, and for their Christmas decorations I'd covered the branches with little white light bulbs, nothing but tiny white lights. I'd first seen those lights in Italy, then I saw strings of them in an electrical shop in New York.

I gave a lot of thought to the decorations for the Seagram Building, did a lot of sketches, but the only idea that pleased me was the use of those tiny white lights on trees. When I returned to Johnson to tell him my plans, I said I had only one idea, and if he didn't like it he'd have to find someone else. He loved it.

October 2, 1960. I used all four of my miniature chandeliers in the window that appears in Breakfast at Tiffany's. *Hanging the chandeliers and the jewelry was the easy part—it was the lighting that had to be redone and redone again.*

The Seagram Building is surrounded by ginkgo trees, so I had nearly 350 firs brought in. My job then was to place each of the trees and direct the stringing of the lights, all told nearly 14,000. It took two days. Pushing those trees around was a wonderful experience. The heavy, sweet smell of fir was everywhere, and with 350 trees around me I sometimes felt myself no longer in New York but lost instead in the Black Forest.

The display worked beautifully, all those little lights made an enchanting sparkle, and I've repeated it for every Christmas since 1959. With the passing of each year, I do a little less actual pushing of the trees, but the chore still takes two days, and the smell is still wonderful. Today, those little white lights have become a common sight, even outside the Christmas season, and even on such trees as ginkgoes.

I created another popular style that year with the opening of the Four Seasons restaurant. Joe Baum of Restaurant Associates asked me to help with the decoration, and along with filling the place with live plants, I put votive lights on the tables and the bar. Another idea from Italy: I'd seen those little glass candleholders in churches and thought they'd provide just the right amount of light for a dinner table. The ones I used at the Four Seasons were red, but the idea caught on fast—overnight it seemed an age-old tradition— and clear-glass versions are now in wide use everywhere.

For Christmas of 1959 I received the gift of a very special tradition. Jean

Audrey Hepburn in Tiffany's during work on the film. I took this picture myself.

Schlumberger designed a Star of Bethlehem for me made of gold, yellow sapphires, and diamonds. In theory, that star was merchandise on sale in the store, but in truth it became part of the Christmas windows at Tiffany's.

Window five, the champagne window, was the most popular that year. I filled the top of the window with large Christmas-tree decorations, nearly twenty of them hanging down like glittering icicles over an ice bucket standing in snow. That year, I had Christmas shining brightly everywhere I put my hands.

This celebrating continued with the windows that went in at the end of December. I recreated period room settings in those displays and think the best was the rococo window, in which I had Amalienburg, the small hunting chateau designed by François de Cuvilliés in the park of Nymphenburg near Munich. I'd never been to Amalienburg and had only seen pictures of it in a book, and the book was in German, so I couldn't read it. Perhaps what I didn't know helped me bring it to life. The room was a turquoise and silver ballroom full of silver leaf. Ron Prybycien and I made the leafy wall decorations by squeezing plaster out of a pastry bag and then silver-leafing it. Ron was particularly adept at squeezing out that plaster. Then I put in Venetian dollhouse furniture that I'd painted, mirrors, and miniature crystal chandeliers. I was soon to use those chandeliers in much more famous windows.

The Valentine's Day windows were four hearts, one of wood, one of flowers, one of sugar cubes, and one of candy; the stationery window had a mailbox with its flag raised and painted with a heart. The wooden heart was best—next to it was a key. It's usually hard to find the key to a wooden heart, and that little joke made quite a few New Yorkers openly grin.

In the Easter windows I had a bird and a squirrel rescuing eggs from grass being mown and leaves being raked. The squirrel looked particularly delighted with his egg, although he held it like a nut. In the last window I had broken eggshells attached to strings hanging in the air. Inside each broken egg was a ring resting on a bit of moss. Getting those strings of eggs to hang straight took patience—and lots of time. In such cases I could, of course, use colorless nylon thread to hold the display in place, but that thread is visible and spoils the magic. It's always better to take the time and have the magic real.

My trips to Italy made their way into my next set of windows. I blew up black-and-white photographs I'd taken during my travels to six by five feet and put them in the windows framed by black window shutters—each photograph became a view from a window in a room in Italy. Merchandise was laid out along each windowsill. There was also a view up into the glass dome of Milan's Galleria. I used it with wineglasses. The other views were of Spoleto, the doge's palace in Venice, the onion domes on top of St. Mark's, and buildings along the Arno in Florence.

Opposite and right: *November 3, 1960. Classical Greeks reveal their thoughts. The heads were from Sarti-Lucchesi. I painted them black, cut out the sections, filled the resulting hole with plaster, painted them black, and used merchandise to give the hints.*

That June I used a series of pin-prick pictures by Nathan Gluck. A good artist, Gluck had worked for Andy Warhol and, in fact, drew just like Warhol. I'd been collecting old pin-prick pictures for years and asked him to make some for me. We set them up with light behind them, creating unusual backgrounds.

Then it was back to Italy. Dan Arje, one of my assistants at Bonwit's, had been over to Italy and brought me back clues of string—the gifts I appreciate most don't come from giftshops. The string was all different colors, and I matched the colors to merchandise. In one window I staged a race among turtles—making them compete against rabbits isn't fair. Each turtle—these were jewelry merchandise turtles—was leaving behind a trail of string from a ball. The resulting stretches of string provided clear clues to the route each turtle had taken.

That fall was particularly exciting at Tiffany's. The rumors we had heard for several months proved true: a Hollywood film company was on its way to the store to shoot scenes for *Breakfast at Tiffany's.* When the company arrived, it was as though Tiffany & Co. had been invaded and occupied by a foreign army. Audrey Hepburn was there, and so were the director, Blake Edwards, George Peppard, John McGiver, camera and technical crews, hairdressers, stylists, cosmeticians, wardrobe mistresses, and hordes of special assistants. The small ground-floor room where salesmen show expensive jewels to customers who wish to shop inconspicuously became Audrey's private dressing room and was cluttered with wigs, makeup jars, and photographs of her infant son. Also present and forever underfoot was her small dog, constantly yapping away.

Opposite: *November 17, 1960. The problem was how to show paper bags and earrings. I created the problem, but I also solved it and filled the bags with sand so they'd stand upright.* Right: *November 17, 1960. The glasses led to the bottles, and if you've got bottles and paper bags you have several opportunities.*

The film crew worked inside Tiffany's and on the avenue outside from a Saturday evening to a Monday morning. The scenes within the store involved several sweeping shots of the jewelry counters and salespeople on the ground floor. Hoving insisted— probably for security reasons—that actual Tiffany's employees be used in these scenes. For the scene in which Audrey and George Peppard have a discussion with a salesman, an actor (McGiver) played the role of the salesman, but changes had to be made in the script to make it conform with Tiffany's standards of how salespeople must behave.

I designed two windows for the film, one using the antique miniature chandeliers and one using wooden cones—actually architectural details off a house—with rings and bracelets. I had to change the windows seven times to meet the needs of the lighting crew. The lighting was particularly difficult for the opening scenes in which Audrey, as Holly Golightly, arrives in a taxi, steps out with her paper bag, cup of coffee, and donut, and walks along Fifth Avenue to gaze longingly in Tiffany's windows. Since the scene is supposed to take place at dawn, it was shot at dawn. The poor filmmakers thought they'd have empty streets at that hour, but Fifth Avenue is never deserted, and several of Tiffany's employees along with members of the film crew had to help the police stop traffic at the corner when the scene was being shot. Watching those technicians manipulate their big lights I remembered my bet with Jean Rosenthal and realized that my lighting problems are small compared to a movie's requirements.

In November, I used some reproductions of classical Greek heads that I'd bought at Sarti-Lucchesi, a store famous for its plaster casts of statues. I painted the heads black, which made them more effective as we're not used to seeing them anything but stony pale. I wanted to show what each of the people was thinking, so I sawed a piece out of

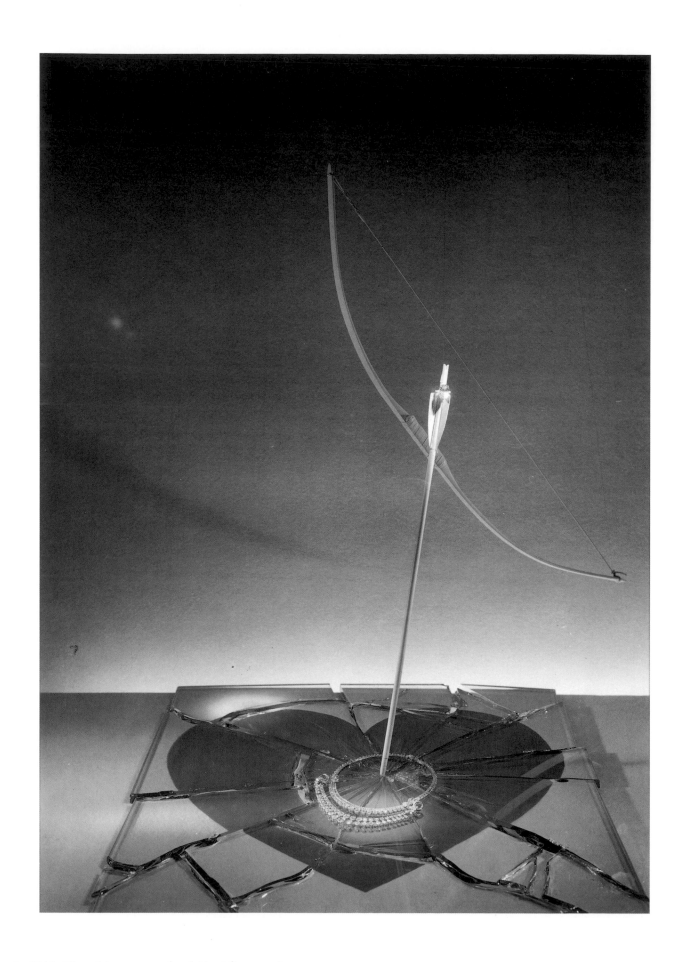

February 2, 1961. The ultimate result of Cupid's unerring aim. Smashing the glass was a trying moment: I had only one chance, and it had to break right. It did.

each head. Since the heads were hollow, I then had to fill in each with plaster to make a solid surface. On that surface I placed a piece of merchandise indicating what was on that person's mind. In one head was a watch—he had time on his mind—one was a female head with a diamond ring—she was contemplating marriage—and one had a butterfly pin—he had butterflies in his head.

As they always do when I need them most, the Muses then deserted me. I felt hollow, absolutely empty. I was sure Hoving would figure I'd finally burned myself out and fire me. This went on for several days. The streets suggested no ideas, even my dark hours of troubled sleep proved barren: no scribbled notes. Then the moment came. I was desperate, I was over at Bonwit's, and I had just come back from lunch. One of my assistants came in from his lunch break eating candy from a small paper bag. Perhaps out of common courtesy, perhaps in the hope the sweetness would calm my troubled mind, he held the bag out to me and asked if I wanted some candy. A common but kind gesture.

It was beautiful, and I thanked him from my heart. I'd never really looked at one of those little bags before. Such a simple, perfect shape, such a reasonable—and eminently usable—color. I knew just where to go—a paper company—and I came back with a few hundred of those wonderful little bags.

In one window I had stacks of the bags with an open bag on top, a necklace spilling out of it. In another were three open bags with pins over them. In the third window I had the bags sealed with earrings—that was my favorite of the series. For the fourth window I had rolls of paper the same color as the bags topped with clocks. For the last window I wrapped champagne bottles in paper bags wino-style and lined them up. Once ideas start they don't stop.

And then it was Christmas 1960. Jeanne Owens had made me a wax angel with wooden wings and a wax Madonna and Child. I used the special Schlumberger star with the angel.

I had problems with those wax figures because of the heat from the lights. The angel kept dropping his wings—they'd fall off, and I'd have to open the window and stick them back on. Even the Madonna acted up. She dropped her baby, and I had to pick him up out of the snow and put him back in her wax arms.

Aside from the Schlumberger star and a crown Ron Prybycien made for the Madonna, nothing was shining in the two Fifth Avenue windows. Except for the star, there was no merchandise.

I created fireworks for one of those windows by cutting holes in a dark background and setting up lights on a wheel behind it. As the lights passed, the holes would glow with color and then fade out.

For January 1961 I took everyone to the beach again, this time with rope in knots. I don't mind repeating a motif if I can improve on it, and just looking at that shining sand seems to make people warm.

That year, following some wonderfully complicated business deals, Hoving separated himself from Bonwit's and came into full ownership of Tiffany's. In reality, bankers, not Hoving, owned the Hoving Corporation, and the day came when those bankers opted to sell. They sold the Hoving Corporation to Maxey Jarman, president of the General Shoe Corporation. Since my days in Nashville painting panels and getting my heart broken, General Shoe had grown.

One day during that period Hoving had Jarman up to meet all the executives at Bonwit's. That included me. I walked over to Jarman and said, "How do you do, Mr. Jarman. I used to work for you way back in 1934. You've certainly come up in the world."

He smiled and said, "Yes, indeed, and so have you."

"Right," I said.

Hoving and Jarman didn't get along, and Hoving soon resigned from Bonwit's and announced he was going to devote all his time to Tiffany's. Even that didn't help. Jarman determined that the only way to rid himself of Hoving was to sell Tiffany's. When he put it up for sale, Hoving was there with a new set of investors to buy it. Beginning in 1961, Tiffany's was really his (and his stockholders'), and Hoving was no longer seen in the halls at Bonwit's.

I had another wooden heart for Valentine's Day, but this one was wrapped in chains sealed with a padlock with no key in sight—just a watch and a pair of earrings. Time has a lot to do with love, usually in a disastrous way, if only because both can pass. Chains, too—I had a window with hanging chains—are part of love. I had fun making the third window, which showed the inevitable broken heart. The heart was painted on a pane of glass, and I climbed into the window, put the heart on the floor, picked up a hammer— and prayed that glass would break right. It did.

The last window, the stationery window, was full of I-love-you notes that I'd written to some of my favorite people: Gardner McKay, Rex Harrison, Bertrand Russell, and Rosalind Russell, too.

There was a Bible in that same fifth window for Easter, in accordance with Hoving's wishes. During that period I used thorns with the Bible. I later got away from the thorns and used a cross of grapevines that I made. In another window I created a pyramid of eggs—their insides blown out, of course—with a glass resting on top.

Flowerpots are like paper bags, with their beautiful but sensible shape and wonderful color. I love the color of terracotta flowerpots, it's a calming color, like the warm orange of rooftiles in Italy. The flowerpots were for spring-planting displays. The merchandise in those windows was the flowers in the pots, flowers made in Mexico of vermeiled silver, very realistic and beautiful.

During this period I made the acquaintance of Robert Heitmann. He came to see me at Bonwit's, and I used some tapestries he'd made in the windows there. Heitmann is from Cincinnati and studied at the Cincinnati Art Academy. He'd served in the navy during the war, traveled throughout Europe on a painting scholarship, studied at New York's Art Student's League, worked in various art departments, and written several children's books. And he's a Gemini. Perhaps that's why I like the way he sees things. Those tapestries in Bonwit's windows were the beginning of thirty years of working together, for he would shortly become the most frequently used artist in Tiffany's windows.

In May I paid homage to one of the most important tools of the window trimmer: the staple gun. When I had my first job in display, making those panels for the General Shoe Corporation in Nashville, there were no staple guns. In those days we used tacks and a magnetic hammer. I'd hold the hammer in my left hand and have my mouth full of tacks. I learned to spit a tack out, raise the hammer, and bang—in went the tack. Once I got the hang of it, I could get going pretty fast, but not nearly so fast as with a staple gun.

The staple guns I used in the windows were from the Bostitch company. I liked them because they look like nothing else but staplers. In one window I had a background wall covered with swirling staples with more loose staples on the floor around a diamond necklace. The necklace looked as if it, too, were made of staples, and to accent that I put a stapler on it (the necklace was then worth $40,000, the stapler $13.95). In another I had diamonds draped over a stapler with the background a patchwork of colored paper rectangles stapled to a wall. In the last window I had two candelabra with candles, the haloes of their glow formed with circles of staples on the back wall.

June weddings called for a set of windows with cakes from Schrafts. In another display at the end of the month I used fruit, real fruit. There, too, I played with repeating patterns: the pattern of a necklace echoed that of a pineapple. The fruit went bad, and I had to change it every few days. During the display's final week, Ron Prybycien had to change the fruit: I was away on a little trip south.

Mohammad Ayub Khan, the president of Pakistan, was in Washington, D.C., to meet with President Kennedy, and the Kennedys wanted to give a dinner in his honor. During a visit to Paris and Vienna, Jacqueline Kennedy had been impressed by the way the French and Austrians use historic landmarks for social occasions, and for this state dinner she'd decided to use George Washington's home at Mount Vernon. Actually, she'd decided to use the grounds of Mount Vernon, and she needed help. Her social secretary, Letitia Baldridge, called me.

After working in Paris as social secretary to the wife of the American ambassador to

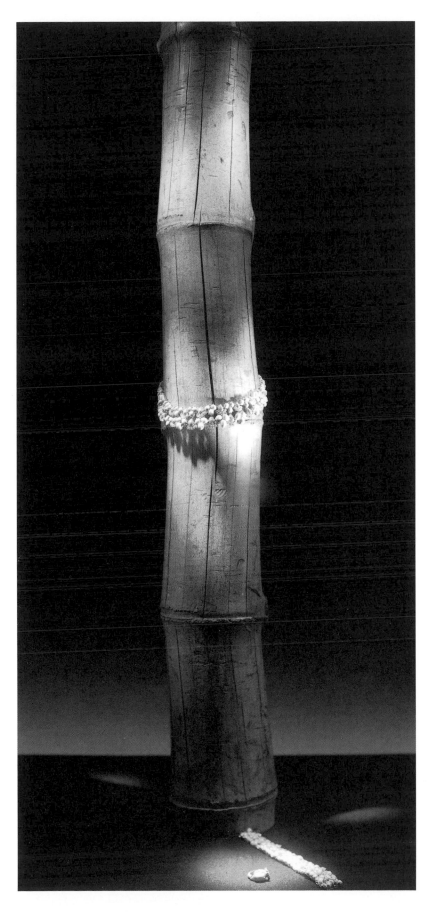

February 17, 1964. This piece of bamboo, the thickest I'd ever seen, was big enough to stand on its own in the window, but I secured it at the top anyway. One might almost wonder how that bracelet got on there.

France and then as social secretary to Ambassador Clare Boothe Luce, Baldridge had become Tiffany's publicity director and first woman executive. She caused quite a bit of consternation the first time she showed up for one of the weekly luncheon meetings of Tiffany's executives: the men didn't know whether to stand for her, remain seated, shake her hand, or bow. She'd done very well for Tiffany's, but in 1961, when Jacqueline Kennedy asked her to come work as her social secretary, she couldn't say no.

With 150 guests invited, this was to be a lavish affair. Philadelphia tentmaker John L. Vanderherchen had been asked to erect a canopied pavilion and serving tent. My job was to decorate the interior of the tent and design the outdoor lighting and decorations.

I spent three days and three nights down there. I was working for the White House, of course, and doing so has definite advantages. If you want something you get it, no matter what. I was working with an electrician on the lighting of the trees. Most trees aren't lighted properly. Ideally, you don't light a tree—the tree shows you its light. Most people make the light too bright and rarely use a filter, and if they do it's green, which is a terrible mistake for it makes the tree look artificial.

I told the electrician I wanted blue filters. "Impossible," he said. "They don't exist in Washington." I walked across the lawn to the head usher—he was always nearby, overseeing everything—and said, "I need blue filters for these lights." He asked how many I wanted and had them flown down from New York that afternoon.

I had my own little army to assist me with my work, a detachment of very alert young marines. I had them up in the trees placing the lights, running out power lines, carrying baskets of flowers. They marched behind me up and down the grounds and waited as I decorated the orchestra bandstand or put together the flower arrangements on the tables. They stood at ease in some nearby shade while I sat in a rocking chair on the porch of Mount Vernon along with Baldridge and the marine commander. The three of us chatted away, swatting at the mosquitoes.

The night before the dinner, I staged a dress rehearsal of the lighting, something truly unheard of. I had several hundred marines in full dress lined up from the dock, where the guests would arrive by boat, all the way along the driveway to Mount Vernon. I lined up the fife-and-drum corps in a courtyard. There were a few awkward moments: eager to take the turn in the driveway gracefully, the drivers ran over the toes of several squads of marines. None of those marines as much as winced. All in all, however, the rehearsal went well, and the next morning I packed my bags and left for New York. Although invited to the dinner, I couldn't stay. It was Tuesday, window night at Bonwit's.

Baldridge was later involved in a contest of wills between President Kennedy and Hoving. Following the Cuban missile crisis, Kennedy wanted to give his aides a gift and asked her to have Tiffany's design a paperweight made of a lucite block over the calendar page for October 1962 with the days of the blockade crisis set off with heavier numerals.

When she relayed the request to Hoving, he directed her to inform the president that Tiffany's had never made anything of lucite or plastic or any other synthetic material and never would. He suggested solid silver for the planned paperweights. When Baldridge reported Hoving's response to Kennedy, she had to bear his furious rage. On his own he had the paperweights made of lucite, decided they would never do, and gave in to Hoving, asking Baldridge to order the silver ones from Tiffany's.

On the Thursday of the week I got back from Mount Vernon, I changed the side windows at Bonwit's during the day and the windows at Tiffany's that night. For those windows I made my first use of bamboo—bamboo together with sand. There's something mysterious and exotic about bamboo and something sensual about bamboo stuck in beach sand. Although made to accommodate the uneven tubes of human bodies, jewelry fits well over bamboo, and diamonds shine wonderfully in sand.

Cameras are wonderful not just for what they can create but for their shapes: slight changes in scale can turn them into enormous or tiny black boxes. I was friends with a woman over at J. Walter Thompson, and one of her accounts was Kodak. Every time a new camera came out I'd lend her a hand and show it in the windows, most of all because cameras are such fun to use. I did my first windows with cameras that August. I bought articulated artist's figures and painted them black. These figures were composed of jointed black squares well suited to being matched to cameras. Putting a real camera in the hands of one of those tiny figures instantly put everything out of scale. In my favorite of that series one of the figures posed, arms akimbo and a glass on his head, while another took his picture.

Articulated artist's figures of another sort appeared in my windows that September. Such figures are sold in unpainted natural wood, but for these windows I painted them to look like Harlequin of the commedia dell'arte. I even made them little felt hats. The hats were essential: without them the figures are just eggheads.

Those figures were having a joyous good time, defying gravity and surviving all sorts of perilous situations. Four of them got together in one window as acrobats, the one on the bottom supporting two on his shoulders who in turn supported the fourth. Absolutely impossible—I had to glue them together—and delightful. People love seeing the impossible succeed, and it always makes them smile.

Another Harlequin figure walked a tightrope, and yet another swung back and forth sitting on a clock's pendulum (I had a motor set up at the top of the window). Certainly the bravest of this troupe was the figure shown resting on a bed of nails—upright forks— holding aloft one of the forks as a symbol of his invincibility.

My next windows were much calmer. These were my Mirandi windows, based on the works of the Italian painter whose still lifes are suffused with a wonderful calm. I found all the bottle shapes I could and sprayed them shades of brown earth tones. There was a tangible silence in those windows.

April 1, 1976. The lily, egg, and jewelry combine and
seem to curve together within their own kind of geometry.

Around the middle of October I did windows with hands holding dried flowers. Those windows were still in when Halloween came around. By then I had made up my mind to leave Bonwit's, not because of Hoving's departure, but because I had so many other things I wanted to do, and I'd done all I desired in Bonwit's sixteen windows. Those big spaces felt empty and old.

On Halloween Day 1961 I went up to see the president, walked into his office and said, "Trick or treat, I'm leaving."

"Where are you going?"

"I'm leaving Bonwit's."

"You can't do that."

"Yes, I can," I said. "I'll stay through Christmas because I've planned the Christmas windows, and then I'll leave and be only at Tiffany's."

He was upset. "What can I do to make you stay? Do you want more money? Just tell me."

"Well, it's very simple, but you won't do it."

"What?"

"Turn the whole main floor into display and start selling on the second floor. Tear out the windows and rebuild them. I want no limitations as to window size. The windows should be totally flexible as well as refrigerated and heated. And I want to be able to use fire, air, and water in my displays."

"But, Gene," the president protested, "you know that's impossible."

"Exactly," I said. "Happy Halloween." And I left.

That November, the artist Ron Ferri provided collages made of newspaper on backgrounds of newspaper. He used foreign-language papers: Greek, Chinese, Japanese. I was pleased with those newspapers and took that thought in as something to remember.

My work with Ron Prybycien reached one of its peaks in the next set of windows. During a trip to Greece earlier that year I'd seen the opening of a show of furniture designed by T. H. Robsjohn-Gibbings, a well-known interior designer. He'd had the furniture made there in Athens by Saridis, a furniture manufacturer. I was so impressed by the furniture that I went to Saridis and asked if they couldn't make miniatures of the pieces for me to use in my windows.

We used those pieces of miniature furniture to create classical Greek room settings. Doing so required a fantastic amount of research. Everything in those sets was authentic. The floor in one room had a sunken pool with real water, but the most difficult thing was the mosaic floors, which we did to scale using tiny pieces of colored cardboard.

For one of those windows on Greece I borrowed a bronze sculpture of a Greek tragedian's foot from Robsjohn-Gibbings. You know it's an actor's foot by the sandal's platform sole. For a backdrop, I took a piece of linen and soaked it in tea to make it look old; its deep shadows brought life to that ancient foot. The merchandise I chose for that window was pins that reminded me of the fastenings Greeks used to secure their cloaks.

Then Ron Prybycien left Tiffany's. He had decided, he said, that I was eternal and he would always remain only my assistant. I'd been giving him some of the freelance jobs I'm always being offered, and he'd done well and wanted a chance to break out and work on his own.

In search of a replacement I asked Ron Smith, who'd been my secretary at Bonwit's, to come work with me at Tiffany's. "But I don't know anything about display," he said. "Why do you think I want you?" I asked.

So I had another Ron, my third, in Tiffany's display department. Many people, used to calling and asking only to speak to Ron, were unaware that during those years they'd been speaking to three very different people.

I'd been planning my Christmas windows for Bonwit's—two sets that would be my

March 1, 1957. Jordan Steckel made the geometric form, I dropped it, and it broke beautifully, perhaps the happiest of accidents. I left it in the window exactly the way it crashed.

final displays for that store—since that summer's trip to Italy. While in Rome I'd visited the Borghese Gardens, and there, amid the tall old trees, the fountains, and the long shady lawns, I'd seen a puppet show. More important, I'd seen children watching the show— they were enthralled. There and then I'd envisioned crowds of children with their noses pressed against Bonwit's glass.

Back in New York I found a puppeteer, a fellow named Jack Bostwick, who also worked as a playwright, and together with him I planned the windows. I decided to set up two marionette theaters, one to relate the story of a little boy's dream of Christmas, the other a little girl's. The two shows were to be presented simultaneously, last eight minutes, and be repeated, with barely a pause for breath, during the morning and afternoon hours.

Bostwick wrote the plots of the two stories, designed the marionettes, and assembled a staff to pull the strings. Jonah Kinigstein designed and made the two theaters, and I made forests of frozen birch trees to serve as backgrounds.

The shows began on November 22, and the response was as expected: crowds of children gathered wide-eyed in front of Bonwit's windows. A few days later I got a call from the store manager—would I please come down to the main floor?

I knew there was trouble as soon as I saw the uniforms. "Well," I thought, "here comes the story of Charley and the police." The police hadn't been fooled by the puppets.

January 18, 1960. A view up into Milan's Galleria. All that glass made the choice of the merchandise simple.

They knew that where there are puppets there are puppeteers, and—as I had not known but soon understood thoroughly—it was then against New York City law to have live people in a store window. The shows stopped.

I then put in my final set of Bonwit's windows, and those displays, too, were unique. I based them on the *Journey of the Magi*, by the Florentine painter Benozzo Gozzoli, with crowds of people, many on horses, moving through the windows toward a Nativity scene. Jeanne Owens made the figures for me out of chicken wire covered with colored confetti. What made those windows so special was that they were absolutely without merchandise.

The response was immediate. Many people called me, and most said the same thing, that it was marvelous, that it made sense.

That was my goodbye to Bonwit Teller. In my sixteen years there I'd turned out some good displays and some not-so-good displays. Any display is the product of the time it's created, and I know that some of my work, particuarly my work at Bonwit's, will look awfully strange a decade from now.

For my Tiffany's Christmas windows that year, Danny Arje made me a needlepoint Madonna. I had him leave it unfinished, with the needle still inserted, and hung the Schlumberger star over it. In the other Fifth Avenue window I created a city full of snow. The buildings were made of plastic children's toys painted black. In another window I had a display showing once again Hoving's *Tiffany's Table Manners for Teen-Agers*, and I used a bird in the champagne window. And that was the end of another year of windows at Tiffany's.

I was already planning windows in my head for 1962. Now I was thinking only of Tiffany's—and my freelance projects—and by then I had a sense of a year's rhythm. There were the holidays, of course, which I knew I had to plan in advance. By April I usually know what I want for Christmas, early in December I like to work out my Valentine's Day theme, and the day comes every year when it's time to start blowing out all those eggs. There's a refrigerator in my office at Tiffany's just for Easter eggs, and in another corner, mixed with props for future windows and pieces of what other people call junk collected from everywhere, are trays of dirt, ready for their grass seed.

Sometime in 1956 a magazine writer asked me to list my favorite things. I started with "Eggs, wind, wire, fire, tree bark, old burlap bags, bows and arrows, stuffed birds, rubber bands, iron girders, sheet music, moss, seashells, shadows, split-rail fences, road maps, the alphabet, yarn, cellos, camera film, ostrich feathers, vegetables, needles, hay, the tops of tin cans cut out using a hand opener, silk, light bulbs, bamboo, pencils, the insides of clocks, dirt, rocks, moving water," and I wasn't even halfway through when that writer put down his pencil.

Another magazine article, also in 1956, reported the response of a teenager to one of my displays at Tiffany's. "Gee, look," the boy had exclaimed. "Diamonds in water. I wonder who thought of that?"

I did. Late at night, half in and half out of sleep, in a mixture of vague worries and memories of old days and old loves I'd remembered something about water and sun and shininess. The diamonds came later. They just happened to be the right color.

UNPRECIOUS OLD GIN

HE TRAFFIC ON FIFTH AVENUE still moved in both directions
during the early 1960s, buses traveling uptown passing those going
downtown and everywhere at once cabs and cars and the usual
honking trucks. Big sightseeing buses often pulled up in front of
Tiffany's, their windows full of faces and cameras aimed out at the
world-renowned jewelry store. Sardi's—that old restaurant on West
Forty-fourth Street was then a sort of unofficial club for theater
people—ran shuttle buses to the theater district that would slow
down before the store, the driver announcing to his load of out-of-
towners, "And on your right, Tiffany's, more famous for its windows
than its jewels."

Now that was sweet, but when I think about those years I
remember best certain shadows, shadows I never saw but thought
about constantly and tried to recreate in my windows. I wanted those
shadows to fill entire windows. There would be no props, just
merchandise, lights, and those shadows. If you think about them long enough, shadows
grow solid, and you begin to sense the kind of light you'll need to shape them. I'd tried for
those shadows at Bonwit's and had had some success. The light all came from the side
and outlined the shadow of the mannequin; I'd stood in the window and made the
shadows darker with charcoal. But I couldn't form those shadows at Tiffany's, didn't have

the space, didn't have enough depth to work with. I could have made it work at night, but there's no combatting sunlight: all those beautiful shadows just disappear with dawn.

Alongside the shadows was always gravity, still my strongest adversary or, perhaps, my most dependable, if unseen, sidekick. Gravity was defied with much success in Tiffany's windows during the 1960s, and each time that I won out—each time that which should have fallen and broken remained suspended and intact—I was thrilled and made New Yorkers and the other members of my audience smile. People adore impossible balance.

During the 1960s I discovered that when I please myself, I please my public. The whole thing—the windows, the art, the shadows, the gravity—is emotional, the whole thing is something I make just for myself. During those years as now, many ideas for windows came to me at darkest night—the Muses won't let you see them and, good Greeks that they are, prefer to find you dressed only in a sheet—but I came on other ideas in the open light of Manhattan streets. I got many ideas during the 1960s while walking to or from work; the city itself was full of ideas during those years. I had a lot on my mind and many things to say to strangers in my windows.

As always, I was eager to do anything different, anything I'd never done before. But during those years, too, the people looking in my windows appeared to want something new. It seemed to me then that people were looking harder through those five panes of glass. Feeling their gazes around me only pushed me harder to force whatever it might be—eggs in a basket, jewelry on a string, an artist's figure balanced on the arm of a chair—to do whatever everybody else said was impossible. I never knew what would happen but did know that if the result were beautiful, New Yorkers would notice.

Between 1961 and 1970 I used works by more than sixty artists. Some I used several times, most only once, and today I remember little of that crowd of artists. From photographs I recognize the art, but I remember few of the faces, few of the voices, of the people who created it. Most of those men and women came once to bring their art and then returned later to pick it up: I saw them twice. The art was with me longer, standing or leaning in some corner of my office for me to look at from time to time, touch, pick up and hold, turn around. I remember the surprising heft of small metal sculptures, the smoothness of stone, the colors—people brought me many shades of blue during the 1960s—the way light changed on paintings. I carried the colors inside me so as to match them to merchandise and know what to do with them. It was the art I thought about, even memorized—the huffy shoulders of an enamel doll, the deep pink of a metal rose. The artists came and then came again, just wanting to thank me and say goodbye.

But I don't forget the past. It stays inside me, and anything inside me eventually makes it into my windows. Few of those who know me were surprised when I put beach sand and seashells in the windows in January 1962. I loved my first winter in New York, still recall my joy when I first saw snow, but even I can have enough of cold. In two of the windows I put rings on fishhooks hanging from lines attached at the top of the windows. I'd gone out to a sporting-goods store to get the hooks—nice, big, shiny ones—and it took forever to get those hooked rings to stay in line properly. The fishhooks kept spinning.

While I was leaning in the window fooling with those hooks I thought of Herman Delman of Delman Shoes. He used to take me fishing down in Florida. He'd say, "Gene, you need a vacation, so you're coming along," and we'd go deep-sea fishing off the Florida coast. One afternoon I caught a shark that didn't want me to make it back to Fifth Avenue. Getting that big fish aboard that tippy boat was quite a battle.

For the next set of windows I worked with Rouben Ter-Arutunian, a theater designer well known for his work in ballet for Balanchine. He loaned me miniature stage designs for his version of *A Passage to India*. Tiffany's small windows are ideal for miniature recreations; I've known that since the room setting I used in my first set of windows back in 1955.

Preceding pages: *August 11, 1966. A watermelon made of Flora Mir gumdrops. The melon was as big as a real watermelon (about two feet long) but, being made of candies and Styrofoam, didn't weigh nearly as much.*

January 18, 1962. One of Rouben Ter-Arutunian's sets for A Passage to India.

For Valentine's Day I used quotations from *Romeo and Juliet* written out, of course, for people will always read handwriting but often overlook printed signs. In one window I stretched a spiderweb of gold thread. The merchandise attached to the web—small pins—looked like trapped insects. The last window, the stationery window, had an arrow piercing cards with hearts.

"Now, Gene," the grade-school teacher would say, "please go to the blackboard and show us how you solved this problem." I dreaded standing up in front of the class, especially as I'd never managed to solve the problems. But I loved drawing with chalk on the blackboard after school. I loved drawing with anything.

I returned to those days in my next windows. Felt-tip markers, chalk, crayons, pastels, and watercolors—I used the five primary mediums of my school days—and in two of the windows I recreated the first kind of portrait I ever made: stick figures, in this case female. I used a marker to draw the stick figure in window one, chalk in window two. I had Ron Smith close me in the windows and then drew the figures so they'd be right in the center. I covered the floor of the chalk-figure window with standing pieces of chalk, each one glued to the felt floor covering. In the last window I set up five crystal glasses as wash basins for watercolor paintbrushes. Each glass held a different color liquid. I used distilled water in the glasses, since regular water leaves a rim, and had to replenish the water every day, since it evaporates.

Right after Easter I was reminded of another old love, Picasso. In April and May nine of the city's leading art galleries exhibited his works simultaneously in a project called "Picasso: An American Tribute." I decided to do something with Picasso in Tiffany's windows and soon learned that other stores were doing the same.

I selected some prints of Picasso paintings and commissioned Ron McNamer and Paul Spradling to reproduce them, to paint them exactly like the originals. Then I had them cut out certain elements—a table, heads, a vase of flowers—and make them protrude, continue right out from the canvas. The idea was to reproduce the paintings three-dimensionally.

On the night the exhibition opened a special bus drove around the city carrying

people to see the various window displays. I still think mine was best and that Picasso would have liked it best.

During that same period I was involved in a different kind of opening involving yet another Spanish artist. James Truax, J. A. Kavanagh, and David Nillo were opening a new Off-Broadway theater at 321 East Seventy-third Street, Stage 73, and for the theater's debut they'd chosen an obscure work by Federico García Lorca, a strange play that had never before been professionally presented onstage. They may have chosen it because Lorca wrote many of its scenes while in New York in 1929 during a self-imposed exile from Spain. Perhaps they had some other reason—the word I got was that they'd searched long and hard to get hold of the work. Its title was *If Five Years Pass*; its subtitle, *A Legend of Time*. It was being directed by the dancer choreographer Valerie Bettis, and I was asked to design the costumes.

Designing the costumes was a matter of pure imagination since the various characters weren't well defined: a young man, a young girl, a stenographer, a cat (dead), a maid, a mask, and seven other characters, among them a talking mannequin. I didn't have to concern myself much with the plot, which is vague, since the events don't occur in sequence, and the entire production is kind of a frenzied dance.

The young man is in love with the young girl, but she's too young to marry him, so he agrees to wait five years. The stenographer is in love with the young man. Crushed by his love for the young girl, she flees. The five years pass, but the young girl then confesses she loves someone else, a cigar-smoking football player (in helmet and shoulder pads). The young man then realizes he has loved another girl all along—this would be the stenographer—goes searching for her, and finally locates her in an enchanted forest. She's glad he's come and agrees to marry him "if five years pass." Sad news for everyone. In the next scene the young man sits at a table with three card players who are wearing dead-white makeup and are dressed in dinner jackets and black capes lined with white satin. The four play cards, the young man shows the card he's holding to the audience and dies. All I remember about the dead cat is that it was played by a young girl and she wore a small, blue-felt cape.

The play had lots of good lines: "She has a figure so fragile you'd like to take a tiny silver hatchet and cut her up"; "My fiancé has icy teeth"; "My father was in Brazil twice, yet he was so little you could put him in a suitcase"; "Her breasts go with tea"; "Some scissors last forever, but my bosom lasts but a moment"; "In the foyer of the Paris opera were some balustrades that went down to the sea"; "He pushes his little nose against the crystal of my heart, but nevertheless he has no air"; "I am like a tiny guitar, burned by the sun." Even the mannequin had a good line: "The fountains of warm milk cover my silks with anguish." This was, of course, a translated work.

Opening night was Thursday, May 10, 1962. The reviews were mixed, with the best coming from those critics who hadn't struggled too hard to understand—and had seen the entire production. Many hadn't, for halfway through the first scene of the final act a curtain had been drawn slowly across the rear of the stage, and at the conclusion of the scene, most of the reviewers, convinced they'd seen the end, had made for the exit. Representatives of the producers and their press agent had rushed to inform everyone that, despite appearances, the play really wasn't over. They hadn't succeeded in coaxing all the critics back into the theater.

The costumes, however, got good notices.

In June, my friend Richard Giglio drew floral backgrounds for wedding windows, and in July I put chairs in all five windows, including a rocking chair that actually rocked (a little motor pushed it up and down). Then those clear summer skies washed away all my ideas. The usual rut: no Muses, no scribbles, no one offering me candy. I had two days to come up with a new set of windows.

I first created this window for a February 15, 1962, display: the version shown here is from the retrospective of May 25, 1978.

July 26, 1962. To create a pasta forest you stick pins into a surface, cut off the tops with pliers, and push a strand of pasta over each one.

I said to Ron, "Let's go downtown and walk around in Little Italy." A nice day for a walk, and I hadn't seen the city's Italian section for a long time. We passed one small shop that had windows full of pasta, nothing but different shapes of pasta. "Now I know what we're going to do," I said.

The woman behind the counter was plump and friendly. "I'd like five pounds of this," I said, waving toward the bins.

"Which?" she asked.

"All of them," I said.

"You're crazy," she said. "Nobody buys five pounds of this stuff."

"I'm going to do a window for Tiffany's."

"What's Tiffany's?"

"A big store up on Fifth Avenue and Fifty-seventh Street. Haven't you ever seen it?"

"Never heard of it," she said, but she sold me the pasta.

Pasta is very popular today, but in 1962 few people had ever really looked at it. I myself had never really looked at all the forms of pasta, and I had great fun putting together those windows, each idea quickly leading to another.

In the first window I made the pasta stand like reeds by driving pins into the floor, cutting off their heads, and then shoving a piece of spaghetti down over each pin. Setting them all at a slight angle gave the sense of reeds leaning in a breeze. For window two I bound strands of spaghetti in sheaves held together with diamond rings—a rare instance of jewelry playing a fundamental role in the idea of a display.

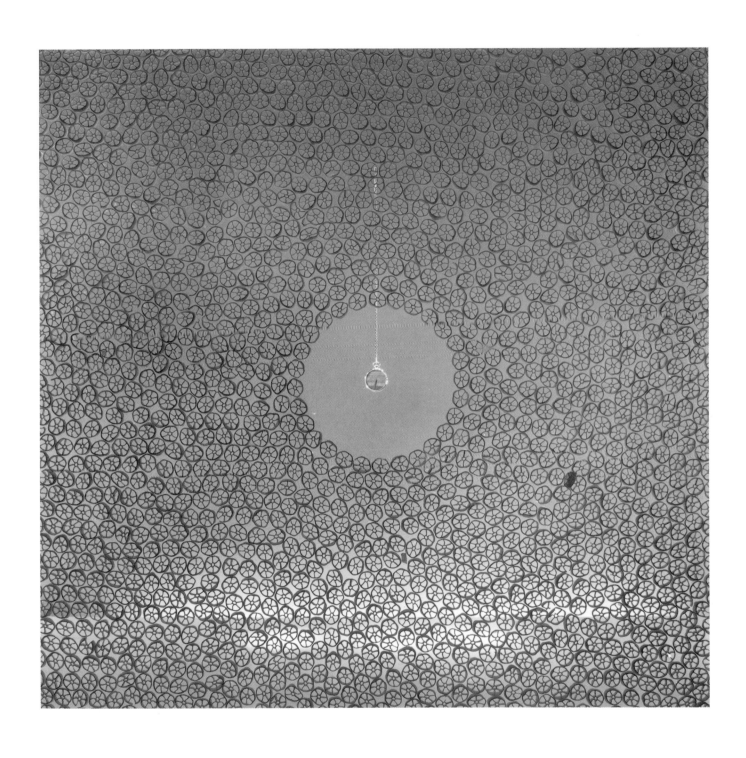

April 16, 1970. The pasta wheels are glued to plate glass.
They reminded me of watch parts, so there's a watch.

Above left: *I watched from my office on the fifth floor of Bonwit Teller as the Duveen Building— once on the northwest corner of Fifth Avenue and Fifty-sixth Street— was torn down. When I took this photograph, they'd gotten around to smashing up the frieze.* Above right: *August 16, 1962. One of the displays from "Disappearing New York."*

In the remaining three windows I put different shapes in glass containers; used pasta wheels, spirals, and twists to imitate the workings of watches—displayed with Tiffany's watches, of course; and filled a bowl with heaped rotelle.

Very popular, the pasta displays even made the cover of a trade magazine, *Macaroni Journal.*

Public reaction was stronger still to my next window displays, probably because they came straight from my heart. I always resent it when one of New York's old buildings is torn down, and I know other New Yorkers feel the same way. We walk around the city and discover holes in the ground where favorite buildings once stood, or we turn a corner to find yet another glass box occupying a city block once alive with small stores. The city we know is forever being knocked down and carted off, so I called the displays "Disappearing New York."

An artist had been collecting sculptural details from demolished city buildings, and I borrowed several pieces and simply arranged them in the windows together with merchandise. People were amazed at what had once been part of city buildings: cornices and moldings and heads with mischievous grins, smiles, or spooky stares. Some of the objects seemed ancient and from another land, certainly another city. Others appeared warmly familiar, and seeing them there in the windows, torn from their homes, was saddening.

I used my next set of windows to celebrate a new New York building well worth celebrating: after sixty-nine years at Carnegie Hall, the New York Philharmonic had been given a new home. Philharmonic Hall, as it was then called, opened September 23 as part of the Lincoln Center for the Performing Arts on Columbus Avenue between Sixty-second and Sixty-sixth streets. To mark this event, I put a musical instrument in each of the windows. Window one had a French horn, its mouth bursting with yellow porcelain flowers. Those flowers were merchandise, made in England and expensive; the bouquet I arranged to fit that horn's mouth was worth several thousand dollars. I thought about that while picking up the pieces. I was in the window, tying the wire that would suspend the horn in the air, and Ron was holding the horn. Someone passing by on Fifth Avenue may have caught his eye, he never said; but he let go of the horn before I had it tied in place— one of the few accidents in Tiffany's windows.

Keyboards were suspended in the air of window two, violin bows floated in window three. The fourth window acted out the power of sound with hands breaking through a kettledrum to beat time on crystal glasses, one of which was broken. There was much deliberate breakage in that window. I climbed into it to break the glass (hit it with a hammer) and sliced through the skin of the drum to make the hole.

I had real harp strings for window five but knew I couldn't just line them up any old way. I took a trip up to the Philharmonic and asked a harpist to show me the correct order of the strings. Then I got in the window and stapled each string in place. The harp strings filled the window. Behind them I placed a candelabra.

Someone will notice if a harp's strings are out of order. A harpist or a harpist's daughter will come in, ask for the store manager, and announce the error. People look hard at store windows—I learned that with the anatomy book in Bonwit's window—and since Tiffany's windows are so small, people look at them even more carefully, examine each detail. I proved that to myself by putting a little test in my next windows.

Rustic scenes for the last days of September: an old water pump and bucket in one window; a coffee grinder in the next; forty-odd rusty old keys glued to a piece of plate glass filling the third window; stemware attached to the inside rim of an old wooden wheel in the fourth; a tureen placed against dark wood in the last.

The keys were the test. All but one were turned to the left. Shortly after the displays were set up, people began coming into the store to point out my error. "Hey," they'd announce, "did you know you have one of those keys backward?" "Oh, yeah?" I'd say. I

September 7, 1962. A celebration of the beginning of a Philharmonic season. This involved a lot of breaking: punching through the drum skin and picking up the glass and banging it against the floor.

knew then that people were really looking at my windows, and that was something new to play with.

The seventy-fifth year of the Metropolitan Opera called for a set of windows, and for these I commissioned Ron McNamer and Paul Spradling to build me skeletons of opera sets. I got photographs of the sets and asked them to build only the bare outlines. I indicated the operas—Verdi's *Otello*, Strauss's *Ariadne auf Naxos*, Beethoven's *Fidelio*—indirectly. On the set of *Otello* was Desdemona's handkerchief, enough of a hint for any opera lover.

My Christmas displays that year included a piece of the past. In the third window I created the interior of an igloo decorated for Christmas, and in one corner was an icy Christmas tree, the glass tree from my first Tiffany's windows, those for Christmas 1955. The Schlumberger star was in window two, suspended over the roof of a church welded by Judith Brown, and in another window I repeated my key test with a wall of candy canes, all but one turned in the same direction. Even frantic last-minute shoppers found the time to inform me of the errant cane.

The champagne window that year had its usual bottle and ice bucket, this time accompanied by a deer head. Ronnie Smith and I had great fun each year putting in the Christmas windows. He and I worked together well, understood each other well. We usually worked in silence, communicating only with glances, and were much like one mind with two pairs of hands. And each Christmas we'd open a bottle of champagne while setting up the displays and merrily toast passersby.

Sometime that December all of New York's newspapers went on strike. I didn't think much of it at first, was sure it wouldn't last long. But it didn't end. What should have been a momentary interruption took on the appearance of a hopeless mess with absolutely no end in sight.

Sooner or later everything washes up on the beach, and wouldn't it be pleasant to come across a few diamonds while hunting for shells? That's what I was thinking while arranging the beach scenes for my January 1963 windows. I've always thought sand was the antithesis of diamonds, and the contrast makes diamonds look even more diamondy. Diamonds really sparkle against that gritty dullness.

I got a phone call one night that winter. The voice at the other end said, "This is John Gielgud. I don't know if you've heard of me."

"Well, somewhere I think I have."

"I've got a proposition for you. I'm coming to New York, and I'd like very much to have lunch with you." He was then in Philadelphia doing *School for Scandal*, and he told me I should give his agent in New York a call. When I did the agent read me a letter from Gielgud in which he said, "I don't know who does the Tiffany windows, but that's the person I want to do the sets for my next play."

When Gielgud got to town, we met for lunch at Dinty Moore's in the theater district. "Every time I'm in New York," he told me, "I always try to drop by Tiffany's to catch your windows. Well, I'm about to do the play of *The Ides of March*, and I'd love for you to do the sets." I told him I really didn't know all that much about theater design but was more than willing to try. He assured me I'd do fine. Then he asked if I knew a good costume designer, someone with whom I'd like to work.

"Yes, I do," I said, "me," and I told him about *If Five Years Pass* and my other work designing costumes and clothes. He agreed. I was to do both the sets and the costumes.

Having made my plans with Gielgud, I had to ask Hoving for a leave of absence. I remembered only too well what had happened with *Auntie Mame* and was determined to put up a battle if Hoving said no. But this time he agreed to let me go—provided, of course, I left Ronnie with the materials for enough sets of windows. I told Gielgud I'd be there for his play and sent over a model of the stage set along with blueprint drawings and designs for the furniture. And I went on with my windows.

September 24, 1962. Rusty old keys glued to plate glass. All but one point in the same direction. "Did you know you have one of those keys backward?" "Oh, yeah?"

I built a wall for Valentine's Day, made it out of sugar cubes. Three cubes thick, that wall filled an entire window except for a heart-shaped opening in the center behind which were hands holding a bouquet. In the next window I spelled out "Love" in sugar cubes. I'd found an old wooden gate out in the country. It had beautiful antique hinges, and the wood looked like a piece of everyone's childhood, even for New Yorkers who'd known only cement walls. Using a child's medium—chalk—I wrote "kiss, kiss, kiss" on the gate and put it in a window.

Among the other items in the last window was a china rhinoceros. He was merchandise, but I loved him because he was homely. I talked a lot to that rhino; he and I got on well because we had so much in common.

Starring in the last window was another favorite animal, my stuffed grackle, a very expressive bird. He was perched on the top of a hat with playing cards falling all around him. He was happy because he'd caught—and was holding in his beak—the ace of hearts. With the sugar and kisses and hearts, some passersby probably wrote me off as a simple old romantic. The more observant looked below the grackle to where I had a joker smiling up. It was all a joke, and maybe love's always a joke, but that doesn't keep it from being sad.

In March the city was still without newspapers—there was no end in sight of that strike. To me, the whole thing seemed silly and childish, and I was irritated and tired of drinking my morning tea without the paper, of never knowing what was going on in the city. After the Valentine's Day windows I did a set using wallpaper backgrounds and then, since the strike showed no sign of ending, I decided to do something about it. Those newspaper people needed a good scolding.

I got some old back issues of New York newspapers from friends in advertising, went over to F.A.O. Schwarz for some children's toys, papered the toys and the floors and walls of the windows with the newspapers, and in just two days had designed the five displays.

There was a show train during the newspaper strike. It ran in from New Jersey—where they still had newspapers and could still know what was being shown on Broadway—so in one of the two front windows I had a wooden toy train. The train, the floor, and the walls were all papered with ads and reviews from the entertainment pages of the *Herald Tribune*, including a big ad for the Bolshoi Ballet. Was it still in town?

In the next Fifth Avenue window I set up a toy steam shovel. It, the floor, and the walls were papered with real-estate pages and apartment listings from the *New York Times*. I thought that was clear enough.

Window three had a toy sailboat in front of sports pages from the *Times*. Wooden blocks were stacked in front of stock-exchange listings from the financial pages of the *Wall Street Journal* in window four, and the last window had letters to the editor from the *New York World-Telegram* as a background to stacked books (papered with newspapers) and pieces of black-china coffee cups. Everything in those windows was black and white.

The response to the displays was great, with many people walking in to say how much they enjoyed them and many more writing me letters. I don't think my scolding did much to end the strike. The windows went in on March 1; the strike finally ended, appropriately enough, on April 1, after lasting 114 days. That strike had a big effect on the city's papers. First to go was the *Mirror*, which expired early in October. In 1966, three of the newspapers—the *Herald Tribune*, *Journal-American*, and *World Telegram*—merged, but after another strike all three ceased publication and then reappeared with different, variously hyphenated names. A year later those papers were gone for good, leaving New York with only three regular daily papers: the *Times*, the *News*, and the *Post*.

All that time I was blowing eggs, Ronnie was blowing eggs, and when we weren't actually blowing, we were poking holes in shells and puffing up our cheeks. Easter was coming. So was my scheduled departure for England and Gielgud, but I was thinking only of eggs.

I wanted to make a hat, an Easter bonnet, and I wanted to make it out of eggs. The idea seemed simple, but constructing that hat took a lot of eggs and a lot of work. I nailed a chicken-wire foundation to a head and then placed eggs on the wire and glued them

December 4, 1962. The scene in window four with a
background of candy canes. How can a candy cane point in
the wrong direction?

Valentine's Days. Below left: *January 28, 1971. The birds give life to the word.* Below right: *January 31, 1963. "Kiss, kiss, kiss" on an old wooden gate.*

together with Duco cement. The eggs weren't glued to the wire foundation, just to one another. Lifting the egg hat off the chicken-wire foundation was a dramatic moment—I was sure the eggs would collapse—but the eggs held together, and I had my hat. It had taken seventeen dozen—204—eggs and was two and one-half feet wide.

The hat still needed something. It was made of eggs: it needed a nest. I collect bird nests—after all, I also collect stuffed birds—so I put one, with real bird's eggs in it and a real stuffed bluebird attached to it, on one side of the hat, along with a large diamond flower.

The other windows were simpler: blue jays together with eggs and real grass and real lily of the valley. In the last window I had colored eggs stacked in a crystal hurricane lamp. I'd used up my blown eggs for the hat, and both Ronnie and I were too weary to poke and blow more eggs, so I filled the lamp with hard-boiled eggs. Some of those eggs, it seems, were cracked, and after a few days the ground floor filled with the unusual—at least for Tiffany's—but unmistakable stench of rotting eggs. We had to take the lamp out of the window, sit down, and blow a few dozen more eggs.

The egg bonnet was very popular and was reproduced—worn by a model—in the April issue of *Life* magazine along with an article about the display entitled "Tiffany Topper Tops Them All."

Before leaving for England and Gielgud's *Ides of March*, I did a set of windows dedicated to the Royal Ballet, with displays for *Sleeping Beauty, Camille, Swan Lake, Giselle* and even a recreation of Margot Fonteyn's dressing table. Richard Giglio had

January 31, 1963. Valentine's Day. The bird has caught the ace of hearts under the knowing gaze of the joker.

designed the Royal Ballet's New York program, and I put a few in the windows.

I left for England while those windows were still in and stayed away the entire month of May. I'd prepared two sets of windows for Ronnie to use while I was gone. The first were spring-planting windows with walls and stacks of terracotta planters. The second were based on twine, the ordinary kind used in the store for wrapping packages. Those are always my favorite kind of window display—absolutely simple but somehow crazy. You look at it and say, "Of course." I made an enormous ball of twine to be used in one of the windows. I wound the ball myself, and only when I'd finished did I realize—what an idiot—that I could have used a hollow center or even wrapped the twine around a baseball. But it looked wonderful. The ball was on the floor of the window, the end of the twine running up and out of sight at the top. A long necklace trailed off the ball and seemed at first glance almost nothing.

I got the idea for the twine windows when I came on a few balls of it upstairs. The color was great, and I thought it would look just marvelous against burlap. For I was thinking of burlap during those days. There was a lot of it in my future.

I was proud and delighted Gielgud had chosen me but soon found that not everyone shared his enthusiasm. I first encountered opposition to my part in the production on this side of the Atlantic, before leaving for England, when I spoke of it to a friend, a New York stage designer. He scoffed at me. "You've never worked in the theater. What makes you think you can design a stage? It's so large compared to what you're doing."

"As far as I'm concerned, a stage set is just an oversized window display," I told him, but that only made him angrier, for he thought I was belittling—very literally—his profession.

On the other side of the Atlantic I encountered opposition of another sort: the people working on the play resented the choice of an American, rather than an Englishman, for the set design. I had constant problems with the scenery people, and my only real support came from Gielgud and a young assistant, Sam Kirkpatrick, who made special props.

I wanted to make the entire set one color and had decided to cover everything in burlap. The problem is, real burlap doesn't look like burlap onstage. It looks like something else, something unpleasant. Straining to make my life miserable, the scenery people didn't let me see the set until it was put up for a dress rehearsal in a theater in Oxford (the play was scheduled to open there the next day). The lighting came on, and I grimaced. The set was awful, just about the worst thing I'd ever seen in my life. When the rehearsal ended, the producer, Binky Beaumont, came over to me and announced, "It's just horrible."

"I know," I said. "I've got to do something."

Beaumont's assistant, barely disguising his glee, whined, "Well, Gene, what do you expect to do? The play opens tomorrow night."

"As you British say, 'Not to worry.' I'll manage. I'm going to stay all night and repaint it."

"And just where do you think you're going to get paints and brushes at this time of night?" asked the assistant and walked off, very pleased with himself. I would have been left standing alone in that empty theater had Sam not bravely offered to stay and help me.

March 28, 1963. The Easter bonnet. The eggs are real (blown), the bluebird is real, as are the nest and the egg in it. And the diamonds are real, too.

The model for the stage set of The Ides of March. *When she saw it, Irene Worth complained about the stairs. "Nobody knows how to build stairs." I knew how: you should have a wide tread and a short riser. Worth ran up and down those stairs like a happy bird.*

Beaumont's assistant didn't know that theater very well. It was a workshop theater, so I knew Sam and I would find paints backstage. The paints were there, but there were no brushes. That seemed like a real problem until I remembered that in theaters there are always bathrooms, and in bathrooms—at least in Britain and Europe—there are toilet brushes. Sam and I went into every restroom on every floor of that theater and gathered the toilet brushes. Then we got to work.

Painting the burlap took all night. We were painting it burlap color, of course, but burlap just drinks in paint, and our brushes weren't the best. The set needed a lot of painting, but when done it looked marvelous. I knew that, and so did everyone else, but the only person to say anything was Gielgud.

The London opening of the play was delayed a few weeks, and since I'd prepared only enough windows for the period of my leave of absence, I had to return to New York. I was back in London on the play's opening night, however, and received a telegram from my New York stage-designer friend: "Congratulations on your mammoth window display."

After the opening, Gielgud asked me if I'd ever agree to do another set design for a play. "Not on your life," I told him. "Too many people have too much to say about something they know absolutely nothing about."

I had a few sets of windows planned for my return to New York: metal flowers with enamel leaves by Nathan Cabot Hale; sculptures made of wine corks by Roger Sammis, a good painter who'd done things for me at Bonwit's; and plaster wall paintings based on Cretan frescoes by Ron Ferri. But all the way home I was thinking not about Tiffany's but about things American—I'd been away for more than a month. I was still vaguely thinking about American products and inventions while walking out of the airport. And then, there in the airport, right in front of me, was a child happily holding and licking an ice-cream cone.

As soon as I got into my office the next morning I nearly shouted to Ronnie, "Call somebody over at Nabisco and have them send us a couple thousand ice-cream cones in a hurry!"

They sent over one thousand, nicely packed in boxes, and we took them out, spread them on a table, and began playing with them, putting them together, cutting them up, and accidentally breaking quite a few, for they're very fragile. They took well to glue—we used Elmer's—and could be stacked easily, just like planters. They seemed to have an endless variety of uses, aside from holding ice cream, and selecting five displays was difficult.

March 1, 1963. The newspaper strike. The sailboat is for the sports pages.

I had a wall of cones with four cones standing in front of it in one window. In the next was an enormous sphere, like a sunburst, made of cones. It was—miraculously, of course—supported on a single cone as base and was topped with a diamond bracelet. In another window I made what looked like a city with spires. It reminded me of Gaudí's architecture. The points of upside-down cones worked wonderfully as holders for rings and bracelets. In the next window I had stacks of cones, and, like planters, they fit into one another perfectly. And in the last window was yet another miracle: standing cones covered the floor and supported a very heavy glass vase (unseen rods held it up).

Some people saw the ice-cream-cone sphere as a bouquet of flowers. I thought it looked more like the moon. Even so, a mother of the bride from Virginia came into the store and insisted on having it for the centerpiece at her daughter's wedding reception. People depend on Tiffany's for weddings. I let her have it.

Around then work I'd done of another sort was on display at the 1963 New York World's Fair. The architect Philip Johnson had called to ask if I'd be interested in designing a show for the fair. A New York dealer named John Wise and Peter Pollack, former director of the American Federation of Arts, had assembled an array of pre-Columbian gold—including pieces from Paul Tishman's collection—for an exhibit in the fair's Travel and Transportation Pavilion. All told they'd assembled five hundred pieces of gold worth $3 million, and they called the exhibit "The World of Ancient Gold." It was

March 1, 1963. The steam shovel is for the apartment listings. The city always needs new apartment buildings.

scheduled to open the first week in June. Johnson was designing the building and wanted me to create the interior and the cases for the gold.

The interior had a low ceiling, and they were planning dark blue carpeting, so I had them do the walls in the same carpeting. That gave the space a rich, cool feeling. The cases, each lined with a special piece of fabric to match the object being displayed, were illuminated with internal spotlights. The gold itself was fantastic: beaten, hammered, and cast miracles of design. The motifs seemed simple but otherworldly, with objects modeled on the creatures pre-Columbian Americans knew best: the frog, snake, shark, turtle, crab, and crocodile. There were golden earplugs, nose pendants, and mustachios made to cover the mouth, golden goblets, and strange baubles hinged to bounce and thus catch light. Some of the forms were abstract, such as a condor turned into a broad-tailed triangle. Some objects had been made symmetrical through repetition—there were many two-headed beasts.

I had a small staff for that job, people being paid hourly rates, and before I started work on the design cases I calculated how much time the job would take and how much money I'd need to pay those people. I then insisted the exhibitor give me that money up front so I could put it in a bank. That was a bright idea on my part, for although the exhibit opened on time and was popular, the exhibitor soon went bankrupt. I was able to pay my staff, but I'd forgotten to include money for my own time and effort. I didn't mind

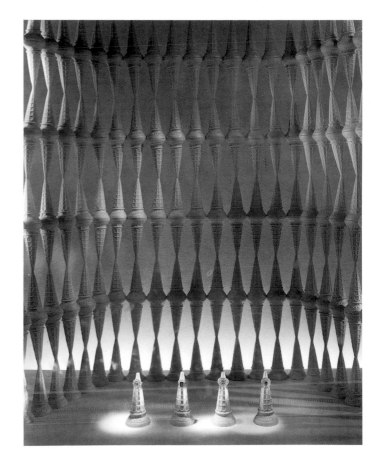

July 30, 1963. Opposite: A metal rod stuck up through the cone supported the sunburst: it wasn't suspended from the top. Above: The vase is sitting on rods that come up through cones. Above right and below right: The shapes came about effortlessly and seemed to have meaning.

all that much, for the gold was thrilling, and I'd learned a lot about primitive art. I'd also met some very nice people and fallen in love with a llama, a beast with incredible eyes.

What I did mind was when Tiffany's store manager tampered with one of my window displays. I'd put together a set of windows dealing with writing: a typewriter (accompanied by a martini) in one window; typewriter ribbons hanging in another; then pencils, a tape machine, and books in the three Fifty-seventh Street windows. A half-written letter was sticking up out of the typewriter in the first window. A woman was writing a girlfriend to explain how she'd come by a diamond bracelet (the window's merchandise). This seemed like another fine opportunity to test my audience. I misspelled one of the words in the letter.

The next Saturday—I don't work weekends—a woman came in, asked to see the store manager, and informed him of the word. A misspelled word in a Tiffany's window was more than that store manager could bear, so he opened the window, took out the typewriter and letter, retyped the letter with the word correctly spelled, and put it all back out in the window.

The following Monday, when the manager boldly informed me of his deed, I was furious. Not only had he mucked up my audience research—he'd actually touched my windows. "If you ever touch one of my windows again, I'll—" He understood.

That was in early September, and the New York Philharmonic was opening on the twenty-fourth in its new home at Philharmonic Hall. Ron McNamer made me figures playing instruments: cello, piano, harp, violin, kettledrum, one for each window.

That year I started doing the windows for the Kenneth Beauty Salon on East Fifty-fourth Street. Kenneth Battelle had made a name for himself with the bouffant hairdo, but those days were far behind him. "Teasing is out," he was often quoted as saying, and he really meant it. With the help of the famous decorator Billy Baldwin, he'd turned all five floors of an old Edwardian townhouse into a salon and commissioned me to do the windows.

Along with other props, I used heads with unusual hairdos for Kenneth's windows: something new for me to think about.

For Christmas that year I used an angel Sam Kirkpatrick, the assistant from *The Ides of March*, made for me out of molded leather. He'd modeled it after an angel in a Hans Memling painting. In the next window was an angel modeled after a Van Eyck.

Valentine's Day means hearts, and hearts beat harder with love. I was thinking of that in my 1964 Valentine's Day windows, which I called "Love and the Doctor." In the first I had an old microscope examining a small jeweled heart; the second had an eye-doctor's tool aimed at an eye—"Love comes in at the eye"; the third had a suspended hand holding a stethoscope to a tiny heart; I put the china rhinoceros in the fourth window amid candy-shop shelves of jars full of hearts; and the last window had a tattooed arm being tested with a blood-pressure device.

The small jeweled hearts—they were made out of various colored stones as well as diamonds—were wonderfully popular, and when the store sold out its supply I had to open the windows and take them out of my displays. In the end, we'd sold every diamond and jeweled heart in the window.

I calmed everyone down with my next windows: bamboo. There's something enormously soothing about looking at bamboo. It's so beautifully designed and yet irregular, as though made with simple philosophy. The space between two joints is never identical. And, of course, it's circular, making it a perfect form for bracelets.

The eggs were ready for Easter—I used far fewer than I had in 1963—as was the grass and clover. In one window a game of croquet was under way, with eggs used as balls. In another, two rabbits stood muzzle to muzzle to support three eggs—with painted designs by Richard Giglio—on top of which was balanced a glass. More impossible still was the balance in the last window's enormous basket of eggs.

Easter and the end of March; the passing of winter and the coming of spring. All those symbolic eggs and thick grass with fertile bunnies everywhere. What fun: spring and rebirth, the shine of a warm summer sun, vacations to far-off lands—maybe Greece again—and yet a dark cloud hung over these pleasant thoughts, and as I walked along the crowded sidewalks to and from Tiffany's I knew that same cloud hung over everyone I passed, over every citizen in our broad republic, from sea to shining sea. The Internal Revenue Service was waiting. By April 15, we all had to do our taxes.

Another year, another decade, I might have let it pass, paid my taxes, and thought only of the next set of windows. But in 1964 I wanted commiseration in my windows, I wanted to display sympathy for the headachy hours of subtracting line 11a from line 9. I also saw an opportunity to tell stories about New Yorkers. Income tax forms are deliciously revealing.

Telling tales with taxes involves much adding and subtracting, and I knew I'd need help with all that math homework—by then I knew very well that people were going to

January 26, 1982. Which makes the strongest heart? And should a heart be strong or sweet?

stand in front of the windows and check my arithmetic—so I made an appointment with my accountant. We worked out IRS stories for four people. I told him how much money each person did or didn't have and how he or she had made or lost it, made up a name for each, and then the accountant worked out the appropriate forms. A calligrapher in the stationery department copied out the forms to be used in the windows; after all, they had to be legible. In truth, the stories in those windows were elaborate, and you had to study them a bit to understand what was going on.

For the first window on Fifth Avenue I blew up a copy of the 1963 Instructions for Preparing Your Federal Income Tax Return Form 1040 to serve as background art and arranged in front of it a timely still life: a bottle of aspirin, ice bag, pile of pencils, erasers, tax forms, and lots of extra red tape. The next window introduced New Yorkers to the hapless Yves Mal Chance, filing a joint return with his wife. Shown in the window was his Schedule A-Exemptions form, on which he claimed medical expenses of $20,159.67, some of it from hospital and insurance premiums and payments to doctors Jones, Smith, and Brown, but most of it ($20,000) a "diamond bracelet prescribed to calm wife's nerves." Near the tax form and more spilled aspirin was a telephone directory open to pawnshop listings. Resting on the open page was the bracelet.

Window three presented the dismal situation of a truly woebegone New Yorker, Ruth O. Astimit. She gave her occupation as taxpayer, her Social Security Number 123-45-6789, her address the impossible "corner of Park and Fifth avenues." Ruth's total income for 1963 was $233,463.76, all of it from "dividends, interest, rents, royalties, and pensions." Her total taxes due ("Pay in full with this return") were $180,071.18. Other articles in the window let on that she had spent all her money on a jewel, a gold bag, and a cigarette case. With four cents left to her improbable name, she had few alternatives. Two were

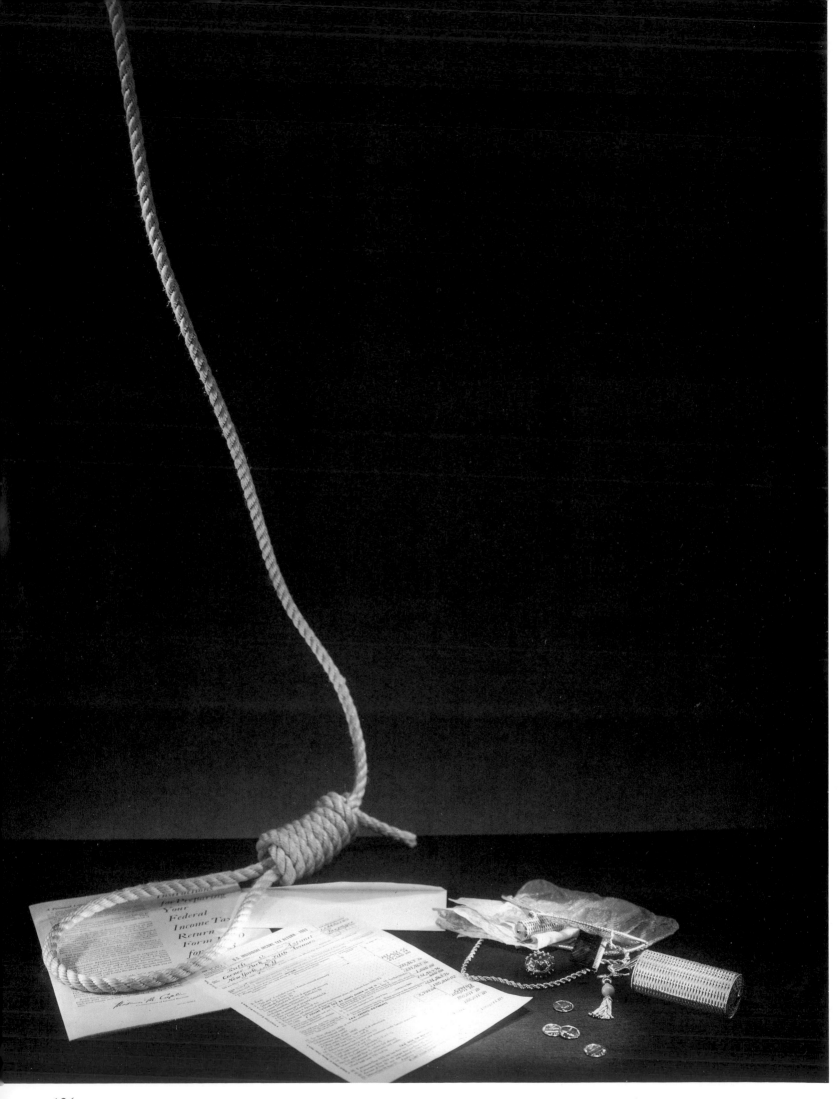

shown in the window: a pistol and a noose hanging nearby. (I didn't know how to tie a noose and was surprised to find that Tiffany's president, the kindhearted, pipe-smoking Farnham Lefferts, was actually quite good at it.)

A. Wastold, president of A. Wastold & Co., a wholesale and general merchandise store, appeared in the next window. Wastold was doing a bit of fancy work with his Profit (or Loss) from Business or Profession form. His gross sales amounted to $284,500, but this he deftly offset by "other business expenses," neatly listed on a Schedule C-1, including small sums spent for stationery, postage, books, and publications; a pearl necklace for his secretary ($10,000); a diamond brooch given a buyer ($7,000); a Tiffany sterling wedding present given a buyer ($1,585); and $1,250-worth of telephone calls and telegrams. In a letter to a friend named Jack he gloated for passersby: "Things have worked out so well this year after taxes that I've decided to take a trip to Europe and will certainly get to Athens to see you and Maria. Perhaps you can get away and we could all do a tour of the islands together. I've always wanted to see Crete and Mykonos and Rhodes."

In the last window, Richard Oilgig of 613 East 51 Street (an address somewhere in the East River) reported that he'd won the Irish Sweepstakes ($150,000) and Aqueduct and Saratoga ($168,532.19). His window was littered with his winning tickets along with a bottle of champagne and two glasses. Oilgig came by his name easily. I simply reversed that of my friend Richard Giglio.

The next month I tried an experiment: windows with nothing but merchandise. The store was then selling crystal cube paperweights, and I just arranged stacks of those cubes and set jewelry on top. The lighting was the entire display, light coming through the crystals and shining off the jewels.

Ordinary objects are the most beautiful, and their beauty is increased by being so thoroughly unexpected. You pick up some commonplace object, something you've lived with or worked with for years, and suddenly you see it in a new way. It's as though you've never really seen it before. Rope, flowerpots, pasta, ice-cream cones—the day finally came for nails.

Nails are endlessly beautiful, each one shiny and sharp, a perfect form. Hundreds of them can become waving swirls or, lined up straight, can form rhythmic rows with a solid gleam.

I used nails in my windows in June. Having discovered their true beauty, I wanted to share it with all the strangers who pass the corner of Fifth Avenue and Fifty-seventh Street. I drove nails into boards and hung jewelry off them, pounded hundreds of nails partway into the floor of a window and rested a hammer on the surface they created, used standing nails to hold up shelves, and to make sure I'd made my point mixed some jewelry into a pile of nails—which was really more beautiful?

In one of the windows I drove a nail through a wineglass, or at least that's how it appeared. A nail was driven clear through one of seven wineglasses, with some loose nails and a hammer lying nearby. Actually, I'd had a glazier drill holes in the glass and then just shoved the nail through them. Since the holes were the exact size of the nail, no one could see they'd been drilled.

In August it was spools, simple spools of sewing thread. Seeing one of the plastic—gold plastic—spools used so much today reminded me of the old wooden spools. I called Coats & Clark, the famous old thread company, and said, "I love your spools, especially the wooden ones. Please send me some." They sent several hundred, both with thread and without. I was so intrigued by matching the colors of the thread to jewelry that I set aside most of the threadless spools to use at another time. For those first displays I had horizontal stripes of spools filling one window, their stripes of color giving the sense of a woven tapestry. A pyramid of spools filled another window, and columns of spools the third window.

Sam Kirkpatrick sent me three beautiful angels for my Christmas windows, two playing instruments and one holding a score of music and singing. All three were dressed in blue robes, their wings an even deeper blue. Since they were based on a painting (by an unknown Flemish artist), I put them in a picture frame. A Madonna and Child by the

March 30, 1964. Faced with "Pay in full with this return,"
Ruth O. Astimit ponders a grim fate.

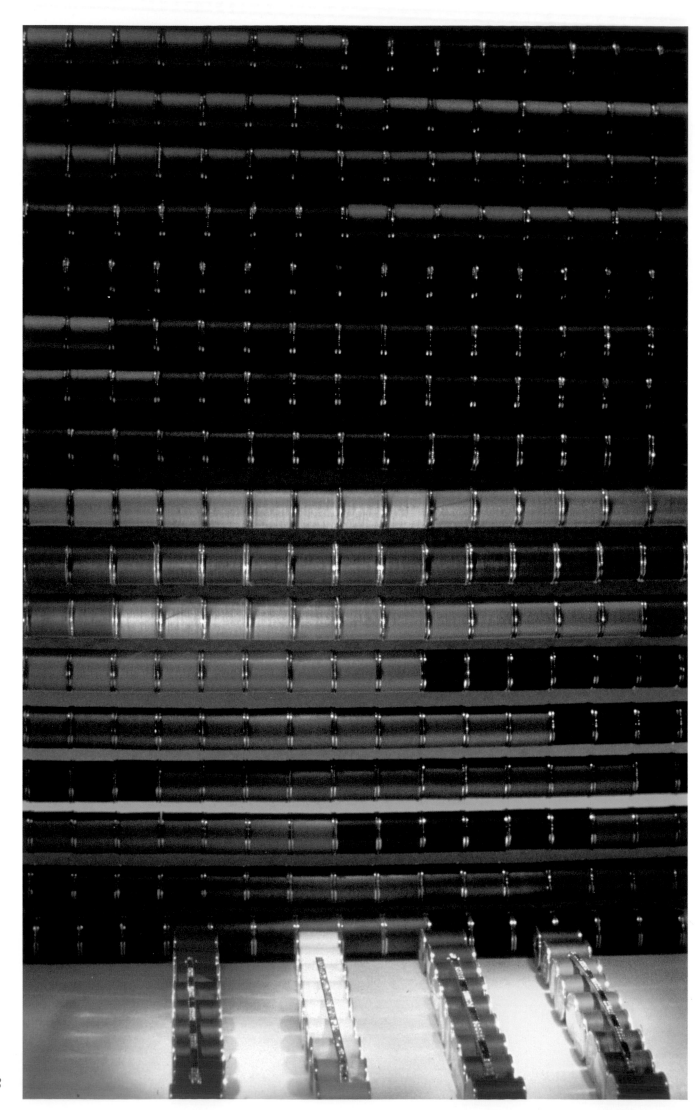

same artist was reproduced inside another picture frame in the next window. I sprinkled the floors of both windows with pretend snow, real spruce needles, and miniature pineapples (instead of pinecones) and tossed in a few star-shaped diamonds.

The first of the windows on Fifty-seventh Street showed emerald-cut diamonds on standing icicles. In the next Santa rode by, his sleigh filled with watches, cigarette lighters and cases, gold and silver pens and pencils, travel clocks, and other small merchandise. The fifth window, the New Year's or champagne window, was the most popular of those holiday displays. I'd made up a story—made it up in my head and certainly not told a soul—about a glamorous lady who goes out skiing in the Alps and falls into a deep snowdrift. She's buried completely in the snow and needs help, so she stretches her arm up through the snow with a glass in her hand—Tiffany's crystal, of course—to a waiting Saint Bernard. Instead of the famous little keg of brandy, that noble dog had a bottle of Moët et Chandon strapped around his neck.

I'd had that dog made for me by a display house. Since I didn't need the entire animal—only his forepaws and head would be visible in the window—I asked for only half a dog. Taking me at my word, those display people cut the papier-mâché dog in half, and where they cut him off they carefully painted his insides. People looking in the window didn't know that the backside of that dog was a true anatomy lesson.

Opposite: *August 2, 1964. Spools from Coats & Clark: the fun was matching the colors of the thread to those of the jewels.* Right: *December 3, 1964. Christmas, and the New Year's champagne window presents the scene of a glamorous lady in deep snow. She was a mannequin's arm, the Saint Bernard only half a dog.*

February 15, 1965. The log that fell off a truck. The bird just flew in the window and stayed there, or at least that was the idea.

For my January 1965 windows I used seashell sculptures by an artist named Carl Malouf. I get along well with Malouf, have always admired his art, and I've used his works several times since that first January display.

Early one morning that winter Ronnie came rushing into the office all out of breath. "I just saw the most beautiful log fall off a truck on Fifty-seventh Street, about half a block down," he gasped. "Well," I said, "let's go get it."

It had fallen off a truck hauling firewood and was big and round, with wonderfully thick bark, and so heavy we couldn't lift it but had to roll it up the street, along the crowded sidewalk, into the store and the elevator. That's how that log came into my life. Since that morning it has made its way into many windows, beginning with that year's Valentine's Day.

The power of love, or at least its weightiness, was on display in window one, in which I placed a pile of stones on one side of an old shop balance and a small wooden heart on the other. As the tilt of the scales clearly indicated, the lone heart—on the left of the scale, and not just because I'm left-handed—outweighed those heavy stones.

February 15, 1965. I bought the cash register out in the country, and being brass it weighed a lot. Someone now owes seven hugs and fifty-four kisses.

The log was in window two, standing amid plants and grass like a real stump in a forest. I'd carved a heart-shaped hole in the bark and then burned the words "I love you" into the exposed wood. To show how the deed was done, I stuck an old pocketknife in the log next to the heart. Perched on the knife was one of my stuffed birds, and from the tilt of his head you could tell he thought that message was for him.

I'd bought an old cash register out in the country. It was in the third window. I'd made some alterations: I'd replaced the numbers on the keys with names—you pushed the name of your valentine—and instead of giving total sales in dollars and cents, the keys rang up hugs and kisses. And in place of cold hard cash, I filled the money drawer with gumdrops and candy hearts.

I had a broken heart that year so put it in the window—along with a jar of glue. Glue doesn't work, of course, unless it's applied by the right person.

People are disappointed if I don't put letters in at least one Valentine's Day window. Letters, particularly upside-down ones, are always successful. That year I had little quotes about love written out, including the sage "Love's a malady without a cure."

The merchandise in most of those windows was the little jeweled hearts I'd used on other Valentine's Days. Anything you put in a window sells—that's a truism of window display—but those little hearts were wildly popular. One Saturday the store ran out of hearts, but the manager knew better than to open my windows and take apart my displays. He very politely called me on the phone, and I very politely came over to the store, opened the windows, and took out the little hearts. I then had to scour the jewelry cases for suitable replacements.

Easter is a time for baskets. I was thinking of baskets full of eggs, which explains how I came up with a basket made of eggs for that year's Easter windows. Another robbery attempt was made while those Easter displays were in, or perhaps someone just drove by and shot at the windows. On my way into the store one morning I noticed two bullet holes in a corner of the glass.

That same April I received a special kind of recognition when Aline Saarinen, the art commentator for NBC-TV's "Today" show, wrote an article about me in *Show* magazine (it turned out to be that magazine's last issue). Attention from a serious art critic was then rare for display people. I was delighted. I was less pleased when she asked me to appear on the "Today" show and demonstrate how I make my windows. That was my first time on television, and I was scared to death, but I went and used a mock window to demonstrate various display techniques, even recreated one of my windows: the Christmas window with the lady's arm and the half Saint Bernard.

Zip into spring. After sixteen years at Bonwit's and eight at Delman's before that, I can't be blamed if I sometimes think of cute mottoes. I don't know where "zip into spring" came from, but I decided to take it literally. I called Coats & Clark again and got them to send over some commercial zippers, the big kind used for tents and curtains. The zippers were attached to pieces of cloth, and I filled each window with a zipper and zipped it open partway to reveal a small vase with a real flower. I had to change the flowers every morning. I was very fond of those windows, had a lot of fun putting them in, and got a lot of mail about them.

Around that time I began another freelance project. Clarence House, a fabric store on East Fifty-seventh Street, asked me to do their window occasionally. Clarence House sells only to the trade, but they wanted their windows to make people appreciate what a professional decorator can do. The merchandise, of course, was all fabrics, but I enjoyed doing those windows for just that reason: it was so different from what I was doing at Tiffany's.

That was a hot summer, all of the northeast was suffering a drought, and right from the start there was talk of a water shortage. At first it was just a lot of talk, warnings about what might happen, but all the talk just added to the heat. In June I used wooden artist's figures to take people's minds off the city's woes. After all, it was time for vacations, so I had the figures doing crossword puzzles, lying on the beach reading, cooling their feet with ice trays, and stepping gingerly across seaside shoals. By then I had quite a collection of those artist's figures. Most of them are genderless—you make them look male or female by the position you put them into—but the one I had stepping across the stones was obviously female. Her carved torso included breasts.

I used backgrounds by Robert Heitmann in the next set of windows, the first time I'd used his work at Tiffany's. For my next windows I'd had Carl Malouf make plaster statues that worked as fountains, two cherubic boys holding seashells from which water could spill. I've often used real water in displays, and I thought fountains with splashing water were just the thing that hot July to cool off New Yorkers.

By then we knew the drought was real, and various measures had been taken to save water, including turning off the air-conditioning in many office buildings. Signs appeared reading, "Save water: shower with a friend," and newspapers were full of instructions for how to brush teeth and shave without wasting water. Unnecessary flushing of toilets was a frequent topic.

Two days before Malouf's fountains were scheduled to go in, the city's water commissioner, Armand D'Angelo, decreed a water emergency. Until further notice, no

April 19, 1965. "Zip into Spring." The zipper filled the entire window. The flowers had to be changed every morning.

Above: *July 29, 1965. One of the famous "gin windows." The trick was getting the jewelry to "float" on the water. I cut a slice from a tube of clear plastic the depth of the water and set the jewelry on it.* Right: *Seagram's placed this "Public Notice" in newspapers to explain the uncommon use of their gin.*

Public Notice

For the next few weeks our gin will flow instead of water in the Fifth Avenue windows of Tiffany & Co., New York.

While we endorse this water saving measure during New York's water shortage, we cannot endorse the use of Seagram's Extra Dry Gin for sprinkling lawns, washing cars, or filling swimming pools.

It does, however, make a perfect Martini:

Seagram's Extra Dry Gin
The perfect Martini Gin

one would be served water in a restaurant unless he or she expressly requested it. The watering of lawns and gardens and washing of automobiles were banned. Although most of the city's fountains recirculated their water, D'Angelo decided to order them shut off as a psychological measure. The Goodyear blimp flew overhead flashing the commissioner's motto, "Save Water."

I didn't know whether my fountains qualified under D'Angelo's ban, but using water during a shortage didn't seem wise. Then I got an idea. All I needed for my fountains was a colorless liquid that resembled water. I knew just the right liquid—gin—but thought I should first speak to Hoving, since he had strong feelings about liquor.

I told him of my planned fountains, my misgivings about using water, and about the gin. He gave me a strange look, thought a moment, and then said it was a wonderful idea, but we would have to put a sign in the window, of course, and he wanted to write the copy. That was fine with me.

Because of my work designing their Christmas displays, I knew several people over at Seagram's, including the woman in charge of public relations. Seagram's was glad to contribute the liquid for my fountains, which turned out to be quite a bit of gin: thirteen cases to get the tanks full, and then one case each day for the ten days of the display to make up for evaporation.

Windows one and two had their splashing fountains. I surrounded the statues in each window with ferns and flowers and put little pools in front of each to catch the tumbling gin. I set jewelry in the pools on clear plastic stands, making those gems appear to float. And smack in the middle of the bottom of each display was Hoving's message, written out by a calligrapher in the stationery department: "No! No! No! this is not precious city water. It's just some unprecious old gin."

I'd expected a reaction, but not the kind of overwhelming response those windows got. People jammed the sidewalks in front of the windows as though they'd never seen gin before. Crowds were there even early in the morning when I'd pour in the new case of gin, which I had to do even on Saturdays and Sundays. Every twenty-four hours those fountains needed more gin. I'd unscrew a bottle and pour in the gin, unscrew another bottle and pour in that one, and all the while people were watching and sometimes applauding. I'd make sure they saw the label on the bottle, of course. The city's newspapers said something about the windows nearly every day. Those windows even made it into foreign newspapers, including one in Russia. Because of their popularity I kept those windows in for nearly a month, the first time I'd held over a display.

The fire department heard about the windows and was not amused. Gin is a flammable liquid. A fire marshal came to the store, and I thought, "Now it's Charley and the firemen." The marshal informed me I would have to shut off the fountains because they were a fire hazard. I went over to one of the windows with him and took out a book of matches. "Don't strike that match!" cried the marshal. "It'll all blow up!" But I'd already lit the match, and waving it in the air I asked, "We're still here, aren't we?"

All five of Tiffany's windows have more than adequate ventilation at the top, so I knew there was no danger of fire. Even so, the ground floor soon smelled like a big martini, a pleasant smell that lingered a few days after I'd taken out the display.

For more than a decade—until my 1978 room settings with Edward Acevedo—those were my most popular and best-remembered windows: the so-called gin windows. Although I was pleased by the response, I soon tired of hearing myself introduced as "the man who put gin in Tiffany's windows." They were nice windows but far from my favorite.

The summer was still hot, so I cooled everyone off with snow in the next windows: an ax and woodpile in snow, an old water pump and bucket with more snow. It was so cold in those windows that water from the pump had frozen in mid-air over the bucket (I made the frozen water out of a piece of cloth covered with Duco cement).

Tiffany's appeared in the city's newspapers again that summer, but this time it was less pleasant. Just as Hoving and I were about to celebrate our tenth anniversary at the store, New York City Markets Commissioner Albert Pacetta ordered all retailers to put price tags on everything they had for sale. Hoving was outraged. He repeated his standard adage, "We don't offer people what they want, we offer them what we want," and stubbornly refused the price tags. For a short while it seemed I'd be forced to put price tags on the merchandise in the windows, but that aspect of Pacetta's plan faded away. The price tags, however, eventually made their way onto Tiffany's merchandise, even though the salespeople on the main floor complained the sticky tags messed up the jewels.

Feeling full of piss and vinegar, I decided to take on the shadows I'd been thinking about so much. To catch the light, I built structures for each window that turned them into corners of a room, and in that closed space I put glassware on the crystal cubes. As I'd done at Bonwit's, I climbed into the window and darkened the shadows with charcoal.

But it didn't work, didn't come out the way I wanted, and after only one week I pulled those displays. Hoving noticed. "Why'd you change the windows?" he asked. "I liked them." "I didn't," I said, and that was that.

I had more success, of sorts, over at Clarence House. The store manager said, "I want you to show leather," and as soon as I heard that word I knew what I wanted to do. Against a background curtain of hanging chains I set a six-foot-long Harley-Davidson motorcycle. I draped upholstery leathers over its seat, laid a nine-foot bullwhip on the floor next to it, and as a final touch placed a long-stemmed rose on the floor beneath its front wheel.

That window attracted a lot of attention. The *Herald Tribune* ran a story about it under the headline "Scandal! Sadism Hits Home Furnishings!" and a gang of motorcyclists more or less camped out in front it for a few days. People have since claimed that window began a trend in sadomasochist displays. I'd be sorry were that true, and it certainly wasn't my intention. It seemed to me that people were then only too eager to do away with innocence, S and M was becoming terribly popular, and I meant that crushed rose as the death of innocence, a death I truly lamented.

The Clarence House window of the summer of 1965 that brought sadism to home furnishings. Barely visible under the front wheel is the run-over rose, a symbol of lost innocence overlooked too easily.

While the window display was in I had another constant worry. I'd used real chains—heavy metal chains—as the background, and I just prayed they wouldn't pull the ceiling down. They didn't.

After the gin and the motorcycle I was a little discouraged, because it seemed a window had to have something scandalous to be popular. Far from seeking to shock, I'm most pleased when my windows make people laugh. I accomplished that in September windows dedicated to the opening of the Philharmonic that used metal sculptures by John Richards of insects playing instruments. People stood in front of those windows and smiled, and every time people smile or laugh at one of my windows I know they've got it, have made it their own.

An artist named Stuart Scherr made fun sculptures using compositor's type and big wooden letters in sculpted type boxes, a lot of playing with words. I put his works in the windows that October and had him make a special display that used Hebrew script to spell out "Diamonds are a girl's best friend."

One month later New York was struck by a big blackout. Just before 5:30 on the afternoon of November 9 all the lights in the city went out. I was sitting in my office at Tiffany's when the city outside my windows disappeared. I soon found myself again accused of being prophetic, because in the display I'd just put in at Clarence House I used candles.

I wanted to use old paintings to create contemporary compositions for 1965's Christmas windows and chose Gerard David's *Nativity* and *The Archangel Gabriel*. I got prints of both from the Metropolitan Museum of Art and had Sam Gallo cut out sections and blow up the sections into different sizes. Hung all together, the repeated sections gave the work exciting life. I got lots of mail asking for photographs of the display.

In another of those windows I built a cave with shiny silver mirrors—part of me is always thinking of caves—and I had water as the floor of the cave, with the mirrors and water moving. I put a small silver deer beside that blue bubbling water, creating a scene I thought had nothing to do with this world. I put one piece of gold mirror in the cave, hard to see but there, a sort of hide-and-seek game I was playing with New Yorkers.

In the champagne window I used a wooden horse with beautiful glass eyes that I'd bought three years earlier in Spain. He was carrying the bottle of champagne. I also put a small photograph of Bert Lahr in that window. I've always liked him, and he was then in New York, being treated for an illness at Mount Sinai hospital.

That January's beach-sand windows didn't last long. I pulled them after just two days, not because I didn't like them but because I had something more important to put in the windows.

The city's transit workers—or, more precisely, Mike Quill, head of their union—had decided to go out on strike. The effect on the city was disastrous, and although the strike didn't bother me personally, since I walk to and from work, I was furious. I wanted to do something about the strike but wanted it to be amusing and not too serious. I came up with the idea while walking to work and had the beach sand and seashells out and the new displays in by that evening.

I went up to F.A.O. Schwarz—I was a regular in that store during the 1960s—and bought alternate forms of transportation. I wanted to show New Yorkers how to get around the city during the strike. As with the newspaper strike, I used children's toys to represent the behavior of the union and the childish—and selfish—way the transit workers were treating the people of New York.

The first window told a story about a New York woman who, because of the strike, was getting ready to start a new life walking to work. In one corner of the window was the pair of dress shoes she'd just taken off. In the middle were an old-fashioned foot bath, pitcher, and towel beside a new pair of women's alligator walking shoes. The window's merchandise was her ring, a hundred-carat star sapphire—its blue matched that of the towel. I reasoned that any woman with a ring that big would certainly remove it to take a foot bath.

I'd found a great bicycle at F.A.O. Schwarz, an old-fashioned bike with a tiny rear

January 6, 1966. A unicycle rolls over a black quill pen, stand-in for Mike Quill. It was a child's unicycle: I wheeled it over to Tiffany's from F.A.O. Schwarz.

wheel and enormous front wheel, and I put it in window two. I knew it needed something when I set it up in the window and sent Ronnie down to Thirty-eighth Street, the center of the notary stores, to buy me a feather pen. He brought back a nice big black quill pen, and I put it under the bike's big front wheel.

A unicycle, roller skates, and pogo stick displayed in the three Fifty-seventh Street windows completed the display.

As I put those windows in I wasn't thinking at all about the reaction they might get. I was thinking only of myself and of how I felt. I was fighting mad, and those windows were my way of expressing the anger.

Everyone understood my little joke on Mike Quill's name, and I was again accused of prophesy when Quill died two weeks after the beginning of my display. I hadn't really meant him any harm. I just didn't like anyone who could cause that much trouble to New York City.

We still live with results of that strike. Many people still walk to work, and morning streets are crowded with women wearing comfortable running shoes while carrying their office shoes in bags. And the subway fare increased. That July it went from fifteen cents to twenty. And, because the traffic congestion caused by the strike was crippling the city, City Hall decided to make Fifth Avenue one-way traveling downtown and Madison Avenue one-way traveling uptown. Hoving fought this decision with his usual ardor, calling its supporters the "lunatic fringe" and claiming it would turn Fifth Avenue into a "superhighway." But on January 14, 1966, while my Quill display was still in the window, the change was made official. The corner of Fifth Avenue and Fifty-seventh Street is still the heart of New York, and the volume of people passing has increased with every year, but it's not the same: to go uptown you have to get off Fifth Avenue. The city's main artery no longer flows both ways.

When I pulled out the transit-strike windows I didn't put back the original January displays, even though they'd been in the windows for only two days. Once I've made a display, achieved the effect I was seeking at that one moment, I get bored with it and want to do something new. In truth, I get bored with the windows after a week and don't want to look at them again.

I did, however, use seashells in the next windows. Perhaps I love seashells so much because I grew up far from the sea. The first time I saw the sea—actually, the Atlantic Ocean—was after I'd just come to New York. Seashells have always seemed like flowers to me, because of both their geometry and their colors, so beautiful and so mysterious. Tiffany's then sold a big glass, about the size of a small fishbowl, and I filled one with water and put shells in it. Other windows had other glasses with water and shells. The water, of course, magnifies the shells, makes them look enormous, and I had people coming in to ask how I'd managed to get those giant shells in the glasses.

For Easter that year I closed down the frame on window three—made it very narrow so that the window became a standing rectangle—and filled that space with eggs, nothing but a thick mass of eggs that almost seemed to be boiling up. Near the bottom of the crowd of eggs was one larger one, a goose egg, with a ring riding on top of it.

I covered the bottom of another window with half eggshells standing upright and open. Standing boldly on that field of shells was my favorite homely rhino.

Kodak cameras then made their second appearance in my windows, this time with squarish artist's figures using the cameras to record events of their vacations.

That June New York celebrated "Swiss Week," an event so well publicized I didn't have to include a credit card in the window in which I placed a small mouse holding a Swiss flag on top of an enormous wheel of Swiss cheese (made of painted wood).

The Flora Mir candy company called me around then to ask if I'd do their windows, but, having too much to do already, I recommended two other window trimmers, first Gene McCabe, a designer I'd known for years, and then, when McCabe left, Howard Nevelow, who'd worked for many years at Hattie Carnegie, a big fashion house. Since I couldn't do their windows, Flora Mir decided I'd be their "creative consultant."

May 26, 1966. The camera is real and actual size, but that fact becomes less believable the more you look at the display.

I never knew what they were going to ask me—candy has lots of possibilities—and one day I got a call from a woman at Flora Mir who said they wanted me to design some edible centerpieces. Interesting idea. I asked her to send over some gumdrops. I had no idea what to do with them, but Ronnie and I started playing around with them, and somehow, without actually wanting to, we created a pineapple. We went on from there, making bunches of grapes, a big watermelon slice, ice-cream cones topped with gumdrop ice cream, a sunburst of gumdrops. Some of these were time-consuming. The watermelon slice, for example, was made by sticking toothpicks into a styrofoam form and then attaching, one at a time, the gumdrops. I couldn't resist putting a little trick in the window with the ice-cream cones. There were six, each with a different color "ice cream" made of gumdrops. Atop five of those ice-cream scoops I put a ring with a stone that matched the color of the gumdrops; the sixth cone was ringless. Sure enough, people came into the store to inform me that I'd forgotten a ring.

I put these candy creations in the window to coincide with the National Fancy Food and Confections Show. Some of the arrangements Ronnie and I designed eventually went on sale all across the country as Designs in Candy. People liked the idea of eating centerpieces.

That September, the month for harvests, I made windows using wheat, which is so very beautiful, so clear and simple. I had separate stalks of wheat, and in one window I tied together bunches of them with string and then spread the bases to create sheaves that could stand on their own. In another I used the old trick of driving pins into the floor, then cutting off their heads and sticking the stalks of wheat down over them. I had a sickle that I wanted to put in that window and also some jewelry.

I solved the problem of where to put the jewelry and sickle by cutting down some of the wheat in the front part of the window. It looked like it had just been reaped. I placed jewelry on the tops of the cut wheat and leaned the sickle nearby. Showing people the tool that has performed the magic is always a good idea.

Opposite: *June 14, 1966. This came about easily: it was a celebration of "Swiss Week," Swiss cheese is Swiss (in theory), mice love cheese, and nothing waves a flag better than a mouse. Right: September 29, 1966. Harvest windows. I loved the shape of the sickle and wanted to find room for it in the window. Cutting down a few rows was the most sensible solution.*

One morning that October Hoving called me into his office and told me I was going to become director of design development in gold jewelry.

I said, "But I don't know anything about making jewelry."

"You'll learn," he said. "You're going to Europe."

I went with Farnham Lefferts to Italy, France, and Germany. We visited manufacturers, and I watched them make jewelry, talked to them, and read as much as I could.

My title, director of design development in gold jewelry, was a tad misleading, since I wasn't working only with gold, but also with gemstones. I eventually had three young designers working with me: Sonia Younis from Beirut, Aldo Cipullo from Italy, and Don Berg from Texas. I put those three kids in an office down on the fourth floor of Tiffany's and started feeding them ideas. I took Sonia with me on a trip to Europe to study gothic architecture because I'd decided to create some gothic jewelry. And in my moments alone, I thought about jewelry designs.

Standing at the counter of a hardware store out in the Hamptons, just waiting my turn to be served, I absentmindedly removed a nut from a large bolt, played around with

it, and finally slipped the nut on a finger. What a beautiful ring. I knew I'd never be able to convince anyone with just a sketch, so I had the manufacturer make a sample for me to show at a design meeting. Everyone loved it, and that ring, made of solid gold, became one of Tiffany's best sellers.

Another idea came to me early one morning while I was dressing. I looked down and saw a safety pin on the floor. I'd never really looked at one before—so efficient, such purity of design. I decided to create a jewelry safety pin—all pavé diamonds—and had Aldo do the drawings. I put a small bow done in gold and enamel on the pin and made it so it could be removed. We had that pin made in large and small sizes (both then sold for under $2,000), and they became quite a hit. Halston saw that pin and used it on a hat he'd designed for Bergdorf's.

From 1966 to 1972 I was director of design development in gold jewelry (I quit the post when a design director was installed with the power to pass on my work). Left: My first jewelry design was the safety pin. Above: Animals that can be worn as pins or used as objets d'art.

Tiffany's windows, Kenneth's salon, Flora Mir, Clarence House—and now designing jewelry. These were busy years, and the freelance jobs I took varied enormously. I was asked, for example, to redesign La Fonda del Sol restaurant, an undertaking I loved because I was supposed to redo the entire restaurant, and I made it all pre-Columbian, from the interior decor—for which I designed pierced-tin screens lit from behind—to the candlesticks for the tables and the flatware. Just when I'd finished my designs, however, the restaurant closed.

National Airlines was opening a new route to Florida and wanted a suitable design. I enjoyed this job, too, because I had so many people to work with and talk to. First I gave them their sunburst corporate emblem. Doing so was trying because the design had to be approved by several hundred executives, and I had to revise it several times before it was finally accepted. I also designed the cabin interiors of the planes, the ticket offices, the passenger waiting areas in airports, and clothes for the stewardesses. Some of those ideas came easily. Since the airline was going to sunny Florida, I used the yellow and white stripes common on beach chairs and umbrellas. They were serving suitable food on the run—Key lime pie, Okeechobee hush puppies, Islamorada stuffed shrimp—and I designed

the menu cover to serve as a souvenir. Turned over, it could be used as a sunshine reflector.

That year I designed costumes for the Glen Tetley Ballet Company at Jacob's Pillow in Lee, Massachusetts. One of the ballets I worked on was called *Chronochromie,* a name made up from the Greek words *kronos* ("time") and *kroma* ("color"): it was usually translated as "The color of time." *Chronochromie* was performed that summer in Central Park's Delacorte Theater as part of the Rebekah Harkness Foundation Dance Festival.

Walter Hoving's son, Thomas, was then the city's parks commissioner. He had a good time as commissioner and tried to bring New Yorkers back into the city's parks, which had become dirty, neglected, and generally unsafe. He installed a Parisian-style restaurant by the lake in Central Park and staged so-called Hoving happenings. On one Sunday he

Above: *More of the jewelry animals.* Right: *The second version of my fish keychain, this one without bones.*

153

December 2, 1976. The water in the vase magnifies the popcorn, and to a person walking by the popcorn seems to move.

had people handing out free paint to strollers in the park, inviting them to apply it as they wished to a 105-foot canvas stretched across a lawn.

In November I helped New Yorkers count down to Christmas by putting big calendars for November and December in the windows showing the days left to Christmas. Each day I got in the windows and crossed off another day.

For Christmas 1966 I used works by Carl Malouf. I'd been to Egypt that year and had fallen in love with Coptic art, so I had him create a Coptic angel and Madonna and Child. That year I introduced popcorn to my Christmas windows. I filled window three with popcorn, had popcorn completely covering the back wall and piled thickly on the floor. Resting on the popcorn was a hibachi with a silver skillet, as though the corn had been popped in that elegant tool. Attaching the popcorn to the wall had taken a great deal of time. There's no easy way with popcorn. You have to put a spot of glue on each piece and then stick it on—and you have to do that hour after hour.

As with every other Christmas, I also did the decorations at the Seagram Building, put a Christmas touch on the windows at Kenneth's salon, and used fabrics in a seasonal way at Clarence House. In that window I put a Santa hurrying off to deliver his presents. He was sitting on a fuchsia Vespa and wearing a nifty suit and boots made of a geranium flower print.

154

Not everyone gets sweet words for Valentine's Day, sometimes it seems there's only a certain amount of love around, so we can't all find or have it at the same time. But during the 1960s I was full of enough gumdrops for everyone on Fifth Avenue, so I put them together to say what everyone wants to hear. In window two was "Love," in one was "You," so looking at the store spelled "Love You." The words were made of gumdrops stuck to Styrofoam forms. In front of each letter was a gumdrop heart, four for "Love," three for "You."

Gumdrops seemed to call for rhinoceroses, so I put two of my homely pals horn to horn—kissing, of course. They were visible through a heart-shaped opening in a screen of gumdrops that covered the face of the window. I used red gumdrops for that screen, with one pink one near the top of the window. Suspended in the air over the kissing rhinos was a heart shaped from other pink gumdrops.

The best colors, however, are real colors, the ones that grow on their own or have been made of the earth. Every year, just before Easter, I get calls from Ukrainian ladies. "I decorate eggs," they say. "Fine," I say. "You keep them." Eggs are perfect just the way they are. An egg is a shape that doesn't need decoration. Even a broken egg is a beautiful thing. Grass, too, is perfect. For Easter that year Jeanne Owens made me a Humpty-Dumpty, and I sat him on a real brick wall. The contrast between the red of the bricks and the green of the grass, as well as between their very different textures, made those windows.

I'm not sure what I believe and what I don't believe, but I like to have all available opinions, so I pay attention to my horoscope and occasionally visit fortunetellers and palmists. The artist Scott Hyde was interested in palmistry, too, or perhaps he thought it was only fun, but for my windows he blew up palms of hands to enormous size and sketched in a few words along some of the thicker lines of the palms. No great truths were revealed in those windows, but people stood still to study them.

After the palms I used rock sculptures by Max Ernst's son James. In the next set of windows I used a real rock, along with real plants and dirt. In one of those windows I even had a real wasp's nest. The wasps had all left it, of course, and I'd found it out in the country on a branch. In the last of that set I had that old piece of firewood, turned on its side to hide its "I love you" brand.

It was then May, and I wanted to reassure New Yorkers that spring would indeed come. So I filled the windows with coal, real coal, and placed real flowers in it so that they seemed to grow right out of it. Coal itself is wondrously beautiful, but I wanted to tell people that out of all that cold blackness would come something alive and real.

That June, just after I'd installed new displays with sculptures by Carl Malouf—busts of such sea gods as Neptune rising from pools, with water coming out of their mouths and hair and running down their cheeks—I found myself promoted. I was now a divisional vice-president. I immediately went to see Hoving. "What does this mean? I get to do more porter work?"

"Probably," he said. But I knew by then that fancy titles are what you get in place of raises. My salary hadn't changed when I'd become director of design development of gold jewelry.

By then, Hoving's son, Thomas, had left his job with the parks department and become director of the Metropolitan Museum of Art, the seventh in the museum's ninety-seven-year history. His approach to the museum was much like his father's to Tiffany's. He wanted to change the displays, do away with the old square glass cases and show things in a way that would make people feel they were holding them in their hands. He wanted, he said, to "weed out the junk. Over several generations, every museum collects stuff which, on reflection, is not as good as it seemed at the time." He couldn't hold a White Elephant Sale, but he could put the objects he didn't like in storage to make room for more interesting exhibits. His opinions were refreshing, at least to me. He wasn't full of love for the museum's most famous Rembrandt, *Aristotle Contemplating the Bust of Homer*, which had been acquired in 1961 for the then record price of $2,300,000. "It's a perfectly fine painting, a beautiful Rembrandt," he said. "But I hate to see people come in and stare at it as if it were dripping with dollar signs."

*Coiffures for the
Kenneth Beauty
Salon. The hairdos
are made of wooden
spools, lightbulbs
(one was lighted),
and wooden balls.*

I was delighted when the Metropolitan Museum, at the suggestion of Thomas
Hoving, invited me to create a permanent display for the Greek and Roman gold and
silver collections. I was particularly pleased by the word *permanent*. I love my work, but
the idea of doing something that would last longer than two weeks—that might even
outlast me—was wonderful. Hoving selected the items to be used but gave me complete
freedom in designing the display.

I planned a large, oval room with a big pool in its center and display cases set around
its perimeter and even suspended over the water of the pool. I needed an architect to help
me and got together with Paul Chen, an architect with whom I'd done some work for
Restaurant Associates. He did all the final drawings for me.

When I showed Thomas Hoving the drawings, he said, "It's wonderful. I knew you'd
do something marvelous, but I had no idea it would be so wonderful."

Hoving's enthusiasm wasn't enough, however. Someone at the museum was against
my plans, and to my great displeasure the project was cancelled.

The heat of that year's July led me to do a set of windows showing ways to survive,
mostly with liquid refreshments: a martini, lemonade, ice water. I also suggested playing
solitaire—the heat had to end sometime—and sitting near a fan.

The terrible heat hadn't ended in August so I had Richard MacLagger make me some
origami snowflakes. I gave him a book of snowflake designs and set up the finished
snowflakes on drawingboard backgrounds.

I used my most popular and agile troupe, the artist's figures, in September windows.
They were playing at acrobats in most of the windows, but in the last display two of the
figures were having a tug-of-war with a watch on a chain. Those wooden bodies clearly
showed the strain and tension of the contest. I didn't have any particular pun in mind,
but I suppose people do steal time from one another, and sometimes they just openly
yank it away.

Chestnut brown was a popular color that year, so in the Kenneth hairdressing
windows in November I designed a mannequin head with hair made entirely of unshelled
nuts. Rows and rows of walnuts, almonds, and pecans were glued to her head. I was
pleased she didn't fall over. I'd tried doing a coiffure of pure coal earlier in the year, but
the head was so heavy it kept falling over.

Just before Christmas 1967 I designed the Terrace Room of the Plaza Hotel for the
wedding of Joan Mailman to Paul Speiller. I'd met Mrs. Mailman through Marilyn Evins,
wife of David Evins, a famous shoe designer. I got to design most of that wedding, from

the room's decor to the bride's bouquet—a three-foot-long white rose with no leaves—and the wedding cake, which I created along with a pastry chef and topped with real lily of the valley.

I was exhausted that year and can remember sitting at a table with Mrs. Evins in the Terrace Room, resting my head on my hands. A wonderful wedding (they later divorced), but halfway through I almost fell asleep.

My most popular window that Christmas showed a Santa Claus fishing. Ice fishing, of course, and making that ice was the hardest part of the display. I made the ice of parrafin, which I'd heated and then poured, layer after layer. I had some blue dye mixed in to add to the cold. Santa had caught a fish: a merchandise fish made of gold and diamonds.

For Easter I broke almost all the blown eggs, which is fun, for no two eggs break alike. I covered a piece of felt with row after row of the broken shells and said a little prayer when it came time to lift that wall of broken eggs and put it in position in the window. The broken eggs stayed in place and created a wonderful backdrop for a field of grass and a single—intact—egg topped with a pin.

All during this period I was playing with places to put flowers. Vases are made for the purpose, but you can weary of putting things where they belong. In September 1967 I'd put porcelain flowers in vases and, for a change, in a Tiffany's bag, which the flowers fit well. In October of that year I'd found locations for dried flowers, including an ordinary cardboard box. Both the flowers and the box benefited. For June flower windows in 1968 I used baskets and vases and also wrapped a bouquet in newspaper. I think I liked that one best of all.

To get lost alone in the woods, to lie down and look up at the trees—perhaps with a bit of Debussy playing—has always been a favorite dream. That dream comes inside music, of course, but I've tried several times to put it in my windows. I don't use dwarf trees. Any small branches will do to create a forest. Just shove them down on those headless tacks. Thus I've made forests even of seed pods. When I made forests that September I also used the strange curly sticks that come from Japan and are called *unyru*. They make an eerie sort of forest.

There are moods in forests just as there are moods in sand. I love what you can do with beach sand: make it smooth, make it miserable and tormented—unhappy. In January 1969 I used sand together with heads made of seashells by James Valkus.

In the Valentine's Day windows that year I had a cardiograph with "I love you" and other messages and names of sweethearts legible in its zigzag scratches. For another window I got a chest X-ray from a doctor and set it up in the window with a jewelry heart hung over it at the right location for a heart. The third window had chains and locks, although I know it's wrong to put them on hearts. In the last window I piled up sugar cubes and had one of my favorite stuffed parrots on top, obviously quite pleased with himself and his perch.

In March I used my wooden spools. In window one I created an entire wall of them: they're perfectly geometric and fit together as smoothly as bricks. That wall's pattern was ideal for catching light. I used the spools to create square frames in window two, smaller frames within larger ones to add perspective to that depthless world. For a display of glassware I made a Leaning Tower of Pisa. Other spools I stacked edge on edge in tall, winding, teetering columns: another impossible balancing act. This one really was impossible. The columns were tied in place at the top of the window, just out of sight of the viewer.

Robert Heitmann looks at the world in much the same way I do. I think that's why I enjoy working with him—it certainly helps me understand him. He, too, often sees what another might overlook. Walking along Sixth Avenue one evening, in an area of old shops, their storefronts dark and dirty, their interiors visibly full of dust, he spotted a window full of old buttons. He went into the store.

"I'd like to buy some of these buttons," he said into the darkness.

The proprietor appeared from the back of the shop. "How many?"

"Two boxes."

December 4, 1969. A Harnett Christmas. Sonny Hawkins made me the unfinished needlepoint in the upper right. Such displays are improvised on the spot: you have to play around to see what belongs with what.

158

In his small apartment Heitmann now had two boxes—who knows how many hundreds?—of old buttons. He didn't know what to do with them until it occurred to him they could be used to make mosaics. He'd always wanted to make a mosaic but had been turned away by the mess involved. So he made some pictures with the buttons, and in June I put them in Tiffany's windows. Every single one was sold out of the windows.

Heitmann did some unusual needlepoint pictures for the windows in October. A needlepoint picture of a man resting on a hammock was made on a small hammock; two needlepointed trapeze artists sitting on a high-wire swing were, of course, sitting on a real swing. I'd asked him to needlepoint me a plate because I wanted to use yarn as pasta, and he modeled the plate after a pattern on sale in the store and completed the place setting with a needlepointed knife and fork, also in a Tiffany's pattern. I heaped yarn on the bowl and stuck a fork in. I then raised the fork so it was suspended in the air over the plate. That worked well and was very popular.

That Christmas I returned to Judith Brown. She made statues of the Three Wise Men and a Madonna and Child. I put them in the window behind panes of a special kind of glass that makes everything blurry. In another of those windows I made a Harnett still life, just as I had done back in March 1956. I set up a wooden background in the window and then brought down a trayful of junk that I'd collected over the years. There was a cowbell along with sleigh bells. There was a wishbone—I have a collection of wishbones—an old padlock, and one of my favorite dolls. There was merchandise in that window, both attached to the wall and set out on the floor in front of it, but the merchandise, too, became part of the picture.

Six rows of stacked wineglasses filled the champagne window. The champagne was there, in a bucket behind the glasses, and the window was closed with a corner created of mirrors that made the whole thing shine with a crystal brightness.

As we'd done for the past nine years, Ronnie and I drank our own bottle of champagne while putting together those displays. Passersby often stopped in front of the window to look at what we were doing and wave hello. We'd wave back to them, call out, "Here's to you," and pause in our work for a while to watch the lights of the passing traffic.

October 30, 1969. Robert Heitmann made the needlepoint plate, placemat, and knife and spoon. He based the design of the plate on a Tiffany pattern and used a Tiffany silverware pattern (that of the fork) for the silverware. The pasta is wool. The fork is suspended.

Neon Sculptures
by
John Tanaka

160

WHAT I WAS UP TO NEXT

A PALMIST NAMED DORIS WAS SET UP in a bar over on First Avenue around Sixty-first Street, and my friend Sondra Lipton, a beautiful woman who worked as a fashion model for many years, decided she and I should go find out about our futures. It was a pleasant evening, cool and just right for a walk, and I was hoping Doris would look in my hand and see love written in at least some of those old lines.

Doris took my hand and felt out its bumps, lingered over a few hard spots, a few dry spots, silently read the lines, and then looked up at me and announced, "You're going to write a book."

I hadn't stepped into that bar to hear about fame or fortune, for I don't care a great deal about either, but I wouldn't have minded word of some future kiss. Instead, I was promised not even a hug: I was going to write a book.

Disappointed and maybe a bit peeved, I told Doris she was crazy. "What are you talking about? I'm never going to write a book."

"Oh, yes," she said. "It's written right here."

I pulled back my hand and looked at it myself. "Why in the world should I want to write a book? Whatever would I write about?"

Sondra, kind and caring woman, tried to console me. "I'm sure it'll be a very nice book, Gene."

"You're all crazy," I said. "It's impossible."

Deciding to have another go at my future, Doris took back my hand. She looked a little harder, or at least looked a little longer, and then corrected herself. "You're not going to write one book"—Sondra and I waited wide-eyed, and Doris knew her art well enough for a lengthy pause before continuing—"No, I see it clearly here. You're going to write two books."

Although I left that East Side bar with doubts about Doris's skills, I didn't forget what she'd told me. That she proved right—this is my second book—stands to reason. Why shouldn't our fates be written in our hands? A good breakfast is essential, and paying attention to the phases of the moon is only prudent, but we should always listen to Dorises.

The notion of a New York window trimmer writing a book wasn't all that farfetched during the 1970s, for window display then reached a kind of popularity it hadn't known since the late 1940s and early 1950s. The primary reason for the renewed interest in display was probably the dreary sameness that descended over so many of our stores. With most of the city's stores selling the same clothes by the same designers, each store's individual image has become of great importance, and the best place to create an image, to give a store a recognizable identity, is right up front by the main doors—in the windows.

Another factor was the entry of women into window display. The regulations against women working after ten o'clock and the fears that display work was too physical for women dropped away over the years. All over this city, and all over the country, more and more women have been working in display and have become famous display directors for major stores.

With lots of new young people in display, lots of articles about it in newspapers and magazines, and even television coverage, I found myself more and more being called the guru of window display—not my favorite word, but then I didn't choose it, and it usually means only that people use my ideas. Flying mannequins, mannequins lying down, mannequins in scenes of dire peril; diamonds in dirt, gin in fountains; windows that startle or amuse and windows that tell stories: I get cited for doing those and other things first as well as for bringing S and M to window display, an honor I could do without.

I've always had fans, get mail from all over the world, and I love that. People write and say that a visit to New York is never complete without a stop to see what I'm up to in my windows. During the 1970s, other city windows attracted fans, and groups of display "groupies" ranged from store to store each week on window nights to check on their favorite "display artists."

Over at Bloomingdale's was Candy Pratts, fond of putting situation comedies into her big windows. She attracted a lot of attention, had a lot of devoted followers—she fed them popcorn on window nights. Film crews were regularly sent over to the corner of Fifty-ninth and Lexington to film Bloomingdale's displays, and she and I appeared on a television program together, talking about our windows. Among the other people then famous for their work in windows were Maggie Spring at Charles Jourdan and Robert Currie at both Henri Bendel and Clarence House.

Having lots of people stare in your windows can lead to misunderstandings and squabbles, and in their attempts to outdo one another some of those eager window trimmers offended certain people. Currie was particularly good at it. In Christmas windows at Clarence House he made the Three Wise Men into women and found himself with irate phone calls from the archdiocese. At Bendel's he created a dramatic scene involving a poisoned mannequin—she was dead on the floor—and several very suspect mannequin onlookers. Not everyone appreciated his humor.

I didn't get any irate phone calls during the 1970s. Those were yet to come. Instead, I got honors, found myself winning awards. It's best, of course, when you don't have to say anything, just go to the dinner, accept the award, say thanks, and leave, but sometimes you have to speak. I didn't have to say much when I was given the 1976 Lumen Award of

Preceding pages: *January 31, 1985. A neon take-out heart by John Tanaka.*

November 20, 1978.
These dolls
assembled to
celebrate
Thanksgiving. The
passerby who
doubted their
sincerity needed
only a glance at the
Limoges turkeys
traveling along the
foreground (one of
which disagrees on
the direction of the
holiday).

the Illuminating Engineering Society, and I was pleased, also because it was the first time that award for lighting had been given to someone in display.

I was also offered many freelance projects, which always pleases me because it means someone has noticed and liked my work. During the fall of 1970 I got another opportunity for the kind of permanence offered by museum displays when I was asked to design and install an exhibit of pre-Columbian gold at the American Museum of Natural History. Called Gold of the Americas, the exhibit involved pieces similar to those I'd worked with at the World's Fair. Dr. Junius Bird, curator of South American archaeology, had put together the collection, which included works from Mexico, Costa Rica, Panama, Colombia, Ecuador, Peru, and Bolivia, ranging in age from 500 to 2,500 years.

I enlisted the aid of my old friend Gene McCabe. Although a great displayman (he was then over at Cartier's), he was never completely pleased with his fate. "I'm a better displayman than you," he'd tell me. "You've just had better breaks."

Since Gold of the Americas was set up to be the first exhibit seen by visitors to the Hall of Mexico and Central America, I wanted it to create a mood. To show off those beautifully savage pieces of ancient gold I used sand—even black sand—and put some of the displays in cases made of mosaics of dark wood. The contrast between the gold and the backgrounds let the viewer discover each piece, suddenly make out its strange, unexpected form.

The exhibit was quite a success and is still up, a fact that pleases me. McCabe and I were donating our services, of course, but a plaque on one of the walls credits our work. Since McCabe seemed to need the boost, I insisted his name come first.

*The Great Heads of Elura,
historic versions of famous
hairstyles.*

Since the late 1950s I'd been designing the windows at the Michel Kazan beauty salon over on East Fifty-fifth Street. One of the beauty editors at *Vogue* magazine did publicity for Kazan, and through her I met Gino di Grandi, a fascinating man always involved in fascinating projects. He was then an international merchandising and advertising consultant, and in 1971 he organized a promotion for a new wig fiber, called Elura, being manufactured by the Monsanto Company. His idea was to show ten female heads with historic hairstyles matched with ten modern versions of those styles. He asked Kenneth Battelle to do the modern heads using wigs of Elura and asked me for the historic versions using the material that's always called horsehair but really isn't. No one has ever told me what it really is.

I was also asked to design the heads, and to call attention to the hair I made them with identical abstract faces.

The project involved interesting research, studying ancient and modern portraits. The ten historic heads I eventually designed included an Egyptian of the Eighteenth Dynasty, a Minoan from 1500 B.C., a Greek from about 420 B.C., an African, a Mycenaean from the fourteenth to twelfth centuries B.C., a sixteenth-century Japanese, a fifteenth-century Italian modeled on Botticelli, a seventeenth-century Dutch modeled on Vermeer, an eighteenth-century English after the portraits of George Romney, and a 1920s style taken from the portraits of Kees van Dongen.

The unveiling of the Great Heads of Elura took place on June 9, 1971, at New York's Museum of Contemporary Crafts. I did the lighting.

Two years later Gino di Grandi got me involved in an even more entertaining project, a promotional campaign for Galliano that involved various celebrities preparing favorite pasta dishes with a few teaspoons of that famous Italian liqueur. I was to go to Rome and create an advertisement with Gina Lollobrigida. Di Grandi paid my way and told me I could have whatever I needed to make the ad.

Lollobrigida is strikingly beautiful. She's also an excellent photographer, even a painter. Her interest in painting created some initial friction between us, for she'd painted a large backdrop and hoped to use it in the advertisement. She was unhappy when I told her I didn't want to use it and indignant when she heard what I did want: chickens, a pig, a goat, lots of hay, and a satin evening dress. Her favorite recipe, a version of carbonara sauce, called for eggs, bacon, and cheese, and I wanted to show the ingredients alive and in their proper element: a barnyard. The dress was for her.

She didn't want to be photographed in an evening dress amid hay. She didn't want to sit surrounded by chickens and a goat, and she didn't want to hold the piglet. She called it a *porcellino*, which can mean "little pig" or can mean something worse, and that day, during that photographic shoot, she meant something worse. But she sat in the hay with the animals and smiled while I took the pictures. When I'd finished, as if on cue, the little pig defecated in Lollobrigida's lap. She blamed me.

She forgave me everything, even the *porcellino*, when she saw the pictures.

A few years later I took part in a much different photography session. Milton Greene was photographing Linda Lovelace, star of the pornography film *Deep Throat*, and asked me to serve as his assistant. Greene wasn't sure what to do with her. I suggested he photograph her as a fashionable lady, not as a contrast to her work in films but because that's how she seemed to me, shy and very nice.

I got clothes for her and furs and prepared all the props. For one photograph we posed her beside a piece of sculpture in imitation of a famous photograph of Sarah Bernhardt.

The three of us worked together for several days on those photographs. Lovelace enjoyed the sessions, but I could see it was hard on her, and at one point I said, "You must be so tired of all this."

She smiled and made me very happy by saying, "I don't think anyone in all my life has ever paid so much attention to me."

In October 1972 I had another experience with museums when I was asked to design a show called "African Textiles and Decorative Arts" at the Museum of Modern Art. Roy Sieber of Indiana University had assembled the 250 items in the show from more than 3,000 chosen by the museum's staff. The show's title was somewhat vague, for the objects included beads, bracelets, anklets, hats, collars, pendants, hairpins, hatpins, combs, belts, many kinds of clothing, carved wood, gold, and brass. Works from twenty-six African countries were there, the oldest from the early nineteenth century.

I wanted to show clothing on mannequins and had Hugh Shearer, an artist and sculptor, carve some for me of dark brown cork. Among the many varieties of carved-wood objects were beautifully painted penis protectors, shapes made to cover the head of the penis, and I had Shearer make me some simple phallic forms of the same cork on which to display the protectors.

"You can't do that." How I hate to hear those words. They said, "You can't do that" when they saw my vaguely penislike cork forms.

"Don't be silly," I said, and that was that. The forms stayed.

In 1977 I lost a similar battle with the *New York Times* concerning a poster I'd designed for the Paul Taylor dance company. I began designing costumes for Paul Taylor during the 1970s—and only then learned that as a struggling artist he'd helped Robert Rauschenberg and Jasper Johns prepare props for my windows at Bonwit's and Tiffany's. My costumes were mostly nude—dance has so much to do with looking at bodies, and I see no reason to hide those beautiful bodies—and for a poster I designed I used bodies—bending forward and back, touching and joined—to form the letters of words.

Some of those letter-forming bodies were joined a bit too close for someone at the *Times*. The poster was declared lewd, and the *Times* refused to run it in the dance company's ad.

I did other freelance projects during the 1970s. In 1974, when Philharmonic Hall became Avery Fisher Hall, I was asked to help redesign the lobbies. All they needed was a little life—plants. In November 1976, Faith Stewart-Gordon, owner of the Russian Tea Room, asked me to help with the restaurant's windows. I did those windows once a month for several years and commissioned several artists, including Roger Sammis, Robert Heitmann, and Richard Giglio, to make works for them.

My favorite project, however, was the exhibit of Joseph Cornell's works I designed for Leo Castelli in 1976. I'd met Cornell, such a shy, quiet man, for he'd come to see me several times at Bonwit's, but I could never use his things, they were just too small for the windows. I liked him and admired his work, particularly his shadow boxes full of found objects, maps, photographs, engravings, and all of it so intensely personal and nostalgic. He died in 1973.

Leo Castelli called me and said he wanted to talk about doing a show on Joseph Cornell. He said Robert Rauschenberg and Jasper Johns had told him I was the only person in New York who should do it.

Flattered, I went to see Castelli.

"I've always admired Cornell's work," I said, "but I don't think I can put together a show of it."

"Why not?" asked Castelli.

"Because I don't think you'd let me do what I'd want to do."

"Try me."

"Suppose I paint the walls and ceiling almost a black brown."

"That would be fine."

"Suppose I tell you the lighting I want to bring in will cost several thousand dollars."

"You can have it."

I had no more excuses. I did the show.

I spent a lot of time at the warehouse where the art for the show was being stored. I'd go in, sit on the floor, and look at all those Cornells to get the feel of them as separate works and as parts of a man's creativity. When I did so I felt Cornell's presence, sensed him there with me. I wanted to make that show beautiful.

I came upon these bodies in an old alphabet. The poster was rejected by The New York Times *as obscene.*

at CITY CENTER 55th STREET THEATRE
MAY 31, JUNE 1,2,3,4,5 1977
Box Office Phone 246·8989

The installation of the lighting took a long time because instead of directing strong lighting onto the boxes, so that the viewer would feel the lighting, I wanted the lighting to seem to come from inside the boxes, as if it belonged to the boxes. I was successful.

People in galleries aren't always quiet, are sometimes quite loud, but the minute the visitors to that show stepped into that dark space with those marvelous boxes with that strange, eerie light coming out of them, they suddenly fell very quiet and barely whispered. There was a wonderful silence in that room, just like the silence in the boxes themselves.

Most of the people who look in Tiffany's windows do so during daylight hours, with traffic sounds all around along with that constant sense—it never stops until you finally shut your apartment door—of someone right behind, anxious to get past. I make my displays to please myself but never forget that audience, all those people who slow down out of crowds and pause in front of my windows.

In truth, however, window display is an art of the night. Darkness sets off the window trimmer's handiwork and invites the passerby to enter a self-contained world that may be sinister, surreal, or merely pleasurable. At best, it may be humorous, and I like to imagine a lone stroller walking along Fifth Avenue in the darkness who pauses and sees something in one of those windows that makes him or her—standing there all alone in this big city—laugh out loud. Or maybe just grin.

Such jokes are best when simple, a little touch in a display that attracts the eye and somehow pleases. For Easter 1970 I filled two of the windows with curtains of eggs with holes broken through each egg from side to side. Visible through the holes in the eggs were ferns, clover, and grass. To break an egg through both sides is a tedious chore: you have to take a needle and make a circle of little punctures and then push along the perforation you've made until it cracks. Holes in eggs are pleasant because no two are alike in their jaggedness, but to make the display work—to give it life—I left one egg unbroken. The passerby somehow knows the black sheep is there and is delighted to discover it.

In April I created a joke of another sort in a celebration of Italian food. One window showed a little barrel from which tumbled breadsticks. The next was a view from behind a wine rack, just a wall of lined-up bottle bottoms (those who read the labels saw the wine was Soave). I covered all of another window with little pasta wheels, which always make me think of watches so I left an opening in the pasta wall and suspended in the opening a small, round watch. The last window had an espresso machine, the fitting end to any Italian meal. The joke was in window three: a place setting with silverware and a dish heaped with nothing but fresh garlic.

The trick in my next set of windows was harder to spot. The windows showed tableware: wineglasses in one, plates in another, and rows of flatware in a third. I wanted to fill a window with flatware, and the only way to do so was to glue the pieces to a pane of plate glass. I closed down the window—made it narrower—to cut down on all that gluing. I had a row of knives followed by a row of forks followed by a row of spoons and so on. One of the forks in the last row was of a different pattern.

Snoopy appeared in my windows twice during the 1970s. I love him because he makes me laugh. In the first set he was enjoying a sunny June, resting on his roof in one window, wearing dark glasses on the beach in another. In 1974 he was joined by his pal Woodstock, the two of them playing with Kodak sound cameras.

When busy having a good time, mice, too, are amusing. I made a popular set of windows using mice and Kodak cameras. Small mice wielding life-size cameras play tricks with size perception. One of those windows concerned an underwater mouse wearing mouse-size flippers, mask, and scuba gear who was focusing a Kodak Instamatic camera, encased in an appropriate underwater housing, on a Rolex watch—waterproof, of course.

March 12, 1970. Each egg is glued to four others around it, and since I didn't use plate glass, I had a moment's anxiety when it came time to pick up this wall of eggs and hang it in the window. It held together.

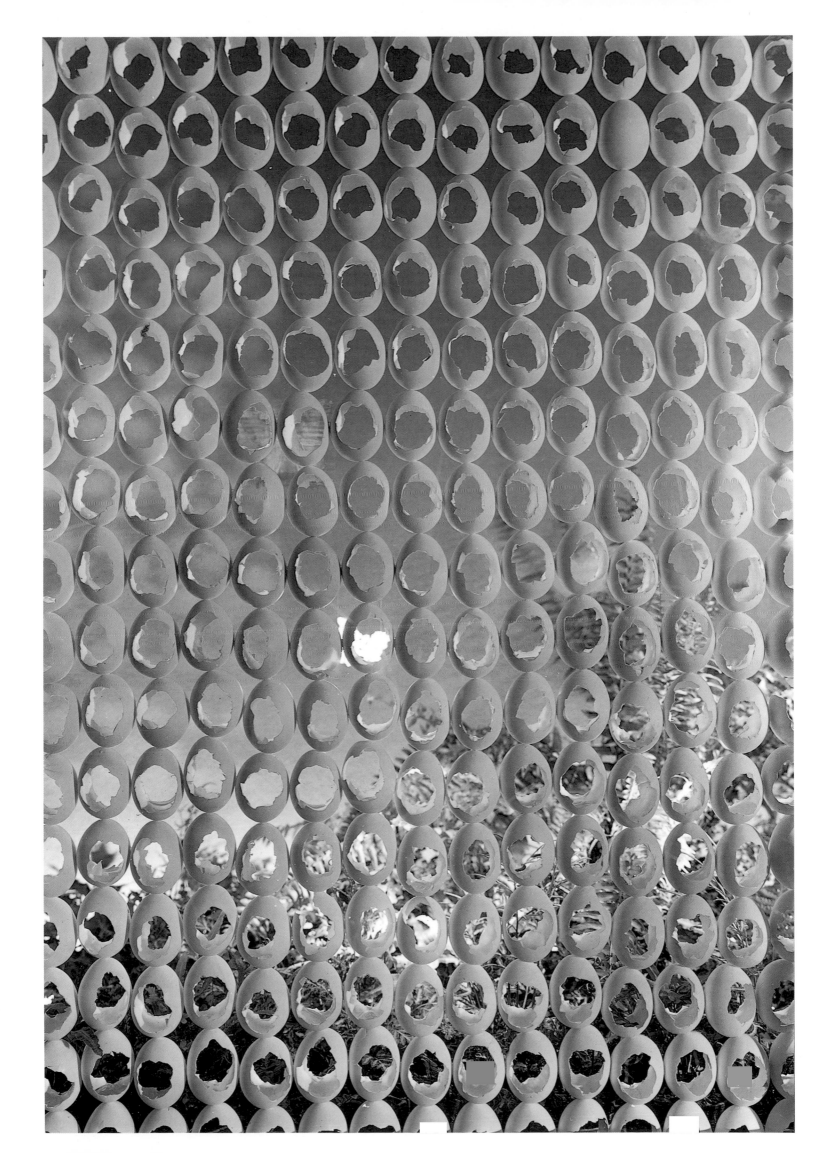

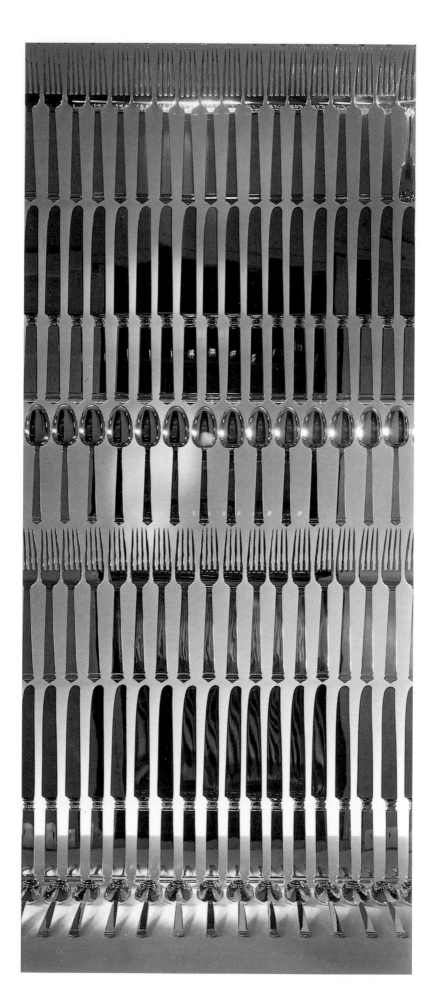

May 4, 1970. Here I used plate glass. One of the forks is of a different pattern, a surefire trick to make passerby study the silverware.

I first used the art of Robin Thew in August 1970. I'd been introduced to her by another artist friend, and she told me about a dream her daughter had had. That little girl loved horses, and in her dream she shared an ice-cream soda with one. I loved the dream and asked Robin, who makes small papier-mâché figures, to create it for Tiffany's windows.

The story in those windows, recounted on handwritten notes placed by each scene, began with "Once upon a time there was a little girl who loved horses," went on to show

August 13, 1970. Artist Robin Thew told me of her daughter's dream, and it seemed perfect for Tiffany's windows. Here she and her horse friend share an ice-cream soda.

the shared ice-cream soda ("a horse would make a true friend"), and ended with the girl turning into a horse ("if dreams could come true").

I used Robin Thew's delightful creations four more times during the 1970s. She's particularly adept at making expressive Christmas reindeer, and I used them three times. For Christmas 1972 she supplied a reindeer making a guest appearance on "The Dick Cavett Show." Speaking in a cartoon-style bubble, the reindeer explained, "Let me make one thing perfectly clear, Dick. There really *is* a Santa Claus."

Her most popular windows concerned the fate of a likable gray mouse. I've always liked jewel thieves, at least those who don't smash my windows or steal diamonds from Tiffany's, so I asked her for a jewel-thief mouse. The five windows related a simple and highly moralistic tale: the mouse robber takes jewels from a safe; brings them home and examines them; sells them to a fence; goes out on the town with his girlfriend (wrapped in pearls and furs); and, in the final window, languishes, head in hands, on a cot behind prison bars.

Most New Yorkers were surprised and delighted to see a jewel heist in the windows of a famous jewelry store, but six days after the displays went in Hoving received a letter from the president of Cartier's, Michael H. Thomas: "Both from the point of view of one in the fine jewelry business and as a resident of midtown Manhattan, I must raise my voice in protest against your recent Fifth Avenue windows. I feel that raising attention to robberies and the hazards of owning fine jewelry are neither humorous nor appropriate." As a reply, Hoving wrote "Nuts, Walter Hoving" across the top of the letter and mailed it right back.

June 3, 1971. Crime story: the mouse cracks the safe, examines his booty, fences the goods, goes out on the town in high style, and laments his just deserts.

Because of their popularity, I held those windows in an extra week, the first time I'd done so since the gin windows.

I anticipated complaints of another sort to my next set of windows. An artist from Germany named Edith Eppenberger baked some mermaids for the windows. Made out of real baked dough painted striking colors, they were, as are all true mermaids, bare-breasted—and those breasts were big, with bright red nipples. No one said a word.

One of the mermaid windows included a piece of merchandise that I'd designed after having lunch one day in the old (it's no longer there) Seafare of the Aegean Restaurant, a Greek place with good fish, if a little expensive. I happened to look up to see a waiter bone a fish. The skeleton of that fish was beautiful, so I motioned to the waiter to come over to my table.

"I'd like the skeleton, please," I said.

"What?"

"The fish bone. May I have it, please?"

From his parting glance I understood the waiter judged me crazy. I called for the manager and expressed my wish to him. He knew me and got me the bone.

I turned that fish bone into a wonderful piece of jewelry with gold ribs, each articulated so the skeleton could bend like a real fish. Available with a choice of eyes—rubies, sapphires, or emeralds—that fish became a popular piece of merchandise, and it worked well in windows, particularly when attached to the end of a fishing line.

The artist I used most during the 1970s—sixteen times, including nine Christmases—was Robert Heitmann. A true Gemini, he's never still, always experimenting, always making something new. Many people were interested in handcrafts during the 1970s, particularly those involving needlework, but only Heitmann mastered them all, even turned around and taught them all, usually after just learning them himself. He has made me tapestries, weavings, quilts, needlepoint pictures, and a remarkably diverse range of other objects and decorations.

For Valentine's Day 1970 he made me valentines that folded out of books. People wondered where I'd found those old-fashioned cards. I used two of his needlepoint pictures, both done all in gold thread, for that year's Christmas. For windows the following October he made miniature Indian loom weavings—made not only the weavings, but had them attached to tiny, historically accurate looms.

Since I wanted to give that year's Christmas an American flavor, I called Heitmann—about five weeks before Christmas—and asked if he could make me two American-style quilts with religious themes. He'd never done a quilt before, but he looked up quilting in a book and called me the next day to say he could do it. He did it wonderfully, creating an angel and a Nativity scene in homespun Pennsylvania Dutch fashion. The angel was dressed in patchwork plaids. The Nativity scene was presented in front of a barn with hex signs, Joseph wearing a farmer's hat and Mary a gingham dress, the couple posed to match *American Gothic*. Those two quilts were bought by Joseph O'Doherty, former director of the American Museum of Folk Art.

In 1972, I decided to celebrate Thanksgiving for the first time in my windows, and Bob Heitmann contributed complete scenes using apple-face dolls. Making dolls with dried-apple heads was then a popular subject in women's magazines. The process involves coring and peeling an apple, carving it into a crude face (cloves serve as eyes), dipping the apple in lemon juice, and then drying it. The resulting shrunken head is surprisingly expressive, with fat pink cheeks that seem wholesome and suitable for holidays.

Heitmann's apple-face dolls have since appeared in many displays, most often for Christmas. For those holiday scenes he makes not only the dolls but builds the sets, the

Above: *June 24, 1971. A buxom baked mermaid by Edith Eppenberger. Swimming by is my original jewelry fish.* Right: *May 20, 1976. A flower with nuns' faces by Robert Heitmann.*

December 4, 1977. Robert Heitmann celebrates New Year's Day. As a stork delivers a baby stork to a stork mother an old man, symbol of the passing year, slips out the back door into the night. I used a baby spot to call attention to the clock.

tiny furniture, and creates most of the props. His resourcefulness is astonishing. If a floor needs a rug, he weaves one. If Mrs. Claus will be shown handing Santa a gift of slippers, he needlepoints them. He molds miniature food for his scenes from clay and then paints and varnishes it and creates his props from whatever he finds that will serve: cut paintbrush handles become table legs, tiny lead pencils are turned into candles.

In 1973, apple-face monks and nuns celebrated Christmas in Tiffany's windows. In 1974, Heitmann brought Santa Claus back to his role as St. Nicholas by creating figures of him carrying a crosier and wearing a mitered cap. Christmas 1975 showed a procession. I set it up so the participants were all moving toward a puppet show in window two. The characters in the show were the Madonna and Child—this was the Nativity scene. Window one's Three Wise Men were journeying toward the Nativity, and in the windows along Fifty-seventh Street other revelers made their way to the scene. As usual, the last window presented New Year's, a baby being carried forward, an old man—the old year—being turned back, and a figure of two-faced Janus in the center.

The angel and Madonna and Child for Christmas 1976 were made of panty hose and stockings. Heitmann is always experimenting with textures, and he'd read somewhere that Germans used stockings to make doll faces. Nylon, he found, is more permanent than silk. In 1977 he created wonderful scenes: in one window a fat bishop spreading his arms in welcome in front of a cathedral; in another the Nativity was part of a wayside shrine being put up by peasants surrounded by their cattle. That years New Year's window showed a stork delivering a stork baby to a stork mother; stepping out a back door in the scene was an old man, the passing year, carrying an hourglass.

In addition to the Wise Men and a Madonna, the 1978 Christmas windows featured Father Christmas as King Winter in one window and the Snow Queen in another. For the New Year's window Heitmann constructed a wonderful three-tiered clock with revolving figures to show changing years, seasons, and holidays. In 1979 Heitmann's figures acted out scenes from children's stories.

Celebration of the nation's bicentennial attracted me to the Fourth of July, and in 1975 I asked Heitmann to assemble some suitable scenes. We both agreed that people, his usual figures, would lack interest in historical stories. Animals fit much better. Thus George Washington became a dog, as did Paul Revere—Heitmann called him Paul Rover. Betsy Ross became a lamb, and in the last window a pair of patriotic monkeys toasted the Fourth with tea.

In a sense, Heitmann's next set of Tiffany's windows reversed this trend. Inspired by a poem he'd spotted in a garden—"I used to love my garden/But now my love is dead/I found a bachelor's button/In black-eyed Susan's bed"—he created flowers with human

December 4, 1975. A Christmas procession by Robert Heitmann. The New Year window (above) shows an old man being turned back, Janus under a wreath, and a baby, the new year, being carried forward.

faces. The petals of lilies became the hats of nuns, a bouquet of daisies wore Indian headdresses, gloxinias were black musicians. He needlepointed the poem for one window, and we recreated the scene, including the button in the bed.

Old gloves inspired a set of windows in August 1977. Heitmann had noticed that women were no longer wearing gloves at Easter, had missed the gloves, and had begun collecting them. He brought by a box to show me and said he could do marvelous things with them. In particular, he could make animals. He had doubts about one idea—using gloves to make a cow's udders—but I assured him no one would mind, and he went ahead. The birds were particularly appealing; gloves make fine feathers.

For "Deviltry," one of Heitmann's most popular sets of windows, he made little devils to celebrate Halloween 1978. In their pitch-black abodes, they used their tails to play jump rope, ran around with pitchforks (one carried a real merchandise fork), climbed out of the mouth of a giant devil. The last window featured a witch flying by on a broomstick, a small devil clutching the broom's straw.

More than one hundred other artists contributed works to Tiffany's windows during the 1970s. Some I used only once, a few two, or even three times. I'd used works by some of these artists during the 1960s or even earlier—Virginia Bascom, Judith Brown, Sam Gallo, Richard Giglio, Carl Malouf, Jeanne Owens—but most were new to me and to

Tiffany's windows. In some cases I used works already created by the artist, but far more often I was more impressed by the artist than the art, and after meeting the artist and looking over his or her work, I suggested changes, asked the artist to try a different approach. You have to recognize the possibilites, and sometimes you have to see what isn't yet there but can be.

Patrick Sullivan, a very creative man, an actor and artist, made peculiar sculptural pieces. I began the decade with some of his architectural sculptures standing in my usual January beach sand. Much different were castles on hills done by Marc Fenyo. William Da Camara called his works kinetic lucite sculptures, but those flowing forms seemed made of glass or even water. Reine Turner, wife of photographer Pete Turner, brought in striking works consisting of watch parts spread across panes of clear plastic. Philip Matthews used flowers and dried vegetables as hair for odd-looking heads. I had Edith La Bate, a Brazilian artist, make stuffed animals using some fabrics I wished to display. She later created big dolls modeled on traditional examples from central Brazil. After La Bate's stuffed animals

I used paintings of snakes by Tom Lyons, an artist who'd once done makeup for Greneker mannequins.

In January 1975 I did without beach sand but not shells. I used faces made of shells by Nino De Faveri, a wonderful man and a fantastic cook. That May I displayed sculptural pieces by Ruby Jackson, a young woman with a small studio in East Hampton, Long Island. She described her works as labyrinths, caves, and tunnels that allow air and light to flow through. I thought they were made of carved plaster and couldn't understand how she made them: they seemed shaped by the wind or water into impossibly intricate windings. In truth, she'd begun by carving solid hunks of plaster but found the plaster cracked. Then she discovered a new method—tying balloons together and pouring the plaster over them. The ballons burst as the plaster solidified, leaving shapes that truly seemed carved.

Hely Lima made dollhouse-size facades of South American movie theaters with every detail in place, including tiny posters announcing the shows. Paul Himmel, a prominent photographer, took up needlepoint during this period, and his works made it into the windows in 1976.

The January 1977 windows had both beach sand and seashells, but you had to look hard to see the shells. Ruth W. Ross used seashells to create sculptures of birds so perfect

Above: *August 25, 1977. Robert Heitmann's cow made of gloves.* Right: *October 18, 1978. A window from Heitmann's Halloween "Deviltry."*

two or three looks were needed to realize they weren't the real thing. I used more sand in the next set of windows to support sculptural forms made of wooden tongue depressors by Edmund E. Niemann. They didn't look much like tongue depressors.

Vicki Romaine made her art with Coca-Cola bottles. She told me she'd looked at an empty Coke bottle one day and suddenly realized it was shaped like a person. All it needed was a head, and a ping-pong ball solved that problem. She painted the bottles with their ping-pong-ball heads white and then filled in the white background with sketches of people and animals. We worked out five scenes using her so-called bottle people, each supplied with a line of explanatory text: "Grace feeds her five cats—and one stray" (the cats were little milk bottles); "My friends waiting for the M27 crosstown"; "Charlie and his Boy Scout troop noticing Rusty talking to a Girl Scout"; "Amy fell asleep in the sun" (a bottle person on its back in sand); and "The fat ballet."

Jill Healy made wonderfully detailed and beautiful art by etching on glass with dentist's tools. Naef Orfaley—his friends call him Nuffy—is an Egyptian who uses silver, jewels, and seashells to create very heavy and very striking sculptural pieces.

In April 1978 I used sculpture by the Russian-born artist Alexander Ney for the first time. Since then I've tried to use his work at least once each year. I had great fun using the work of Hella Hammid, big blowups of color photographs of crushed tin cans. The photographs were beautiful, but to make certain they'd be understood I crushed some tin cans and put them in the foreground of the windows.

John Tanaka made neon-light sculptures for the windows in August 1978. Neon had long fallen out of favor, but while sign makers had dropped it, designers were beginning to appreciate it, and Tanaka's works were exciting, particularly the piece in which tubes of neon paint poured from an overturned bucket.

September 22, 1977. Etched glass by Jill Healy. She uses dentist's tools to scratch into the glass.

I celebrated Thanksgiving—only the second time in Tiffany's windows—in November 1978 using dolls from the collection of Richard Rheems. In one window the dolls—a motley crew from all over Europe and the United States—stood together, leaned against one another, or sat on the floor of the window and stared out. Or perhaps waited. I was unclear about what all those dolls wanted in that window. One was smoking; another was too young to be there that late. But I made it all Thanksgiving by setting out white Limoges turkeys in front of them.

Holiday spirit was clearer in the next window, in which I created a shooting gallery, with more porcelain turkeys on a moving conveyor belt. A Pilgrim doll was in the window, but he was paying no heed to the turkey-shoot targets, choosing instead to rest on the floor with his gun—made for me by Ron McNamer.

That I'm known for using real fruit in my windows made it easier for me to fool people with Anne M. Cembalest's trompe l'oeil baskets and bags of fruits and vegetables. Nothing in those displays was real: even the baskets and bags were part of the sculpture. I had her make separate pieces for me to put beside the baskets, a few loose onions for a bag of onions, and so on. People had to look more than twice at those windows. They also did doubletakes at the dramatic, if not spooky, dolls and puppets by theatrical designer E. J. Taylor. I used them in three sets of windows during the 1970s.

January 31, 1974. From left to right, the Valentines read: "Dear Nora: Have a heart— Have a martini—See you later. Love, Nick"; "Dearest Leo: I want to be alone—with you, my darling! Ever, Felicitas"; "Golly gee, Andy—You're swell and so very generous. Love, Betsy"; "Flower Belle, my Angel: Be my little Chickadee. Be mine to woo—Your devoted servant, Cuthbert J. Twilly"; "Ahoy Min, You tug at my heart. Ha Ha, Bill."

I had a lot to say for Valentine's Day during the 1970s. In 1971 I used 7,000 sugar cubes to spell "love" in English, Greek, Japanese, Swahili, and Spanish, one language to a window. The words weren't bare—you have to help words have meaning—but were garnished with jeweled hearts and, occasionally, stuffed birds.

For the Valentine's Day windows in 1974 I got five black-and-white movie stills of famous screen couples from the Museum of Modern Art's Film Stills Archive. I blew each photograph up to eight square feet, put one in each window, and wrote out a suitable valentine message for each couple. Nick (William Powell) wrote to Nora (Myrna Loy); Felicitas (Greta Garbo) to Leo (John Gilbert); Cuthbert J. Twilly (W. C. Fields) to Flower Belle (Mae West); Betsy (Judy Garland) to Andy (Mickey Rooney); and Bill (Wallace Beery) to Min (Marie Dressler). Those windows were very popular, and I was very fond of them myself.

The next year's Valentine's Day windows were more elaborate. In each window I made a background of clear-glass, heart-shaped paperweights set in cutouts in a background wall. Behind the wall I hung a piece of china silk dyed red. A fan moved the silk, making it appear the glass hearts were flaming with passion. In front of this I placed a vase with a single rose accompanied by a handwritten poem. The poems were about roses: "Rose Leaves," by Henry Austin Dobson ("Rose kissed me to-day/will she kiss me to-morrow?"); "A Red, Red Rose," by Robert Burns ("My luve's like a red, red rose"); "My Love's a Match," by Alfred P. Graves ("My love's a match in beauty/For every flower that blows/Her little ears a lily/Her velvet cheek a rose"); "The Passionate Shepherd to His Love," by Christopher Marlowe ("And I will make thee beds of roses").

The reading matter in the 1977 Valentine's Day windows was less serious. Next to vases of flowers (by Ray Kohn) were brief valentines from four famous people and one famous gorilla. The first was addressed from Lorelei to Tiffany's: "Dear Tiffany, You surely know the way to this little girl's heart." The Lorelei here is Lorelei Lee of *Gentlemen Prefer Blondes* and "Diamonds Are a Girl's Best Friend." There was a diamond bracelet in the window.

The second valentine, addressed to Dwan, said only "you drive me bananas" and was signed "Kong." So much for the gorilla. Kojak's well-known "Who loves ya, baby" supplied the third note. Understanding the fourth took a moment's thought. Beside an envelope addressed to Mrs. Anna Whistler lay a note that read, "My Own Darling Mother, Your portrait is an enormous success! Will you be my Valentine? Your loving son, Jamie."

The last window displayed a recipe for "Coeurs Flambés," signed Julia. The bouquet in that window was all vegetables, radishes and onions and carrots.

The sugar cubes reappeared in 1978, forming a big heart in one window and a wall with a heart-shaped opening in another. Red filters on the lights gave the cubes an almost lacy look. In the third window a large wooden heart held a smaller heart on a leash.

Easter had its eggs, of course. I have yet to run out of things to do with eggs. In 1973 I treated them geometrically, horizontal and vertical rows in one window, slanting rows in another. The eggs were glued to plate glass, the only way to get so many eggs to stay together and fill a window. Plants were visible through openings in those geometric walls of eggs. Looking through one thing to see something else is a pleasant activity.

In 1978 I filled a window with more than fifty eggs that seemed to be falling. Each was suspended by nylon thread so fine it's practically invisible. The eggs were hanging at varying heights and, thanks to a small fan, moved slightly. Although obviously falling— some were sure to hit the window's floor in the next fraction of a second—there was no sense of imminent disaster.

The articulated artist's figures appeared in the 1979 Easter windows along with some small eggs I'd found—real eggs, but small. In one window the figures balanced the eggs; in another a figure deftly juggled some along with a jewelry pin. I broke out the backs of seven eggs, placed them over the heads of figures, and formed a leg-kicking chorus line of eggheads.

March 9, 1978. Each of these eggs was suspended by nylon thread. A small fan trained on the eggs moved them ever so slightly.

My Easter displays during the early 1970s didn't always include the Bible and cross. Window traditions are good only if they work, and I sometimes tried for other effects. I brought back the Bible on a regular basis in 1975, but I included a butterly in the window, usually resting on the cross, for there should always be a spirit, something alive, somewhere.

Hoving had become extremely religious, and seeking to share his faith with others he'd taken to wearing a little vermeil pin that formed the words "Try God." He'd had that pin made and put on sale in Tiffany's and was quite enamored of it. It was always there, shining from his lapel button.

"I don't see you ever wearing a 'Try God' pin," he'd say to me when we ran into each other, and I'd respond, "Nope, not me."

One day he decided to investigate my beliefs and asked, "What's your religion?" a question I really didn't appreciate. "First Church of the Heathen," I offered.

"There's no such church," he protested.

I'm as religious as the next person, but I've never seen the need to go to church; there's so much beauty in the world and good—if not God—in everything.

I decided to have my own pin, had a jeweler make it for me in the jewelry department. It was identical to Hoving's except that it read, "Try Dog." I wore it in my lapel. I'm sure he noticed it, but he was too clever to say anything.

I didn't wear Hoving's pin, but that was a matter of personal religion and had nothing to do with my feelings for him. He and I understood each other perfectly in the most important sense: our feelings for Tiffany's. For both of us, that old store came first, and we both did whatever we could for it.

I had the opportunity to celebrate the store's history in August 1973 in windows dedicated to the publication of the paperback edition of Joseph Purtell's *The Tiffany Touch*. The store's publicity department gave me wonderful things to put in the windows, pieces of Tiffany's history, including Mrs. Lincoln's pearl necklace, presidential chinaware, and old photographs.

One year later I celebrated the arrival at Tiffany's of Elsa Peretti, the Italian-born former fashion model who'd already made a name for herself designing for Halston and Bloomingdale's. With her fervent opinions on jewelry, she had a noticeable and immediate impact on the store. She broke with twenty-five years of Tiffany's tradition by designing jewelry in silver, and her designs in both gold and silver became—instantly—wildly popular classics. Among her first creations were tear-shaped perfume flacons made to be worn around the neck on a chain, lopsided hearts on chains, a horseshoe-shaped belt buckle, lima-bean earrings, and, most popular of all, "diamonds by the yard," tiny diamonds set every few inches along a delicate 18-karat-gold chain and sold by length, a wonderfully simple idea that was soon considered one of the great merchandising coups of the century. In 1974, the first year of "diamonds by the yard," Tiffany's sold 3,520 yards of the stuff.

For those windows, I let the jewelry suggest the displays. In the first window I built a fence with yardsticks and draped over it lengths of "diamonds by the yard." In the second, a Peretti-designed jeweled snake bracelet rose, charmed, from a basket. I hung the tiny perfume vials in the third window, impaled some of her ivory bracelets on elephant tusks in the fourth, and used her horseshoe belt buckle to hold up the tail of my glass-eyed Spanish horse in the fifth.

Almost exactly one year later, in October 1975, I celebrated another of Tiffany's jewelry designers, but this time the displays were more personal, inspired most of all by my feelings for the designer. Angela Cummings, the daughter of a German diplomat, trained in Germany and Italy as a gemologist, goldsmith, and designer. In 1967, at age twenty-three, she walked into Tiffany's carrying her portfolio and looking for a job. She was taken on to work with jewelry designer Donald Claflin. In 1975 she began designing her own collection.

Leaves, seashells, rose petals, and the wings of birds in flight have been her sources of inspiration, and her colors—such as blue chalcedony, rose quartz, and green and pink

October 9, 1975. A piece of driftwood celebrates the jewelry designs of Angela Cummings.

tourmaline—come from sunsets and the bottom of the sea. I've always been delighted by her creations and, even more, by the wonderful person she is. I've even managed to inspire her. She'd always associated spiderwebs with evil and darkness, but I made her really look at them and see they aren't mean at all, just strong and beautiful. She turned a spiderweb into a beautiful necklace.

My window displays for her were of driftwood, one piece for each window to set off her jewelry. Only the most attentive passersby will have spotted the name Angela carved into one of those quiet shapes of pale wood.

During the 1970s, the city and its day-to-day affairs provided fewer causes for celebration—or lamentation—than they had during the 1960s. Heavy rain, real April showers, in April 1972 gave me the idea for windows using umbrellas, which I discovered work wonderfully with watches; not just that watches slip over umbrellas, but that they seem to mean something similar, something that has to do with rushing through rainy city streets. In June 1973 I acknowledged the Belmont 1973 Renewal, won by triple crown winner Secretariat (the trophy was made by Tiffany's). I had wonderful material to use in those windows. I'd been sent samples of a new sponge-rubber material used under carpeting. Its dimpled surface let me create views of other worlds, with pyramids and rolling dunes (populated by Schlumberger jewelry camels).

In November 1973 I saluted the publication of Lincoln Kirstein's book on the New York City Ballet, which coincided with the company's twenty-fifth anniversary. I got original scale models of the company's stage sets from Rouben Ter-Arutunian and put one jewel in each. In other windows I hung ballet slippers and posed my artist's figures in dance positions.

October 25, 1973. Judith Brown asked me to come look at five new pieces she'd made. They were all wonderful, including this version of the Trojan Horse, and I used them in the windows.

June 24, 1976. Celebrating the Fourth of July with paint cans that spill the flag.

Such ballet windows are rare. Because of my many friends in ballet, and because I so often design sets and costumes for ballet, I avoid the subject in my windows. If I spoke of one company, I'd have to speak of them all.

In 1976 I celebrated the opening of the American Museum of Natural History's Hall of Minerals with windows displaying blocks of stone—hematite, quartz, topaz—matched to jewelry.

The Fourth of July celebration in the summer of 1976 was extravagant and included Operation Sail. For that event I used works by Gary Grant—his real name—that played with the components of the flag: paint rollers that spread fields of stars, paint cans that poured stripes.

Only the Arab oil shortage raised my ire. By 1974 I was irritated by all the warnings and dire threats of impending doom, and that March I put my own sermon in the windows. In the first a single lightbulb hung from a wire over an Arabic newspaper; in the second was a pile of nearly one hundred lightbulbs, with only one lit; in the third was an old kerosene lamp; in the fourth a candle; and in the fifth an old railroad lantern.

In 1978 Hoving asked me to do a retrospective show in the windows: to recreate five of my most popular displays. This was in May, too soon after Easter for me even to consider reproducing the Easter hat or any other window calling for eggs. The five I

March 1, 1974. The Arab oil shortage inspired this window, which implies that dark times are ahead.

ultimately chose were the ice-cream-cone sphere of July 1963, the "Ice on Ice" window of July 1957, the horizontal rows of spools of August 1964, the Harlequin figure sitting on the bed of forks of September 1961, and the chalk stick-figure of February 1962.

I have photographs of all the windows I've done, not for pride or posterity, but to avoid repeating myself: I often get a wonderful idea for a display only to remember I've already done it. I used the photographs to recreate the five windows, but I don't believe those recreations were completely accurate. As you make a display you discover it, build it but also unearth it from your imagination. Things go wrong and become wonderfully right, or go wrong and require rethinking. And, anyway, once I've done a display I don't want to see it again. But I was flattered that Hoving had asked, and the windows were popular.

By then, Dirk Luykx, a book designer who works with Harry N. Abrams, had begun telling me I should do a book of my windows. Remembering the palmist Doris, I knew saying no would be fruitless. The project grew to include Lena Tabori, Ruth Eisenstein, and Judith Goldman. There was a lot of work to do, I didn't always enjoy having to remember the past, but I did like talking about the windows.

That November, just after Robert Heitmann's "Deviltry," I put in what became some of my most popular displays. Edward Acevedo and I had the idea of creating miniature

October 24, 1979. Miniature room settings by Edward Acevedo. Above: *A home for Baryshnikov by Mel Dwork.* Opposite: *Rooms for Dorothy Loudon by Cronin-Stempler.*

rooms designed by famous decorators and invited five top New York decorators to submit blueprints and drawings for real or imagined rooms. The five decorators were Kevin McNamara, Mario Buatta, Angelo Donghia, Vladimir Kagan, and the Parish-Hadley firm. Acevedo recreated their plans on a scale of one inch to one foot.

The five rooms were astonishing, perfect views of other worlds. Kagan's southern California mansion included a miniature painting by Frank Stella; tiny impressionist paintings were hung in the living room designed by Buatta. Miniature bulbs glowed from lamps on miniature tables. Pat Tornborg, one of Acevedo's assistants, had fashioned tiny ceramic pieces for the rooms from Play-Doh; another, Nancy Hoffmann, petitpointed a miniature version of an antique Dhurrie rug for the McNamara living room. I placed a piece of jewelry in each room, and those jewels wrought havoc with size perception.

The unveiling of these windows was made an event—"Breakfast Outside at Tiffany's"—my first big opening since Bonwit Teller days. On the morning the windows were unveiled, half the sidewalk in front of the store was marked off with white satin ribbon and bows, and tables were set up to serve coffee and pastries—in Tiffany-blue paper cups and plates—to 150 guests.

Well before the guests had left and the tables had been taken down, those five windows had attracted crowds. Each room setting offered much to look at, and people just couldn't get enough of them. For the third time in my years doing Tiffany's windows, following popular demand and a request from Hoving, I held the windows over for an extra week.

We repeated the magic a year later, but this time each of the five decorators designed a room for a particular person: a room for Bill Blass by Mac II; Zubin Mehta by Easton-LaRocca; Dorothy Loudon by Cronin-Stempler; Audrey Hepburn by Macmillan; Baryshnikov by Mel Dwork. It worked again, and again the windows were held over another week.

By 1979, Tiffany's was doing well. Its business had reached $84 million, a ninefold increase since Hoving's takeover in 1955, although some of that was the result of the nation's generally improved economy. Hoving himself certainly never took credit for the turnaround. "God runs this business," he'd say, "so I don't have much to worry about."

Prosperous stores attract attention. In April 1979, when Hoving was eighty-two years old, Avon Products, a company best known for door-to-door sales of cosmetics, bought Tiffany & Co. Many people were dismayed, and many joked, "Ding-dong, want a diamond?"

190

MAKE THEM STOP

THERE ARE CERTAIN ORCHIDS I've never seen but have heard about and thought about a great deal. They're white, I think, but their color isn't what makes them special. Those orchids hold my interest because they have an even number of petals, and most often in nature, such numbers are odd.

I can teach tricks, but that doesn't mean I'll use them myself, and I certainly don't think of them when working out a display. Odd numbers are one of those tricks: it seems to me that most forms in nature grow in uneven numbers, and I always strive to agree with nature. But you shouldn't stand in the window counting Easter eggs. You should sense the right number, recognize when you have enough or too many without actually counting.

Tricks, rules, and guiding theories. Display has become a subject taught in schools—it's usually called visual merchandising. Students studying visual merchandising probably learn a lot about the basics of display, but such information will never be enough to make them competent and make them enjoy their work, and I sometimes worry those students come away with nothing but rules.

I volunteered once to teach a class in window display at one of New York's design schools. I knew I'd have to face some initial nervousness about standing up in front of a class, but I imagined that would pass and that being around all those kids would be fun. The directors of the school expressed delight, were overjoyed to have my services, but time went by, an entire summer, and I heard nothing from them. Then I received instructions to attend a faculty meeting and learned that certain rules strictly determined what could or could not be done when teaching at that school. That was enough for me. I never went.

My list of rules ends with the first: make people stop. You can't cram windows full of merchandise and expect to generate excitement. You've got to make windows interesting.

A simple rule, but I have to add that you should make people stop with taste, not vulgarity; you should startle people, but shouldn't frighten or outrage them. What you put in a store's windows is that store's image. Outrage may suit some wares, but not those of Tiffany's, and not those of most stores. Mannequins posed as though urinating on white marble floors will make passersby pause but won't create interest in purchasing what lies within the walls of the store. Store windows speak to strangers and should thus be polite.

Make people stop. Show them what you're really selling. Piles of clothes in a window indicate a clothing store; a single beautiful gown says fashion. Rows of sapphire rings laid out on a piece of cloth mean this store sells jewelry; a single sapphire ring set casually among live flowers against a background painting of cloudless sky reminds the passerby of blue, of how beautiful all colors are, of how much life has to offer.

A store's windows open on another world, the world of possibilities offered by the merchandise. No one is likely to buy everything on sale in the store, however, so there's no reason to try to display everything. One item will do, just one sent into the window together with an idea. The fewer the distractions, the stronger the effect.

Surprise is a wonderful tool, people love to be pleasantly surprised, and humor is an essential of display. Humor is often little more than the surprise of the truth. When I was at Bonwit's I wanted to show a woman—a mannequin—in a marvelous evening dress scrambling eggs. Other display people would show her all dolled up to go to the opera, but maybe she first has to scramble some eggs. The store's fashion buyer would say, "How dare you show that beautiful dress in front of a stove? Who would ever do that?" The truth is, probably everyone. Scrambled eggs and evening dresses are parts of our world and will sooner or later come together. Why not in a window?

Like diamonds in dirt, it's a matter of contrast. Contrast can help achieve the double take, the turned head and suddenly awakened curiosity that you want to create in the passerby. Diamonds never look so diamondy as when they're in dirt. The contrast is dramatic, and there's something humorous about seeing something so valuable tossed in something so ordinary.

Make them stop by showing them something they've never seen before, or by showing them something they've seen every day but never thought about. In that sense, the display person is doing what every artist does: showing people the way he or she sees things, making people see something differently from the way they've seen it before. Behind all of it is beauty, which has nothing to do with money. And not the beauty of the merchandise itself so much as the beauty of what the merchandise suggests. Thus to make people see, the display person must see first, must have beautiful dreams and then admit that all those dreams are shared by each of the strangers shuffling by on the sidewalk.

Like most New Yorkers, I walk a great deal. New York is one of the few cities left in our country where people get where they're going by walking, and that's why this city has always had the most exciting window displays. People in other cities get in cars, drive to stores, and then drive home with their purchases. Window displays in those cities can give stores identity but aren't necessarily made to pull in passersby, simply because there are no passersby.

But I walk, I do a lot of my thinking while out walking alone, and I look in the windows I pass. I'm rarely impressed. I can't remember ever looking at a display and saying to myself, "I wish I'd thought of that." Many windows are just stacked goods, too

Preceding pages: *The "Broken Heart" from Valentine's Day 1990 by Judith Brown.*

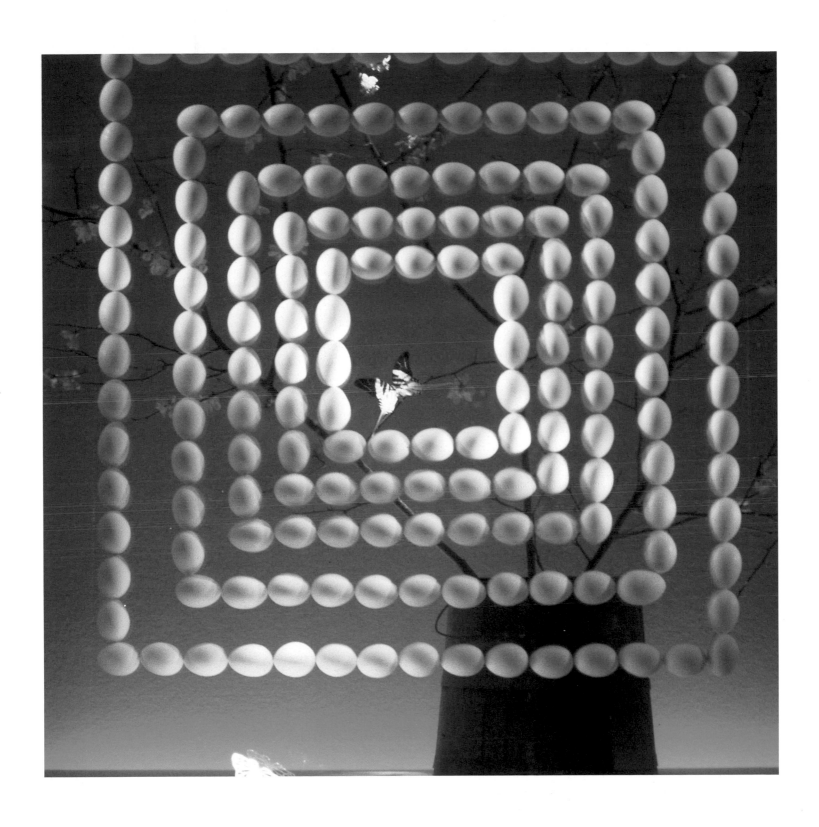

March 6, 1986. Eggs glued to plate glass. Like many simple and pure shapes, eggs are beautiful alone but also lend themselves to major group activities.

many places seem to store goods in their windows. Some windows give the impression that the owner ran out of shelf space and merely stuffed the rest in the windows.

Bookstores are among the best examples of bad window display. I love books and rarely walk by a bookstore without going in, but bookstore windows are almost always dull. Very rarely do they even attempt anything resembling display. All they do is show lined up books so the passerby understands that within is a bookshop, should he or she ever need a book. But such rows of books don't sell anything. Even when booksellers try to make their windows attractive, they usually create something full of amateurish touches, something that smacks of the loving hands of home.

For more than sixteen years I've been designing the window of the Madison Avenue Bookshop, so I've had the opportunity to explore the possibilities of books in displays. The founders of the store wanted their window to be special and asked me for advice even before the store opened, in May 1973, so I was able to make suggestions about the lighting installation. I also had time to think about how to give the store an image.

I thought of my wooden man, the big artist's model I bought in Italy in 1957. I've always liked him. He's calm and very expressive, very versatile. He's made of brown wood and is big—five feet six inches tall, nearly as tall as I am. At the time I thought of him for the Madison Avenue Bookshop, he was over at Gloria Vanderbilt's. She'd had him for quite a long time, had borrowed him to use as a model back when she was doing a lot of painting. I'd let her have him because when he wasn't in a window he was always getting in the way. I called Gloria, asked if she still had my man and if I could please have him back. She was willing to part with him.

He was standing in the window when the Madison Avenue Bookshop opened, and within a few months he'd given that store a personality. People were purposely crossing the avenue on their way to work in the morning or on their way home in the evening just to pause before the window and see what the big wooden man was doing, for he was always up to something, something tied to a book.

I decided to avoid the usual librarylike bookstore displays, and rather than fill the window with fifty different titles, I usually use one hundred copies of a single book. Involved in some way with each book, the man has proved his versatility. With the addition of a few props he can be anything or anyone, with gender no obstacle. Over the years, he's been Leonardo da Vinci, Julia Child, Paul Bocuse, Michel Guerard, a chorus boy, a CIA undercover agent, Somerset Maugham, Picasso, an undersea diver, a beach bum, a skier.

My wooden man has helped me come up with ideas that have made the Madison Avenue Bookshop's displays stand out from those of other bookstores. A while ago everyone was selling a new book of Richard Avedon's photography, and every other bookstore in the city did the obvious: opened a copy of the book to show the photographs or blew up some of the photographs. I turned the man into a photographer and equipped him with an antique camera on a tripod. People stopped at the window and stayed there to study the camera and then look at the book. Avedon himself was thrilled with that window, for it sold his book without showing even one of his photographs.

People look carefully at my man, and I try to dress him well. I usually make his clothes out of tissue paper, just that paper held together with pins and spit. For a book by Deborah Tourberville of photographs of Versailles I made him into an eighteenth-century lady with a pleated paper dress. A woman came in and asked if she could please buy that wonderful dress in the window.

After about three years I grew a little bored with the man, with shoving him around and dressing him, and I decided to see if anyone would say anything if I did the store's window without him. The reaction was immediate. On the second day of the manless window Arthur Loeb, who runs the store, called me and said, "Gene, you've got to get the man back in the window. We've had nothing but complaints. Where's the man?"

I designed this dress in 1984 for the Resources Council. All
in all, I used more than 2,000 peacock feathers.

He was resting in the back of the shop. I went up, hauled him out, and stood him back in his place in the window.

The man works because he's enjoying himself, because he's amusing and fun, and because he puts everything at a human level. Too many store displays either talk down to passersby or are cold and humorless. Without speaking a word that wooden man invites people to stop, and without moving he offers to share his every enjoyment. And people recognize the wooden man in the bookstore's window: he becomes part of their lives.

Mice, too, have fun. There's something humorous and delightful about busy little mice. A few years ago I decided to add a small papier-mâché mouse to the bookstore's window. I put him in a display with snow. Loeb fell for the mouse and asked me to put him in the next window display. For that display, I just about hid the mouse, placing him on a shelf behind a book, only his head and part of his body visible. From then on, he was in every window, but always in an inconspicuous location.

After all those performances, the poor mouse wore out, and I had to have another made. He disappeared from the next window display. The phone rang, people walked in: everyone wanted to know what had befallen the store's adorable "mascot."

An old Italian wooden man and a mouse made of paper have brought that bookstore's window to life. Other bookstores sell the same books, but do so as newsstands vend newspapers: anonymously. Giving people something to look for in a window adds a moment's pleasure to their lives, and such gestures don't go unnoticed.

Nick Lecakes made a train of wood and brought it up to show me at Tiffany's. A fun little train, it gave me an idea, and I asked him to add some boxcars to make it longer. He did, and when I put it in Tiffany's windows in January 1980 I had the locomotive in window one, passing cars in windows two, three, and four, and the caboose in window five. Such displays awaken curiosity. Having seen the locomotive, people walk window to

Left: *August 21, 1980. Acrylic sculpture by Walter Verdick.* Opposite: *January 29, 1981. Freesia seen through walls of eggs. Like looking through a hedge into a garden or peering over a wall, a little bit of effort makes what you see more interesting.*

window and around the block to watch the train pass and see the caboose, just as children sitting on a country fence wait through a freight train for a glimpse of the caboose. The only difference was that there was no signalman to wave a friendly hello from the caboose's back rail.

Jeffrey H. Packard, a painter, made me some paintings of different kinds of sky—cloudy, clear, gray, stormy—that made wonderful backgrounds to jewelry in displays that February. I wanted to use his work again, but I wanted him to put something in those skies. When people look up at the sky, they're usually looking for something. I myself look for the moon. "Jeffrey," I said, "I would love to do phases of the moon." He made the paintings, and I used them in August 1982.

Later in February 1980 I made displays using Woodson fabrics. I've used fabrics made by the Woodson company several times in windows because I like the colors and patterns. The fabrics serve as background. In this case, I put clear-glass vases full of water in the foreground. The water magnifies the pattern, which also seems to move as you walk by. Lena Tabori chose one of those windows for the cover of my book with Harry N. Abrams. I think she chose it not just because it's pretty, but because it gives the eye something to do, jumping back and forth from the fabric's pattern to that of the vase.

By then, we'd spent more than two years on that book project. Judith Goldman had taped about four months of interviews with me, and we'd gone over not just the windows I'd done for Tiffany's, but also my earlier work all the way back to Jim Buckley and I. Miller. A difficult task and not always pleasant. Many of the people with important roles in the stories that together make up my life are dead. Many dear friends are dead, many wonderful artists.

The book went on sale in October, and I was sometimes embarrassed but most often pleased by the attention it attracted. When people asked, I said no, I certainly did not intend to write another book. I swore I would never write another book.

I didn't put my book in the window at the Madison Avenue Bookshop and didn't put it in the windows of Tiffany's, but at Hoving's request, I prepared my second retrospective to coincide with the period of the book's release. This time I repeated the "Zip into Spring" zipper windows of April 1965, the Woodson fabric display used on the cover of the book, the paper bags closed with earrings of November 1960, the big ball of twine of May 1963, and the six ice-cream cones with gumdrop ice cream, five of them topped with rings, of August 1966.

Walter Hoving, one of the most important characters in the story of my life as well as a central figure in any history of Tiffany's, was still chairman of the board of Tiffany's. He remained for about one year after Avon bought the store. A few months later in 1980 he resigned, and Tiffany's president, Harry B. Platt, a great-great-grandson of Charles L. Tiffany, took over. He was later replaced by Anthony Ostrom.

There were other changes. Van Day Truex, already in semiretirement, had died in 1979 and been replaced by John Loring. Loring soon made his mark on the store. A graduate of Yale and former professor of art at the University of California, he's an artist himself, with prints and paintings in the Museum of Modern Art, the Whitney Museum, the Chicago Art Institute, and the Boston Museum of Fine Arts.

In October 1980, while my retrospective was in the windows, he introduced a new jewelry designer to Tiffany's: Paloma Picasso. The youngest daughter of Pablo Picasso and the painter Françoise Gilot, she was named for the dove of peace Picasso designed in the year of her birth. She'd begun designing jewelry while working as an assistant costume and scenery designer on a play in Paris. The main actress had needed a lot of jewelry, and Paloma had made it. She then studied jewelry design in Paris and made jewelry collections for Yves St. Laurent. Loring had met her in Paris and asked her to come to Tiffany's, where she joined Angela Cummings and Elsa Peretti as jewelry designers. Aside

August 10, 1978. Glassware against a background of Woodson fabric.

from Jean Schlumberger, who still had his own department in the store but was no longer active as a designer, those three women are the only designers in Tiffany's history whose names are stamped on their pieces.

By 1981, Tiffany's had five branches—Houston, San Francisco, Beverly Hills, Chicago, and Atlanta—and more were planned. (Tiffany's merchandise was also being sold in branches of the Japanese department store Mitsukoshi.) Each new store has meant a new set of windows, and no matter where a Tiffany's is located, people expect it to have special window displays. I go to the opening of each store and create the first window displays. Sometimes I recreate windows I've done in New York, sometimes I make something new. After the store's opening, I leave, and the store's chosen window trimmer takes over.

The image created in the New York windows never changed during the period Tiffany's was owned by Avon. No one suggested I alter in any way what I'd always done. The only minor change was one I made myself when I decided to let the late summer windows, those for July and August, occasionally run three weeks instead of the usual two.

There has never been enough time. The props and art from last week's windows lean against those being prepared for next week, and all around them are objects used, perhaps, eight years ago and objects planned for windows eight months from now. With each spring my first thoughts turn to Christmas. Grass growing in boxes for Easter reminds me I have to think of something new to do with eggs.

With the passing years I've used less and less merchandise in Tiffany's windows. To me, the store's image is tied less to what is actually on sale than to a way of life and a way of looking at life—mine. What I've done in Tiffany's five windows over all these years has changed, of course, as I've changed and as art has changed, but I like to believe that the windows have presented a coherent image, have made an intelligible statement.

I make my statement, but I also use art created by other people. I've always used the newest art, art just created by artists just beginning to find their way. New York is still the center of artistic creativity. It often seems there are no movements, no movement at all in art, but when a movement starts it usually starts here, and I try to know about it. I read the art sections in magazines, go to galleries and openings, and, of course, artists come to see me to show me their work. I don't always like what I see, and I've even told artists that I don't like their work but want to use it in Tiffany's windows because I want to show the public what's going on.

Thus, like the windows of Bonwit Teller in the 1950s, the windows of Tiffany's are often an art gallery, an art gallery open to the public at all hours. Some of the artists I've used over the years have become familiar, and attentive passersby may have noticed changes in their styles with passing time. Judith Brown's metal sculptures, for example, have become more representational. I used her works twice during the 1980s, along with works by such familiar artists as Roger Sammis, Sam Gallo, Walter Verdick, Richard Giglio, Hans Van De Bovenkamp, Edith La Bate, Anne M. Cembalest, E. J. Taylor, Edward Acevedo, Alexander Ney, and Robert Heitmann.

More than 120 other artists contributed works for Tiffany's windows during the 1980s. Paintings and sculptures, assemblages and collages: artists often have their own descriptions for their work, and deciding what to call a medium can involve much discussion.

Some of the mediums were truly new. Handmade paper appeared often in art galleries during the early 1980s, and I thought it was strange and interesting and that the public should be made aware of it. I chose the work of Gertrude Simon, an artist who achieved particularly interesting forms by manipulating paper pulp and embedding pieces of wood in the resulting sculptures. She called the series of sculptures "Paleocene Fossils."

Needlework, so very popular during the 1970s, was less so in the 1980s, and one of its only appearances in Tiffany's windows was in April 1981 when I used three-dimensional representations of houses by an artist named Lisa Regal Druck. Three feet long and two feet high, these needlepoint structures showed five of the Preservation Society's mansions: The Elms, Kingscote, Château-sur-Mer, Rosecliff, and The Breakers.

This carousel is a recent creation. The seven animals—giraffe, zebra, two horses, Bengal tiger, rabbit, and camel—go up and down as the carousel turns, which it does to the tune of "The Carousel Waltz" from Carousel.

July 22, 1982. Shining eyes in a photograph by Arthur Swogger.

In May 1980 Lawrence Lacina attracted attention, including magazine reviews, with five gilded collages playing tricks with *Mona Lisa*. In April 1982 I used collages he'd made, representations of mandalas that were both beautiful and fascinating. Cile Bellefleur-Burbidge makes cakes, enormous, amazing, multilayered cakes perfect for wedding windows. I used them in May 1983 and then again in May 1987, and the response both times was a kind of hushed awe. People don't expect to see cakes in a jewelry store's windows.

In January 1985 neon light appeared in Tiffany's windows for the second time. Once again, these were the creations of John Tanaka. This time the colored light was bent into hearts for Valentine's Day. Far different was the art of Jacob J. Kass: rural scenes painted on the blades of old saws.

I used photography several times during the 1980s. The most popular windows of the summer of 1982 were probably those using Arthur Swogger's photographs of animals, photographs made striking because the animals' eyes were brightly shining. Swogger went into zoos at night and flashed a light in animals' eyes to get that shine. In September 1983 I used five of Ken Duncan's portraits of famous female dancers: Natalia Makarova, Carmen de Lavallade, Suzanne Farrell, Twyla Tharp, and Liliane Montevecchi. In March 1984 it was Greame Outerbridge's photographs of Bermuda, which are so unusual—angles of buildings, shadows against clear sky—that many people thought them paintings.

For holidays I often turned to Robert Heitmann. He has a special understanding of traditions, and his creations seem familiar, like shared memories, and are full of the wonderful details that thrill children. For Christmas 1980 he made an Annunciation and a Madonna and Child. For Halloween 1981 it was witches and fairies and nursery-rhyme scenes, such as Jack jumping over his candlestick. For Thanksgiving 1982 he made pictures with clothespins. His Thanksgiving windows for 1983 told a charming story about a cook, spreading his arms to indicate the size of the turkey he wants in the first window, cooking it in the second, carving it in the third, serving it in the fourth, and in the fifth resting in bed reading *500 Ways to Use Leftover Turkey*.

For Christmas 1984 he created scenes that altered the traditional views of Christmas. The crèche scene was located in front of a subway station with city dwellers taking the roles of the Three Wise Men, Mary, Joseph, and the Child. In the next window nuns atop a steeple looked at a star through a telescope. His Christmas windows for 1986 were international, historic scenes of Christmas in Belgium, Italy, Germany, France, and the United States. In 1988 his Christmas windows related the story of Christmas trees, trees being gathered, sold, trimmed, and finally discarded, to the delight of birds. His 1989 Christmas windows were again international, scenes of historic Christmases from around the world.

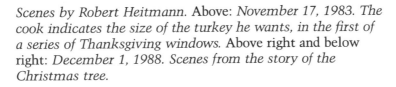

Scenes by Robert Heitmann. Above: *November 17, 1983. The cook indicates the size of the turkey he wants, in the first of a series of Thanksgiving windows.* Above right and below right: *December 1, 1988. Scenes from the story of the Christmas tree.*

December 2, 1981. Santa's helpers assemble a toy horse in a display by E. J. Taylor.

Other artists contributed Christmas windows. For 1981 it was E. J. Taylor, whose figures aren't as innocent as Heitmann's. There's something eerie about them, but they're marvelous. The 1983 Christmas windows were by Dale Payson and were more homey: houses of real gingerbread peopled by painted wooden dolls.

The only difficult Christmas was 1982, which involved me in one of the only arguments I've ever had with an artist. That year, I wanted the Christmas windows to feature the beautifully evocative dolls of Abigail Brahms. An Israeli, Brahms didn't grow up with Santa Claus and Christmas trees and had never heard of Tiny Tim. She's also a headstrong woman. I spent many hours explaining Christmas to her; she didn't always want to accept what I told her, leading to some lengthy discussions of religion, philosophy, and folklore. She understood fairies and angels and children with toys, and she grasped enough of what I said to create recognizable scenes, but some of them teetered on the edge of tumbling into some other mythology.

Window one had a wonderful scene of children and toys, including a ballerina that turned on a stand. I'd wanted a Madonna and Child for window two, and Brahms's interpretation was touching: a little girl looking up at a framed Madonna and Child with the child crawling out of the frame toward the little girl. The other windows showed more little girls with fairies, her recreation of Tiny Tim, and an angel flying low over children in a snowy forest.

During the 1980s I also experienced the most upsetting days of my career.

In May 1981 I first used the work of Robert Keene McKinley, an artist from Alabama who'd come to New York and found work as a designer of children's fashions. He made small, very realistic, exquisitely detailed clay sculptures of people. I wanted to use his work and asked him to make me a series based on a common theme. He thought of the city's park benches and decided to make five typical park scenes. He told me his plans for four of the scenes but refused to discuss the fifth. "It'll be a surprise," he said.

I was surprised and not particularly pleased. The fifth park scene showed me sitting alone on a bench sketching. There was nothing I could do about it—the displays had to go in—but I put myself in window five.

The other four windows were more amusing. In the first, McKinley had two tourists sitting on a bench agog over a red-lipped, red-booted woman passing on roller skates—none other than Diana Vreeland, the famous editor of *Vogue* magazine. The second scene had two women sitting at opposite ends of a bench, one well dressed and well to do, the other a homeless woman, one of the so-called bag ladies. Both women sat surrounded by shopping bags from famous stores—Valentino, Tiffany's, Saks—the same bags in the same arrangement, the only difference being that the bag lady's were torn and battered. In the third window a young couple sat at one end of a bench, the girl gazing at her new engagement ring; at the other end an elderly woman examined hers. The fourth window showed three cheerful winos drinking out of paper bags. All were scenes one might expect on a walk through Central Park—except for that of me sitting on a bench sketching. I haven't done that since my first years in New York.

Each scene was matched to a piece of jewelry, including a silver flask in the scene of the winos and a diamond bracelet coming out of one of the bag lady's bags.

Vreeland, who died during the winter of 1989, was delighted to see herself roller-skating through the park, something she was just crazy enough to have done. The window with the engagement rings attracted much attention for its poignancy. I later discovered that the scene of the bag lady, without my knowledge, had been made into a postcard. Someone had stepped up to the window, taken a photograph, and made it into a card. A friend sent me one from the West Coast.

In May 1982 I again used works by Robert McKinley, this time large doll-like figures

May 7, 1981. Scenes on New York city park benches by Robert McKinley. Opposite left: *Diana Vreeland skates past astonished tourists.* Opposite right: *A bag lady and well-to-do lady with identical shopping bags share a bench.* Left: *Contented winos.*

representing female characters from Shakespeare—Ophelia, Titania, Lady Macbeth, Juliet, and Kate—each accompanied by a quotation from the play.

In April I put in a set of windows called "Urban Entomology," by Mark Borow. Dark and grim, these were miniature scenes showing metaphorical insect figures in city settings. At the bottom of each of the five windows was a written description of the scene. Window one showed the black widow ("The webs of this deadly female can be found primarily on Eighth Avenue in midtown, where they often ensare philandering worker ants") and the worm ("The worm acts as an agent for the black widow and is widely considered to be one of the lowest forms of life"). The other windows displayed, and caustically described, the cricket, the monarch butterfly, the boozebottle fly, and so on, each insect shown in its "natural" environment.

There were complaints. A few people were offended by the black widow window, saying it was racist. Tiffany's president received an extraordinary letter from someone complaining that we had a picture of a vagina in one of the windows. As background to a bar scene, the artist had made a tiny picture of a jack-in-the-pulpit and even labeled it as such. The flower was part of the story. Seeing it as a vagina required a certain imagination. Others complained about one of the insects, the JAP beetle ("These ostentatious beetles tend to infest fashionable sections of the city, where their fathers have installed them in nesting grounds with doormen").

I'd received complaints before, of course. There was the man who spied female reproductive organs in Bonwit's windows, and following the "Great White Robbery" windows at Bonwit's I'd received a letter from a woman indignant that I'd used white— "the color of purity and innocence"—for an evildoer. And when I did a window with a hammer resting on a bed of nails, a man wrote complaining the window was violent.

Those complaints had seemed silly, but the "Urban Entomology" complaints surprised me. People were seeing things in my windows that I certainly hadn't put there.

Tiffany's wasn't the only store receiving complaints concerning its windows. While doing the windows of Saks, Donald Nowicki placed an eyepatch on a female mannequin and was astonished to receive letters complaining he was making fun of Israeli leader Moshe Dayan. When Guy Scarangello, then display director at Barneys, did a series of Christmas windows in which he showed a man and a maid standing together in a kitchen, a group of local women complained that the maid was being sexually abused. They'd seen an entire drama in that one scene: the maid was poor, needed her job, and couldn't refuse the advances of the evil man. Responding to such complaints can be very difficult.

On July 21, 1983, I put in my third set of windows with figures by Robert Keene McKinley. Once again, he had created vignettes of New York, this time remarkably detailed street scenes. The first recreated a moment of New York history: Gloria Swanson being photographed in the rubble of the old Roxy Theater. The second showed a bag lady, based on a woman who lived in a box on a street near McKinley's home, and a bum. The bag lady was sitting on the ground between two garbage bags reading *House and Garden* magazine; over her head was a No Loitering sign. The bum was standing at the corner, holding a bottle of scotch in one hand, a cigarette butt in the other; behind him was a poster advertising gin. The scene was made more realistic with crumpled beer cans and graffiti.

In the third window Greta Garbo was shown walking by some astonished tourists. On a background wall was a poster for *Camille*, the 1936 film in which she starred with Robert Taylor. In the fourth window Helen Hayes walked away from some astonished card sharks, evidently having won all their money. Window five featured a nameless New York street performer, revealing in his hands his broken heart.

I placed a piece of merchandise—jewelry—in each of those windows, just as I do with all Tiffany's windows, except those for Christmas.

These July windows were scheduled to stay in three weeks. Thirteen days after they'd been installed, a reporter for the *Daily News* attacked them, calling them "a pretty grim

July 21, 1983. A New York scene by Robert McKinley. This window led to a controversy, and I finally decided to remove the bag lady and the wino. I left the woman's slippers, and I also left the necklace.

joke in a city where 36,000 men and women live in boxes and doorways and in the hidden corners of railroad stations."

As a result of this article, the displays became a subject of controversy. I received phone calls and letters condemning the windows as heartless and phone calls and letters praising them as realistic views of New York. People blamed Tiffany's and were saying terrible things about the store, but no board of directors had chosen that piece of art. The windows were my doing. The major cause of the anger was the contrast between the jewelry in the window and the plight of the homeless woman and wino. No one claimed McKinley's art was inaccurate.

After three days of anguish I met with Anthony Ostrom, then president of Tiffany's. He told me to do whatever I wanted. "Whatever you do will be all right," he said.

On August 4 I removed the bag lady and bum from the window but left the rest of the scene intact, for it still presented an artist's view of a New York street. That was the first and only time a display has been changed because of a complaint.

I hope to someday use Robert McKinley's work again. In October 1983 I used figures by Mark Borow—he of "Urban Entomology"—for the second time, scenes entitled "Backstage at the Metropolitan Opera" showing furious activity on the part of very small stagehands and assistants.

One morning in January 1982, in the middle of a snowstorm, I had a visit from a friendly Canadian named Carmine David Gallo. I never understood why he'd come, and what he had to show me wasn't art but bundles of false $1 million bills. They looked remarkably real, and I told him so. He gave me a few handfuls, then continued on his way. I later learned he'd gone to the top of Rockefeller Plaza and dumped hundreds of the bogus bills into the snowy air. When they hit the streets those bills caused a terrible traffic jam and a small riot. People thought they were real and, slipping and sliding in the snow, chased them up and down the avenue and streets. I put my $1 million bills away for future use in a window.

I first used the bills in June 1983. Brookie Maxwell, daughter of William Maxwell, the writer and former editor of *The New Yorker*, made five portraits of cats, and I placed one of Carmine David Gallo's $1 million bills in the fifth window.

For Father's Day 1985 William Bodenschatz made me father-figure sculptures: a rock star made of sheet music, a father and son of wrapping paper, a businessman made of dollar bills, a jogger made of maps. Gold money clips seemed the right merchandise to display with the businessman, and I put into each a few folded $1 million bills left over from Mr. Gallo's visit.

A would-be thief mistook those bills for legal tender and tried to break into the window and steal them. He was still banging his way through the thick glass when the police stepped up beside him.

Valentine's Day and Easter I usually reserve for myself. Those holidays please me and challenge me. And throughout each year, from time to time, a sleepless night—or a remark overheard, something remembered while walking alone down one of this city's streets—leads to an idea for a set of windows.

For Easter 1980 I put butterflies in a circle around a single egg in one window, and eggs in a circle around a single butterfly in the next. It worked: the eggs flew as convincingly as the butterflies.

One way of surprising people is to play tricks with materials. I'm sure many of the passersby who glanced at my Valentine's Day windows in 1981 thought the displays were simply frilly valentines. You had to stop and look closer to see that those valentines were made of pasta, uncooked pasta glued to plate glass. The pasta pictures included hearts, a unicorn, a pope's coat of arms, and an eagle bearing the word "Amour."

Mustaches suggested a set of windows that March. Mustaches were very popular during the early 1980s. I found them on friends and noted them on passing strangers. I also found that Tiffany's sold gold mustache combs. Such a classic item deserved special treatment.

Black and gold were the colors I chose for those windows. The background in all five windows was black to set off gold men's jewelry. In window one were gold barbell-shaped cufflinks and, to call attention to the shape, a real barbell, which I'd gold-leafed. The mustache comb was in window two. I'd gold-leafed a Greek head, attached a mustache on his upper lip, and gave him the gold comb. In window three I hung real chains, painted gold, behind men's gold chains. I painted a big rock gold and put it in window four along with gold nuggets on chains, and for window five I painted some bamboo to set off the store's bamboo-style gold pens.

The Optical Manufacturers Association and the Museum of the City of New York

Opposite: *June 13, 1985. One of five figures William Bodenschatz made for Father's Day displays. This gentleman is made of real torn dollar bills glued to a clay frame. The fake $1 million bills in the billfold were taken as real by a misguided soul.* Above: *March 13, 1980. In this window butterflies encircle a single egg. In another window of this display, it's the eggs that fly around a single butterfly.*

celebrated Eyecare Week in March 1981 and asked me to prepare a display showing the history of eyeglasses. I got my friend Gene McCabe to help with the project. Eyeglasses need faces as props, so I asked Robert Heitmann to recreate famous portraits of people, but to make the subjects animals, mostly dogs and cats. We hung the portraits on the walls, and I just poked real eyeglasses through the canvases over the animal faces. At either end of this little art gallery we placed audiences of soft sculpture figures wearing antique glasses. The earliest pair of glasses dated to 1690; the most expensive was the pair that marked the debut of designer eyewear frames in 1955, the work of Elsa Schiaparelli, with nearly 200 diamonds.

That exhibition was Gene McCabe's last job. While we were working on it he complained he wasn't feeling well, and shortly after we finished he was hospitalized for a few months and then died. I had lost another friend, another person who knew and understood my world.

Visual puns have inspired many of Tiffany's windows, and for Valentine's Day 1982 I

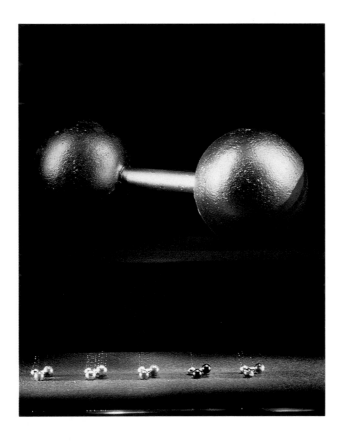
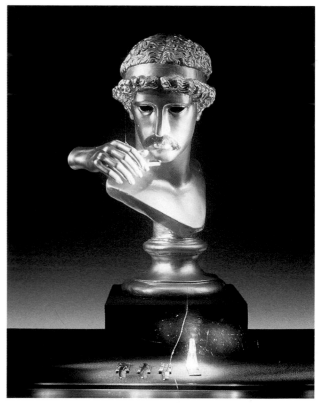

March 19, 1981. Black and gold were the colors I used here for a series of windows on men's accessories.

formed five hearts, each of a different material glued to a pane of glass: a heart of nails, of ice (plastic cubes), stones, candy hearts, and the special crystallike forms you get when you smash a mannequin's base.

By gluing eggs to plates of glass I made geometric forms for that Easter: a triangle of eggs that filled half a window; two vertical rectangles at either side of a window that left a windowlike opening; two horizontal rectangles of eggs that left open only a strip of open glass.

The birds and the bees. I don't remember whether someone said it or I just thought of the phrase, but I decided to base the 1983 Valentine's Day windows on the birds and the bees. Birds in window one with nests and branches; a beehive—an old one I'd bought out in the country—in window two with jeweled bees; birds in branches for three; a view through a honeycomb-covered window in window four; a lone bluejay sitting on a branch in window five. From birds to bees to birds I hoped people would get it, and many did.

Insects up against a screen are a common summer sight, so that June I suspended in each window a framed piece of screening—chicken wire, regular screening, and so on—

and placed butterflies and jewelry on them, making them small summer windows within Tiffany's windows.

In January 1984 I took a little trip to South America with Gino di Grandi. I used to wonder about that man. I thought nobody could really be that nice, that selfless, but through the years he's been exactly the same, and he brings out the best in other people. Having done well for himself in the business world, he'd gotten together with a group of like-minded souls to form a nonprofit organization, New Ideas for Export Development Aid, dedicated to teaching people in disadvantaged countries how to plan, make, and market products. The idea was to identify those products with the best export potential in underdeveloped countries and show the people how they could make them themselves, using their own materials and their own manufacturing.

Working with the U.S. Agency for International Development, we went to La Paz, Bolivia, and spent two weeks there studying their handcrafts and making suggestions. At times I felt uncomfortable down there, both because of the change in altitude and

 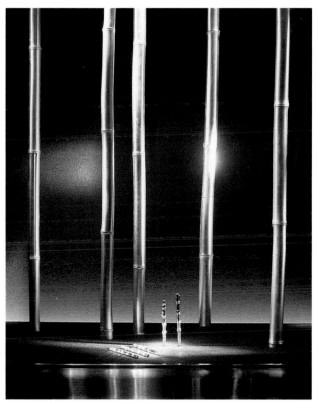

because it all seemed like a Graham Greene novel, with several demonstrations each day and the constant sense of violence. We visited wood carvers, weavers, clothing makers. I made sketches and had samples made.

One day we went high into the Andes to a ranch where llamas, vicuñas, and alpacas were being raised in captivity. There were hundreds of those beautiful animals, and I discovered vicuñas are even sweeter than llamas and have eyelashes like Louise Nevelson. I wanted to stay there forever.

In 1988 I did the same thing as part of a World Bank project for Senegal, but this time no travel was involved. I was shown the crafts and asked for my suggestions. It was like looking at the work of an artist, but this time it was a country. Di Grandi is involved in wonderful projects, efforts aimed at helping people all over the world, and I'm always delighted and honored when he asks my assistance.

My 1984 Valentine's Day windows used telephones, the first time I'd dedicated a display to phones since my days at Bonwit Teller. I had receivers suspended in the air with cartoonlike balloons indicating the conversations. Thus the windows had "Yes, Mark, it's

214 William Bodenschatz made these figures for me to help celebrate
the opening of Tiffany's new London store. One shows the British lion greeting the
Statue of Liberty; the other Uncle Sam and Britannia.

215

Cleo. If it be love indeed, tell me how much"; "Oh Romeo, Romeo! Wherefore art thou, Romeo"; "Hello, Kermit, this is *moi*. I didn't know you cared so much!"—I've always loved the Muppets; "Dear Robert—It's Elizabeth. How do I love thee? Let me count the ways"; and "Yes, this is Priscilla—Speak for yourself, John!"

In July, following another set of windows using Ruby Jackson's plaster sculptures, I again created the kind of scenes for which Tiffany's windows are ideally suited: miniature interiors. Each of these windows was a view into another world, some through archways, some through doorways leading to other doorways leading to yet another darkened door.

In August I played with glass, light, and shadows in a series of windows. One window showed a porcelain rooster seen from behind chicken wire beside an egg he obviously hadn't laid. In the last window I set up seventeen glasses in rows with a hammer and a broken glass—I smashed it myself—in the foreground.

It worked. No sooner had that display gone in than I began receiving helpful phone calls. "Did you know you had a broken glass in the window?" And I said to all of them, "Did you happen to notice the hammer?"

The September 1984 windows featured "Dramatis Personae," figures of famous film characters created by Van Craig. Along with the lion from *The Wizard of Oz* and Gloria Swanson, there was Theda Bara, star of the first movie I ever saw.

In October, while the windows were showing "Models of the Future," futuristic views of cities, by Hans Carl Clausen, Tiffany's broke from Avon and became again an independent company. The man responsible was William R. Chaney. President of Avon from 1977 to 1983, he'd moved to Tiffany's board in January 1980, had become chief executive officer in August 1984, and had led the successful attempt to gain control of Tiffany's.

When he took over Tiffany's, Chaney began restoring the store to its former stature and reasserting the store's superiority. A fine man, a true gentleman, he reminded me of Hoving. "You can't be all things to all people," he said. "Our goal is to be the most respected source for fine jewelry and other luxury products." And once, when a bureaucratic executive asked him to whom I answered, he replied, "I think his name is God."

For Valentine's Day 1986 I said "love" in a different language in each window: Hebrew, English, Arabic, Spanish, and Russian. The fun was in the props for each language, an oilcan for Arabic, caviar and bears for Russian.

That April Paul Taylor's dance company performed *A Musical Offering*, for which I'd designed the costumes and set. Taylor had turned Bach's baroque offering to Frederick the Great into a native ritual, and the costumes—leather loinclothes—were the result of hours spent studying the African costumes and artifacts exhibited in the Metropolitan Museum.

That September Tiffany's opened a London branch, the first Tiffany's in Europe since World War II. The Tiffany Diamond was brought there and exhibited, and I went to do the first set of windows. The store has two windows, and I put in them figures I'd had Bill Bodenschatz make: the British lion greeting Miss Liberty in one, Uncle Sam saluting Britannia in the other.

I used my own blue blazer for the Valentine's Day windows in 1987. In window one I had the blazer with a red heart sewn on one sleeve. Window two showed an extremely fragile heart packed in a wooden crate and hanging by a block and tackle. For window three I made an archery target with concentric hearts instead of circles. In window four I formed heart paperweights into the shape of a heart. There was a broken heart in window five, alongside it the guilty hammer.

On September 18, 1987, Tiffany's was 150 years old, and four months of events were dedicated to the celebration. There were fancy balls in those cities with Tiffany's branches, the publication of *Tiffany's 150 Years*, by John Loring, the exhibition "Triumphs of American Silvermaking: Tiffany & Co., 1860–1900" at New York's Metropolitan Museum of Art, the exhibition "The Silver of Tiffany & Co., 1850–1987" at Boston's

January 29, 1987. A fragile heart is loaded aboard a ship.

January 29, 1987. A smashed heart and the hammer that smashed it.

January 29, 1987. Cupid's target practice. If you aim at the heart you can sometimes do great damage.

Museum of Fine Arts, and, in 1988, "Tiffany: 150 Years of Gems and Jewelry" at New York's American Museum of Natural History. In Japan, Mitsukoshi commemorated the anniversary with a traveling exhibition of Tiffany objects.

The five New York windows celebrated the anniversary with miniature recreations of Tiffany's stores by Robert Heitmann. One window showed Tiffany's first two locations, 259 Broadway and 271 Broadway; the next 550 Broadway in 1854, with Atlas over the door; then the Union Square store, with figurines of Lillian Russell with her silver bicycle and Diamond Jim Brady; then Fifth Avenue and Thirty-seventh Street; and finally the Fifty-seventh Street store and next to it the small farmhouse that had occupied the site in 1837.

Tiffany's celebrated its anniversary by introducing its first original fragrance, called Tiffany. I used bottles of the perfume in displays that October. In some windows the bottles were located on rocks amid tumbling water. In others, my articulated artist's figures were photographing the bottles or painting their portrait.

By then Tiffany's had seven branch stores, with seven distant sets of windows. I have the people who design Tiffany's windows in other cities come to New York so that I can talk to them and they can work with me. Some are students just out of art school, some have had experience in other display departments, a few have come to window display after working in the theater.

Over the years I've occasionally had bad reports on the window displays in some of those stores. I talk to the store managers, go to the stores. Most recently I gave all the store managers Polaroid cameras and asked them to send me photographs of their displays.

My involvement in the windows of Tiffany's branch stores has put increasing pressure on the New York window display department—a title that sounds grandiose but in fact means only me, my assistant, and two crowded little rooms. Since my assistant and I couldn't possibly design Tiffany's New York windows and respond to the needs of the store's branches, including those overseas, Sam Kirkpatrick was taken on as associate director of display in January 1988. In theory, Sam's job involves only the branches and the international stores, but we are still too few, and we all work together on almost everything. In the summer of 1988 Ronnie Smith left and was replaced by Brian Johnson—for the first time in thirty-five years, Tiffany's display department was without a Ron.

Of course, each time a new store is built from the ground up, the opportunity comes—and is passed by—to create better display windows. Sam and I even made a scale model of a window to be used, if possible, wherever Tiffany's opens a new store. Perhaps architects will begin to listen. Thus far they never have.

The 1987 Christmas windows were a particular joy. The publicity director for Jim Henson, creator of the Muppets, had reported to me that Henson was interested in doing a set of windows at Tiffany's. I told him I'd always wanted to work with Henson but thought he was much too busy and important to bother with me.

"That's funny," said the publicity director, "that's exactly what he says about you."

Thus I met Jim Henson and the people who work with him as well as the Muppets. The display had to be for Christmas, the special Christmas that marked Tiffany's anniversary. We put Big Bird in place over the main door to welcome everyone. The windows showed the Cookie Monster, Gonzo, Scooter, and Fozzie sorting Christmas mail; Bert and Ernie as Santa and a snowbound Rudolph; Muppet Babies around a fireside; and Kermit popping the question to Miss Piggy, offering her a diamond ring (from a Crackerjacks box).

The Valentine's Day windows for 1988 played a spelling game. Window one had a revolving globe, two the letter E, three V, four O and five L. This was easier than spelling the word in different languages and meant the same: love makes the world go 'round.

I played a similar game in that year's Easter windows. Floating in the air over grass, clover, and azaleas in window one were a single egg and a single butterfly. The same grass, clover, and azaleas appeared in window two, but in the air were two eggs and two

January 1990. Papier-mâché forms by Penny Carter. It took her so long to make these that she refused to sell them at any price.

221

February 1988. "Love makes the world go 'round."
The globe revolved.

butterflies. Having seen those two windows, the passerby knows what must come next—three eggs and three butterflies—but can't just walk away without being sure, without actually seeing and counting. Sure enough, window three had three eggs and three butterflies, and there were four of each in window four, although you had to look hard to see the fourth egg and butterfly because they were mixed in with the plants. For the first time, I moved the Bible from its traditional place in window four to window five: I didn't want to break the set's rhythm.

If you want to see some things, you have to make them yourself. From time to time I get ideas for jewelry. I talk to someone, have sketches made, and the object is brought into existence. A few years ago I decided to design scarves and toys, the scarves because I thought the stained-glass designs of Louis Comfort Tiffany would make marvelous scarves, the toys because I love toys. The toys, made of silver and enamel, were popular, and I followed them, in the summer of 1988, with a line of circus animals and performers, also made of silver and enamel.

A portrait of me appeared in Tiffany's windows for the second time in August 1988.

Again, I was tricked by an artist, this time Alexander Ney. He prepared five sculptures, and the fifth showed me, seated, with a large, rectangular form in my arms: a Tiffany's window.

For Valentine's Day 1989 I wanted to use the art of Konstantine Kakanias, a Greek who lived for many years in Paris and has done many window displays since coming to New York, including several over at Barneys. I met with him, and we discussed his plans. He wanted to tell a story using small cutout silhouettes against a background: a woman alone looking at herself in a mirror, a man appearing and offering her flowers, the two embracing. A large velvet heart was to be suspended over each scene.

I liked the idea but wanted him to change the final scene. We argued and argued, but I finally won him over, and his silhouette tale concluded with the woman crying, the man walking away, a piece torn from the suspended velvet heart. That's the truth of love as I've seen it, as I've known it.

Another cold December day, mist in the air, and I was standing alone in front of the

Seagram Building, watching the first trees of another Christmas being put into place, when I received word that Walter Hoving had died.

The smell of those trees is always wonderful, and standing there in front of that towering building I can close my eyes and imagine I'm alone in a distant forest, far from all traffic and all voices. All the work that Walter Hoving and I did together we did in big buildings, in offices and hallways. He always gave all he had to make Tiffany's the store he believed it should be, as I've always given all I have to make Tiffany's windows what they should be. And we were lucky because what we wanted, what we were struggling to do, was so often the same.

What I originally wanted, of course, was to paint. I came to New York to become a famous painter. But in my work at Tiffany's I think exactly the way a painter thinks, I deal with the same basics—composition, color, design—and I work hard to make those windows express what I want to say. Jim Buckley used to say designing a window display was like painting a picture through the rear of the canvas, so perhaps I did become a kind of painter, for Jim Buckley was always right.

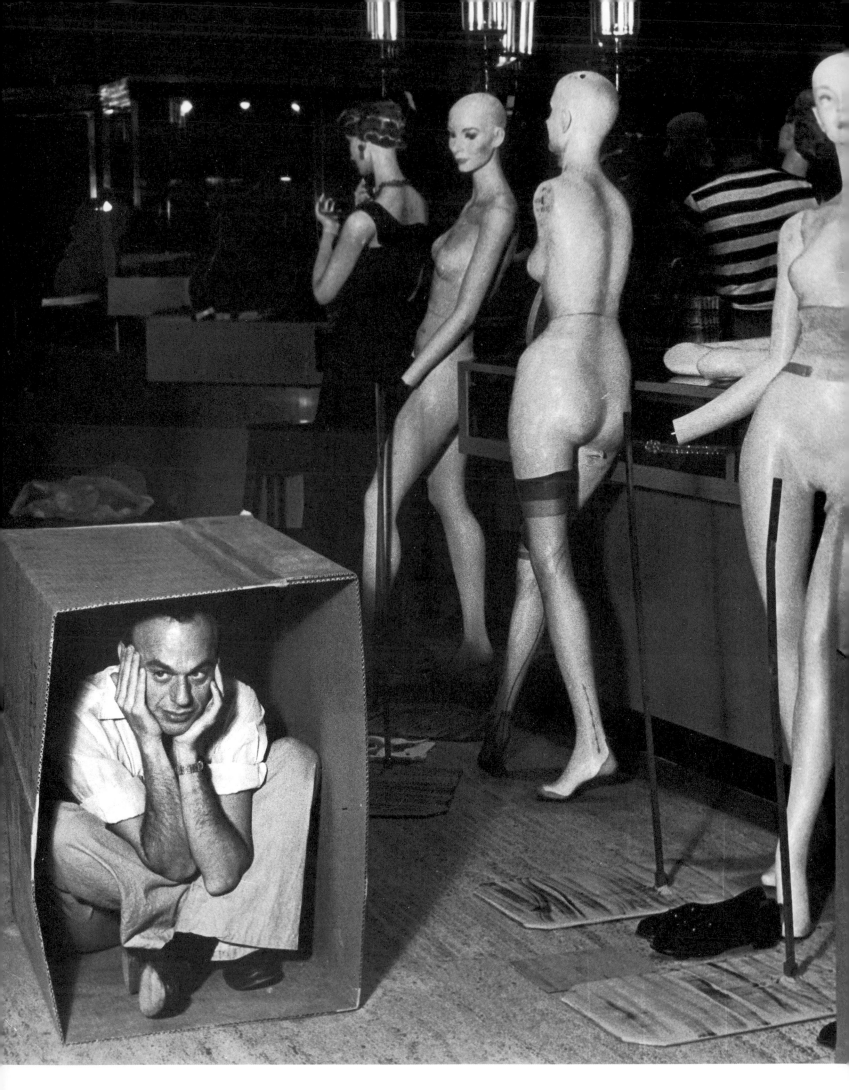

THANKS

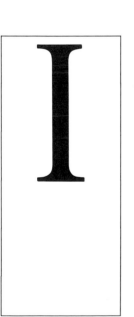

I FIRST SAW VENICE from a gondola by moonlight, an experience everyone should have and no one ever forgets. While I was there that first visit I was determined to see St. Mark's Square without a soul in it, not even a pigeon. So I stood and waited for the bars to close, the locals to go home, the tourists to tire and wander back to their hotels. Finally, around three in the morning, I found myself alone on that most perfect of stages. So I danced, danced all over the square until I was too tired to dance a step more.

Being alone to see and to think, to experience, has always been important to me, but that's not something I'd stress: everything I've created or tried to create has involved other people. All the people with whom I've come in contact over the years have had an influence on my life, and I've been wonderfully lucky, for so very many of the people I've met—for whatever reasons of work or art—have become my friends. To all of them I wish to offer certain words, not really of gratitude—it seems foolish to thank people for being who they are—but of recognition.

First and last are always the artists, those hundreds of men and women who have inspired me and worked with me, who have listened to me and understood my wishes, helped me shape and color my statements. To name even one would be unfair, and to list them would take away all my breath along with all the pages left to this book.

I've had the joy of knowing many people in the performing arts, in show business: Gloria Swanson, Rosalind Russell, Vivien Leigh, Audrey Hepburn, Blanche Thebom, Victoria de Los Angeles, John Gielgud, Irene Worth, Melina Mercouri. With some of those

Another window night at Bonwit Teller. Nude mannequins, raw fashion, and nerves. Cris Alexander dropped by and wanted to take my picture. "Take it the way I feel," I said, and showed him.

people I've shared moments of wonderful understanding and moments of insanity. One evening at rush hour, riding with Mercouri in a limousine along Sixth Avenue back to a hotel, she turned to me—perhaps she had tired of the car's pace, perhaps the evening light attracted her—and said, "Let's get out." We opened the door of the car, stepped out into the honking traffic, and walked up the avenue to the hotel. I'll never forget how sensible it then seemed to walk hand in hand in the middle of Sixth Avenue.

People from ballet, dancers and choreographers, have always played important roles in my life. David Nillo, Alicia Markova, Alexandra Danilova, Muriel Stuart, Leon Danielian, Rosella Hightower, Simon Semenoff, John Butler, Valerie Bettis, Antony Tudor, Maria Karnilova, Martha Graham, Paul Taylor, and Glen Tetley are among those who have thrilled me with their talents and with whom I've enjoyed working.

Many businesspeople have supported me, aided me, or graciously put up with me. Herman Delman found his way to my heart, as did Walter Hoving, although by a different route. The many other people with whom I've enjoyed working include William Chaney, Harry Platt, Suzanne Macmillan, Andrew Goodman, Luana Cinti, Simone Racine, Lucetta Carboni, Arturo Grimaldi, Joan Freeman, Arthur Loeb, and Nora Brennan.

During the seven years I was director of design development in gold jewelry—as well as before and since—I've had the pleasure of working with many manufacturers and designers of jewelry: Joe Schwartz, Marcello Falai, Johnny Schlumberger, Donald Clafin, Gabriel Kraus, Werner Sonn, Henri and Elin Stern, Farnham Lefferts, Charles Dishman, Robert Swanson, Ed Wawrynek, and, of course, Angela Cummings.

Publicity people, too, have helped further my career and have been good friends: Dorothy Killgallen, Nan Robertson, Louis Ufland, Peter Carlsen, Fernanda Gilligan, Patricia Rousseau, Barbara Corvino, Martin Feinstein.

I've had wonderful associations with such cloths designers as Pauline Trigere, Norman Norell, James Galanos and such decorators as T.H. Robsjohn Gibbings, Billy Baldwin, Melanie Kahane, and Mel Dwork.

There are also the models Phyllis Cook, Sonny Harnett, Georgia Hamilton, Suzy Parker, Dorian Lee, and Sondra Lipton.

And there are those with whom I've worked side by side, sometimes in silence, sometimes in laughter, sometimes in chaos of the most absolute beauty: Jim Buckley, Robert Riley, Walter Hazeltine, Guy Kohn, Dan Arje, Layton (Sonny) Hawkins, Ron Prybycien, Ron McNamer, Ron Smith, Paul Hensley, Sam Kirkpatrick, and Brian Johnson. I also want to mention Gene McCabe, Simon Doonan, Guy Kohn, and Thomas Beebe.

Other friends and sometime accomplices in my undertakings are Michel Ateyeh, Joe Baum, Tom Margittai, Gino di Grandi, Dr. Aldo Selvi, David Dale, Cris Alexander, Babs Simpson, Lee Anne Taylor, Dirk Luykx, Mark Neider, Hughes DeMontalembert, Pablo Manzoni, William Rondina, Barry Walker, Carolyn VanNess, Silvia Wild, Tony Weinberg, Edward Acevedo, John Lykos, Lawrence Lewis, III, Louise Cone, and Mark Davis. Nor can I not name Stephanie Guest, without whom I would never be properly nourished.

Many people deserve my thanks for their contributions to this project. In particular, there are Sandra McCormack, Ruth Nathan, and Bob Weil.

I can't begin with Venice and not move on to other places that have made their way into me and thus into my work and the windows of Tiffany's: Padua, Vicenza, Verona, Florence, Volterra, San Gimignano, Siena, Spoleto, Rome, Naples. And Paris and London and Delphi. The most beautiful sky I've ever seen is at Delphi, illuminating an atmosphere of spirituality that I try hard to hold near me. I should also add Mykonis, or at least the Mykonis I once knew, and New York, the New York of fifty years ago and, sometimes, the New York of today.

Such places are good for understanding the people, long since dead, who left works that inspire us still—Palladio, Giotto, Shakespeare—as well as for the dreams to be found on hillsides during the moments in between. Dreams of wind and water, autumn leaves and sand, the tops of tin cans cut out using a hand opener, silk, bamboo, the insides of clocks, dirt, birds, rocks, shadows—and after all those possibilities have flashed by, you can usually find room for a diamond.

CHRONOLOGY
OF TIFFANY'S WINDOWS

1955

December 2. Christmas. Angel with Tiffany Diamond by Mary Terhune; glass angel by Marianna Von Alesch.

December 30. Miniature 18th-century gardens.

1956

January 16. Animals from the American Museum of Natural History.

January 27. Valentine's Day.

February 13. Geometric forms.

March 1. Still lifes based on William M. Harnett.

March 21. Easter.

April 2. Magnifying and reducing glasses.

April 20. Palladian buildings and columns.

May 10. Flowers painted on two panels of glass.

May 25. June weddings.

June 8. Layers of torn paper.

June 25. Caves.

July 19. Cutout fish paintings by Jonah Kinigstein.

August 9. Rope knots.

August 30. Cave scenes with Robert Rauschenberg and Jasper Johns.

September 20. Fashion: feathers and furs.

October 11. Plastic constructions.

October 18. Dried plants.

October 25. Colored transparencies.

November 9. Recreations in dimension of 18th-century still lifes with Robert Rauschenberg and Jasper Johns.

November 29. Christmas. Angels and reindeer head by Judith Brown; Notre Dame in balsa wood by Jordan Steckel; forest with trees by Robert Rauschenberg and Jasper Johns.

1957

January 2. Seashells on beach sand.

January 18. Fantasy buildings.

January 31. Valentine's Day. Trees by Robert Rauschenberg and Jasper Johns.

February 15. White ferns. Tic-tac-toe with flatware; composition with flatware and nails; hopscotch with glassware.

March 1. Geometric constructions of balsa wood by Jordan Steckel.

March 20. Miniature furniture; The Hamilton typeface.

April 22. Musical instruments with flowers.

May 8. Easter. Rabbit by Jeanne Owens.

May 15. Building boom: dump truck and steam shovel with diamonds in dirt; children's blocks, cinderblocks, bricks.

June 5. Sports: baseball, golf, archery, fishing, badminton.

July 20. Landscapes with Robert Rauschenberg and Jasper Johns.

July 26. "Ice on Ice."

August 29. Webs with Robert Rauschenberg and Jasper Johns.

September 18. Blowups of 18th-century constellation charts.

October 10. Piles of leaves and falling leaves with Robert Rauschenberg and Jasper Johns.

October 25. Potbellied stove and other light and heat.

November 20. Autumn branches.

December 5. Christmas. Doge's Palace and St. Mark's by Jordan Steckel.

1958

January 2. Vases with flowers with pastel backgrounds.

January 30. Valentine's Day.

February 13. Cut-paper sculptures by Sam Gallo.

March 3. "The Five Senses."

March 20. Easter. Rabbit by Jeanne Owens.

April 7. Orientalia.

April 24. Spring planting.

May 15. Hands and string.

June 5. Sculptures by Judith Brown.

June 26. Sports: horseshoes, bowling, croquet, baseball, scuba.

July 17. Wire-and-paper weather elements.

August 14. Caves of glass.

September 8. Dimensional cutouts of birds with Robert Rauschenberg and Jasper Johns.

September 25. Fallen autumn leaves.

October 9. Fashion windows. Terracotta sculptures by Jeanne Owens; hat by Toby Coppock.

October 30. Men's accessories.

November 13. Colored transparencies by Henry Reis.

December 1. Christmas. Three Wise Men and Madonna and Child by Judith Brown.

December 31. String constructions.

1959

January 15. Nautical items on beach sand.

February 2. Valentine's Day. Knitted heart and crocheted heart by Sonny Hawkins; embroidered heart and needlepoint heart by Dan Arje.

February 13. Collage paintings by Jeanne Owens.

March 2. Wooden forms.

March 16. Easter.

March 30. Plastic panels and porcelain flowers.

April 17. Collages by Ron Ferri with cut-paper designs.

May 13. Building windows.

June 11. Ice-cream cones and cold drinks.

July 7. Winter scenes with snow.

July 24. Plastic backgrounds.

August 13. Metal and enamel flowers by Nathan Cabot Hale.

September 3. Harvest windows: wheat, hay, grapes.

September 30. Backgrounds with jewelry and lightbulbs.

October 22. Fashion drawings by Richard Giglio.

November 5. Italian scenes in pasta by Helen Watkins.

November 19. Star bursts made of pins.

December 3. Christmas.

December 30. Cut-paper backgrounds by Sam Gallo.

1960

January 21. Seashells and bamboo.

February 4. Valentine's Day.

February 18. Building spires by Judith Brown.

March 3. Colored boxes.

March 17. African sculptures.

March 31. Easter.

April 18. Blown-up black-and-white photographs of Italy.

May 12. Dimensional panels.

May 26. Painted metal flowers.

June 30. Pinprick backgrounds by Nathan Gluck.

July 22. Stained glass.

August 11. Italian colored string.

September 1. Cutout paper backgrounds by Ron Ferri.

September 22. Wooden objects.

October 2. Miniature chandeliers in window one especially for *Breakfast at Tiffany's*.

October 13. Hands cutting paper to match designs in jewelry.

November 3. Greek heads revealed thoughts.

November 17. Paper bags.

December 3. Christmas. Wax angel and Madonna and Child by Jeanne Owens.

1961

January 5. Rope in sand.

January 20. Cut-paper constructions by Sam Gallo.

February 2. Valentine's Day.

February 16. Spring.

March 2. Glass constructions by Priscilla Manning Porter.

March 16. Easter.

April 3. Terracotta flowerpots.

April 20. Stage designs by Charles Brandon.

May 11. Staplers and staples.

June 1. Schrafft's wedding cakes.

June 22. Fruit (real).

July 13. Sand with bamboo.

August 3. Artist's figures with Kodak cameras.

August 30. Autumn leaves.

September 14. Commedia dell'arte figures.

October 5. Still lifes based on Morandi paintings.

October 19. Dried flowers.

November 2. Newspaper collages by Ron Ferri.

November 16. Recreations of Greek interiors with miniature furniture by T. H. Robsjohn Gibbings.

December 1. Christmas. Needlepoint by Dan Arje.

1962

January 2. Seashells with rings on fishhooks.

January 18. Stage sets for *A Passage to India* by Reuben Ter-Arutunian.

February 1. Valentine's Day. Mask from Frederick P. Victoria.

February 15. Stick figures and drawing and painting mediums.

March 1. Architectural forms of pasta by Helen Watkins.

March 22. Painted constructions by Vin Giuliani.

April 5. Easter.

April 23. Dimensional Picasso paintings by Ron McNamer and Paul Spradling.

May 9. Brass sculptures by Sam Gallo.

May 31. Hats.

June 14. Wedding backgrounds by Richard Giglio.

July 5. Backgrounds of Woodson fabrics.

July 26. Pasta.

August 16. "Disappearing New York."

September 7. Celebration of Philharmonic season with musical instruments.

September 24. Old water pump, coffee grinder, keys, wheel, gate.

October 15. Celebration of Metropolitan Opera season with skeleton sets by Ron McNamer and Paul Spradling.

November 1. Corrugated paper designs by Ron Ferri.

November 15. Brass constructions by Sam Gallo.

December 4. Christmas. Carved Nativity from Fred Fredericks; sculpture by Judith Brown.

1963

January 2. Beaches.

January 17. Fruit (real).

January 31. Valentine's Day.

February 14. Backgrounds of Woodson wallpaper.

March 1. Newspaper strike.

March 14. Background screens by Gary L. Smith.

March 28. Easter.

April 17. The Royal Ballet; *Sleeping Beauty.*

May 2. Terracotta planters.

May 16. Balls of twine.

June 6. Metal and enamel trees by Nathan Cabot Hale.

June 20. Sculptural forms made of wine corks by Roger Sammis.

July 9. Grecian frescoes by Ron Ferri.

July 30. Ice-cream cones.

August 22. Fountains and metal sculptures by Hans Van De Bovenkamp.

September 5. Forms of communication.

September 20. Salute to the New York Philharmonic with figures playing instruments by Ron McNamer.

October 4. Pinprick Rorschach tests by Nathan Gluck.

October 21. Celebration of Dick Button's Ice Travaganza at the New York World's Fair.

October 31. Geometric forms by Lance Kazarosian.

November 19. Greek art from the Metropolitan Museum of Art.

November 28. Christmas. Angels by Sam Kirkpatrick.

1964

January 2. Seashells.

January 28. Valentine's Day. "Love and the Doctor."

February 17. Bamboo.

March 11. Easter. Painted rabbit and eggs by Richard Giglio.

March 30. Income tax stories.

April 16. Pueblos by Ron Prybycien.

April 30. Collages by Ron Ferri.

May 14. Merchandise.

June 4. Nails.

June 25. Large playing cards by Bernard Wolff.

July 16. Fruit and animal pinprick pictures by Nathan Gluck.

August 6. Backgrounds of Woodson fabrics.

August 26. Spools of thread from Coats & Clarkes.

September 11. Celebration of Mexico week with pieces from the Mexican Tourist Office.

September 24. Celebration of Philharmonic season with wire sculptures of musicians by John Richards.

October 8. Celebration of Metropolitan Opera.

October 22. Buildings by Ron McNamer and Paul Spradling.

November 5. Metal sculptures by William Accorsi.

November 19. Drawings of houses by Hubbel Pierce.

December 3. Christmas. Angels by Sam Kirkpatrick.

1965

January 4. Fossil sculptures by Carl Malouf.

January 21. Plaster sculptures by Ron Ferri.

February 4. Valentine's Day.

February 15. Geometric sculptures by Roland Carter.

March 4. Metal sculptures by John Richards.

March 18. Lead and silver-leaf sculptures by Walter Meade.

April 1. Easter.

April 19. "Zip into Spring."

May 6. Cut-plaster sculptures by Sam Gallo.

May 27. Birds.

June 17. Artist's figures on summer vacation.

July 6. Colored tin-foil pictures by Robert Heitmann.

July 29. Water-shortage gin windows with sculpture by Carl Malouf.

August 24. Wintery scenes for a heat wave.

September 9. Shadows.

September 16. Celebration of Philharmonic season with metal sculptures of insect musicians by John Richards.

October 7. Wooden type by Stuart S. Scherr.

October 21. Hanging glass sculptures by David Whittemore.

November 4. Thread pictures by Luba Krejci.

November 18. Sculptures by William Accorsi.

December 2. Christmas. Compositions by Sam Gallo.

1966

January 3. Beach sand with coral and shells.

January 6. Transit strike. Bicycle, unicycle, roller skates, and pogo stick from F.A.O. Schwarz.

January 17. Glasses filled with water and seashells.

January 27. Valentine's Day. Floral displays by Sylvia Davis.

February 15. Cookie-cutter forms by Clint Hamilton.

March 8. Paper constructions by Sam Gallo.

March 24. Easter.

April 11. Greek vases from the collection of Joseph Noble of the Metropolitan Museum of Art.

April 28. Merchandise.

May 12. African sculptures from the collection of John Butler.

May 26. Artist's figures using cameras. Metal accessories by John Richards.

June 14. Merchandise and celebration of Swiss week.

June 28. Fantasy buildings by Patrick Sullivan.

July 21. Sculptures by Patricia Peardon.

August 11. Edible centerpieces made of gumdrops.

September 1. Faces on bottles by Charles Saint Amant.

September 15. Metal sculptures of birds by Silas Seandel.

September 29. Harvest windows with grain.

October 13. Designs for *The Magic Flute* at the New York City Opera at the New York State Theatre by Beni Montresor.

October 27. Wood sculptures by Mary Gardner Preminger.

November 15. Counting off the days to Christmas.

December 1. Christmas. Coptic sculptures by Carl Malouf.

1967

January 3. Sand castles.

January 17. Plastic and metal sculptures by Feliciano Bejar.

February 1. Valentine's Day.

February 15. Fantasy wire constructions by John David Stokes.

March 9. Easter. Humpty-Dumpty by Jeanne Owens.

March 27. Drawings of palms of hands by Scott Hyde.

April 13. Rock sculptures by James Ernst.

April 27. Objects from the woods.

May 18. Flowers blooming out of coal.

June 1. Painted backgrounds by Edward Ghossn.

June 15. Fountains by Carl Malouf.

July 17. Pitchers and glasses of ice water.

August 3. "Homage to Rousseau," paintings by Virginia Bascom.

August 24. Snowflakes by Richard MacLagger.

September 15. Porcelain flowers.

September 25. Artist's figures.

October 12. Dried flowers.

October 26. Wooden sculptures by Mary Gardner Preminger.

November 24. Scenes from the book *I Saw a Ship A-Sailing*, by Beni Montresor.

December 8. Christmas. Angel by Virginia Bascom.

1968

January 3. "Beach Creatures," found pieces by Trudy Jeremias.

January 18. Constructions by Vin Giuliani.

February 1. Valentine's Day.

February 15. 1920s dolls by Roger Selchow.

February 29. Wire sculpture by Aijiro Wakika.

March 14. Neon lights by Ron Ferri.

March 28. Easter.

April 15. Light sculptures by Chuck Prentiss.

May 2. Paper figures by Virginia Bascom.

May 17. Sculptures of body parts by Merle Edelman.

June 3. Porcelain flowers.

June 27. "Targets," by Karen Brown.

July 18. Thread sculptures by Gerald Quick.

August 8. "In the Park," figures by Virginia Bascom.

August 29. Sculptures by Don Hedin.

September 12. Metal sculptures by Joe Bascom.

September 26. Dried-plant forests.

October 3. Metal sculptures by Charles Sorel.

October 17. Fantasy machines by Joel Ettelson.

October 31. Plastic sculptures by Feliciano Bejar.

November 7. Metal sculptures by John David Stokes.

November 15. Metropolitan Opera, *Das Rheingold.*

November 29. Sculptures by Virginia Bascom with *Mother Goose*, illustrated by Gyo Fujikawa.

December 10. Christmas.

1969

January 2. Seashell masks by James Valkus.

January 16. "New York Impressions," by Bob Bednarski.

January 31. Valentine's Day.

February 14. "Acrobats," by Karen Brown.

March 4. Wooden spools from Coats & Clarks.

March 20. Easter.

April 7. "Light Sculptures," by Earl M. Reiback.

April 24. "Tuscan Towns," by Helen Watkins.

May 15. Metal sculptures by Silas Seandel.

May 29. Macramé sculptures by George Pfiffner.

June 19. Button pictures by Robert Heitmann.

July 10. "Shell Mobiles," by Brad Jernigan.

July 31. Sculptures by Sam Gallo.

August 21. "Maquettes," by Ron Ferri.

September 4. Metal sculptures by Raúl Zuniga.

September 18. Merchandise with real flowers.

October 2. "Glass Constructions," by Carlo Andreoli.

October 16. Sculptures by Judith Brown.

October 30. Needlepoint constructions by Robert Heitmann.

November 17. "Shadow Boxes," by Charles Rain.

December 4. Christmas. Three Wise Men and Madonna by Judith Brown.

1970

January 2. "Facades," architectural sculptures by Patrick Sullivan.

January 15. Kachina dolls by Robert T. Worman.

January 29. Valentine's Day.

February 16. Real fruit in bowls.

March 12. Easter.

March 30. Metal sculptures by Stephan Edlich.

April 16. Italian food and drink.

May 4. Merchandise.

May 20. Rope.

June 11. Scenes with Snoopy.

July 2. Mice, by Bill O'Connor Associates, with Kodak cameras.

July 23. Paintings by Edward Ghossn.

August 13. Figures by Robin Thew.

September 4. Merchandise.

September 24. "Castles," by Marc Fenyo.

October 8. "Zoos," by Virginia Bascom.

October 22. Metal sculptures by Lillian Weinberger.

November 5. Assemblages by Patrick Sullivan.

November 19. Paintings and painted sculptures by Vasarely.

December 5. Christmas. Metalic needlepoint by Robert Heitmann; reindeer by Robin Thew.

1971

January 4. Seashells on beach sand.

January 28. Valentine's Day.

February 15. Wooden figures by Thomas Freund.

March 4. "Kinetic Lucite Sculptures," by William Da Camara.

March 18. Paintings by Norman Sunshine.

April 1. Easter.

April 12. Merchandise.

April 23. Backgrounds of Quadrille fabrics.

May 13. Figures of yarn by Domenica Guarrana.

June 3. "The Mouse Robbery," by Robin Thew.

June 24. Mermaids of dough by Edith Eppenberger.

July 19. Papier-mâché acrobat figures by Virginia Bascom.

August 5. Masks of seashells by James Valkus.

August 26. Dried-branch arrangements.

September 10. Merchandise.

September 23. Watch-part constructions by Reine Turner.

October 12. Cut-paper designs by Kent Bedient.

October 28. Indian looms by Robert Heitmann.

November 16. Masks by Philip Matthews.

December 1. Christmas. Quilts by Robert Heitmann; reindeer by Robin Thew.

1972

January 3. Seashells in sand.

January 18. African masks by Perry Smith.

February 2. Valentine's Day.

February 15. Rope.

March 2. Constructions by Raymond Izbicki.

March 16. Painted metal flowers by Trailer McQuilkin.

April 3. April showers windows with umbrellas and wristwatches.

April 20. Sculptures by André Harvey.

May 4. Constructions by Chris Thee.

May 18. Figures using Woodson fabrics by Edith LaBate.

June 1. Paintings of snakes by Tom Lyons.

June 23. Paintings of faces by Edward Ghossn.

July 20. Sculptures by Carl Malouf.

August 17. Chicken-wire sculptures by Virginia Bascom.

August 31. Soft sculptures by Barbara Demaray.

September 14. Greek sponges.

September 28. Silver plastic springs.

October 19. Rocks.

November 9. Thanksgiving. Figures and constructions by Robert Heitmann.

November 30. Christmas. Figures by Patricia Peardon; reindeer by Robin Thew.

1973

January 2. Stone assemblages by Reine Turner.

January 18. Constructions.

February 1. Valentine's Day. Soft sculptures by Barbara Demaray.

February 15. Mirrors by Hank Reis.

March 13. Grasses and African animals.

March 22. Metal sculptures by Martin Newman.

April 5. Easter.

April 23. Constructions by Robert Salleroli.

May 10. Decorated screens by Donald Green.

May 24. "Fantasies," sculptures by David Barnett.

June 14. Celebration of the 1973 Belmont; backgrounds using rubber under-carpet material.

June 28. Sculptures by Loet Vanderveen.

July 12. Artist's figures with backdrops of Woodwon fabrics.

August 2. Celebration of the publication of the paperback edition of *The Tiffany Touch*.

August 23. Paper sculptures by Richard Etts.

September 13. Sculptures by Richard Schmidt.

September 27. Tapestries by Lya De Ruiter-Wolkowiski.

October 11. Figures by E. J. Taylor.

October 25. Sculptures by Judith Brown.

November 9. Salute to New York City Ballet's 25th Anniversary; stage designs by Reuben Ter-Arutunian.

November 23. Masks by Nicki Hitz Edson.

December 6. Christmas. Figures and constructions by Robert Heitmann.

1974

January 2. Wooden sculptures by John Osgood.

January 17. Sequin paintings by Pat Kurz.

January 31. Valentine's Day. Photographs from the Museum of Modern Art's Film Stills Archive.

February 15. Fiber optics sculptures by Tom Tiffany.

March 1. Arab oil shortage.

March 14. Wooden structures by Stuart John Gilbert.

March 28. Easter.

April 15. Puppets by Robert Anton.

May 2. Paintings by Steve Dudko.

May 16. Photographs by Henry Reis.

May 30. Constructions by Jean Nicolesco.

June 13. Metal sculptures by Ray Hurst.

June 27. *Mona Lisa* variations by Sam Gallo.

July 11. Vice Versa fabrics designed by Richard Giglio.

August 1. Snoopy, Woodstock, and Kodak cameras.

August 22. Assemblages by Augusta Grumborg.

September 5. Bird sculptures by Silas Seandel.

September 20. Celebration of Elsa Peretti opening.

October 3. Quilts by Eleanor Loecher.

October 17. Sculptures by Patrick Norado.

October 31. Figures by E. J. Taylor.

November 14. Papier-mâché sculptures by Marge Gehm.

December 5. Christmas. Figures and constructions by Robert Heitmann.

1975

January 2. Heads of shells by Nino De Faveri.

January 16. Glass sculptures by Robert Teitelbaum.

January 30. Valentine's Day.

February 14. Plastic sculptures by Frank R. Baresick.

February 27. Wooden sculptures by Katalin B. Moser.

March 13. Easter.

March 31. Sculptural forms by Richard Schmidt.

April 17. Mother-of-pearl pyramids by Roberto Estevez.

May 2. Bowls with fruit (real).

May 15. Sculptures by Ruby C. Jackson.

May 29. Weavings by Patricia F. Rohrer.

June 12. Facades of movie theaters by Hely Lima.

June 26. Fourth of July celebration with figures and constructions by Robert Heitmann.

July 17. Indian dolls from central Brazil by Edith LaBate.

August 7. Glassware with twine.

August 28. Paintings by Mario Nania.

September 11. Geometric forms by Roy Hoggard.

September 25. Sculptures in silver, semiprecious stones, and shells by Naef Orfaley.

October 9. Celebration of Angela Cummings.

October 23. Merchandise.

November 6. Paintings by Ray Hurst.

November 20. Woods in winter.

December 4. Christmas. Figures and constructions by Robert Heitmann.

1976

January 2. Beach sand with sculptures by Barbara Ziegler.

January 15. Needlepoint designs by Paul Himmel.

January 29. Valentine's Day.

February 16. Marble sculptures by Ruth Zuckerman.

March 4. Acrylic sculptures by Clarence Bunch.

March 18. Masks by Tom Fitzpatrick.

April 1. Easter.

April 19. Assemblages by Jacqueline Veloso.

May 6. Salute to opening of the American Museum of Natural History Hall of Minerals and Gems.

May 20. Flowers with faces by Robert Heitmann.

June 3. Metal sculptures and fountains by Hans Van De Bovenkamp.

June 24. Celebration of Fourth of July.

July 8. Coral and shells in vases and glasses.

July 22. Sculptures by A. Corday.

August 12. Metal sculptures by Domenikos T.

September 2. Plastic sculptures by Jean Nicolesco.

September 16. Artist's figures balancing chairs.

September 30. Paintings by Robert Cramer.

October 14. Figures by E. J. Taylor.

October 28. Paintings by Jeanne Owens.

November 11. Scenes by Marge Gehm for *Oh, What a Busy Day!* by Gyo Fujikawa.

December 2. Christmas. Figures by Robert Heitmann.

1977

January 3. Bird sculptures made of shells by Ruth W. Ross.

January 18. Sculptures made of tongue depressors by Edmund E. Niemann.

February 1. Valentine's Day. Flowers by Ray Kohn.

February 15. Kinetic sculptures by Robin Thomas Grossman.

March 3. Constructions by Carl Malouf.

March 25. Easter.

April 11. Sculptures by Ray Hurst.

April 28. Masks by Robert Sherman.

May 12. Paintings of faces by Curtis Ether.

May 26. Paintings by John Lanphear-Costello

June 9. "Bottle People," by Vicki Romaine.

June 23. Stained glass butterflies by Dave Bradshaw.

July 14. Merchandise.

August 4. Paintings by George Grammer.

August 25. Figures made of gloves by Robert Heitmann.

September 8. Painted wood sculptures by Tali.

September 22. Glass etchings by Jill Healy.

October 6. Sculptures of pearl, silver, and stone by Naef Orfaly.

October 20. Printers' and publishers' marks by Priscilla Manning Porter.

November 3. Noah's ark and animals in wood by Nick Lecakes.

November 17. Dolls from the collection of Richard Rheems; paintings by Richard Giglio.

December 2. Christmas. Figures and constructions by Robert Heitmann.

1978

January 3. Masks by Carol Anderson.

January 19. Collages by Marc Scott.

February 2. Valentine's Day.

February 15. Egyptian antiquities from the collection of Sam Haddad.

March 9. Easter.

March 27. Flexible statuary by "Toshi."

April 13. Sculptures by Alexander Ney.

April 27. Soft sculptures by Vlada Rousseff.

May 10. Retrospective.

May 25. Paintings by Philip Read.

June 8. Soft sculptures by Gini Hamilton.

June 22. Photographs by Hella Hammid.

July 6. Assemblages by Jacqueline S. Veloso.

July 20. Nail sculptures by Olaf Gravesen.

August 10. Fabric backgrounds of Woodson fabrics.

August 30. Neon light sculptures by John Tanaka.

September 14. Nail sculptures by Patrick Bairado.

September 28. Kinetic sculptures by Robin Thomas Grossman.

October 18. Halloween and "Deviltry," by Robert Heitmann.

November 1. Interiors by Edward Acevedo.

November 20. Thanksgiving. Dolls from the collection of Richard Rheems.

December 4. Christmas. Figures and constructions by Robert Heitmann.

1979

January 2. Hourglasses on beach sand.

January 18. Models of vehicles by Vincent E. Murray, Jr.

February 5. Valentine's Day. Hearts by Kent Bedient.

February 15. Sculptures by Judith Brown.

March 1. Acrylic sculptures by Brennan Reid.

March 15. Flowers in vases.

March 29. Easter.

April 16. Papier-mâché sculptures by Alexander Ney.

May 3. Sculptures using tongue depressors by Edmund Niemann.

May 17. Houses and castles by Daniel Martin.

May 31. Collages by Marc Yankus.

June 14. Paintings by John Deckert.

June 28. Totem-pole carvings by Louis V. Fischer.

July 19. Gazebos by Ann Gatto.

August 9. Paper sculptures by Sally Vitsky.

August 30. Art Deco sculptures.

September 13. Trompe l'oeil fruit and vegetables by Anne M. Cembalest.

September 27. "New York in Color," photographs of the city.

October 11. Terracotta sculptures by Gundi Dietz.

October 24. Room settings by Edward Acevedo.

November 15. Sculptures by Alexander Ney.

December 3. Christmas. Figures and constructions by Robert Heitmann.

1980

January 2. Seashells.

January 17. Wooden train by Nick Lecakes.

January 31. Valentine's Day. Cut-paper valentines by Kent Bedient.

February 15. Sky paintings by Jeffrey H. Packard.

February 28. Backgrounds of Woodson fabrics.

March 13. Easter.

April 7. Clay sculptures of cities by Tom Lollar.

April 24. Photographs by Michael Schapiro.

May 7. Collages of *Mona Lisa* by Lawrence Lacina.

May 22. Cities by John S. Winkleman.

June 5. Stuffed animals of J. P. Stevens sheets by Edith LaBate.

June 19. Paintings by Roger Sammis.

July 10. Metal constructions by Sam Gallo.

July 31. Papier-mâché constructions by Ian Leventhal.

August 21. Acrylic sculptures by Walter Verdick.

September 4. Sculptures by Alexander Ney.

September 18. Sculptures by Michael Parkinson.

October 2. Trompe l'oeil baskets of fruit and vegetables by Anne M. Cembalest.

October 16. Retrospective.

October 30. Carved wooden horses by Taal Mayon.

November 13. Masks of silver, mother-of-pearl, shells, and stones by Naef Orfaley.

November 26. Sculptures by Judith Brown.

December 8. Christmas. Figures and constructions by Robert Heitmann.

1981

January 5. Pipe-cleaner constructions by Don Silberstein.

January 15. Sculptures of buildings by Daniel Martin.

January 29. Valentine's Day.

February 16. Sculptures of handmade paper by Gertrude Simon.

March 5. Soft sculptures by Linda Novack.

March 9. Gold on black; men's accessories.

April 2. Easter.

April 20. Needlework buildings by Lisa Druck.

May 7. Park benches, sculptural scenes by Robert McKinley.

May 21. Paintings by Fred Wehmer.

June 4. Marble sculptures by Ruth Zuckerman.

June 18. Merchandise.

July 2. Ship models by Frank Armstrong.

July 23. Dolls by Caryn Ostrone.

August 13. Assemblages by Philip S. Read.

September 3. Paintings by Richard Giglio.

September 17. Sculptures by Hans Van De Bovenkamp.

October 1. Acrylic sculptures by Vivian Richmond.

October 15. Nursery tales. Figures and constructions by Robert Heitmann.

October 29. Paintings by Chi Watts.

November 12. Paintings by Robert Heitmann.

December 2. Christmas. Figures and constructions by E. J. Taylor.

1982

January 4. Suns of dough by Miriam Rabinowicz.

January 26. Valentine's Day.

February 15. Paintings by Steven Auger.

March 4. Wood sculptures by Simcha Tomer.

March 22. Easter.

April 12. Mandalas by Lawrence Lacina.

April 29. Paper sculptures by Victor Amador.

May 13. Figures from Shakespeare by Robert McKinley.

June 3. Marble sculptures by Irma Mitchell.

June 17. Seashell flowers by Jacqui Manoff.

July 1. Paper sculptures by Amalia Hoffman.

July 22. Photographs by Arthur Swogger.

August 12. "Phases of the Moon," paintings by Jeffrey Packard.

September 2. Acrylic sculptures by Walter Verdick.

September 16. Bronze sculptures by Patricia Peardon.

September 30. Assemblages by Tomas Stephens.

October 14. Sculptures of horses by Tom Martin.

October 28. Terracotta sculptures by Olenka Bachinska.

November 11. Thanksgiving. Clothespin assemblages by Robert Heitmann.

December 2. Christmas. Figures and constructions by Abigail Brahms.

1983

January 4. "Force Fields," by Art Spellings.

January 27. Valentine's Day.

February 15. Terracotta sculptures by Alexander Ney.

March 3. Buildings by Tom Lollar.

March 17. Easter.

April 4. Wooden cars by Nick Lecakes.

April 21. "Urban Entomology," by Mark Borow.

May 5. Figures of J. P. Stevens sheets and towels by William Bodenschatz.

May 19. Cakes by Cile Bellefleur-Burbidge.

June 2. Assemblages by Ralph Romano.

June 16. Summer screens.

June 30. Cats by Brookie Maxwell.

July 21. New York scenes by Robert McKinley.

August 11. Paintings by Rupert Deese.

September 1. Photographs by Ken Duncan.

September 15. Assemblages by Lawrence Lacina.

September 29. Marble sculptures by Michael Esbin.

October 13. "Backstage at the Metropolitan Opera," by Mark Borow.

November 3. Needlepoint paintings by Cecile Dressman.

November 17. Thanksgiving. Figures and constructions by Robert Heitmann.

December 1. Christmas. Figures and constructions by Dale Payson.

1984

January 3. Paintings by T. T. (Tom) Mallow.

January 17. Sculptures by Alexander Ney.

February 1. Valentine's Day.

February 15. Three-dimensional paintings by Tomas Stephens.

March 1. Photographs by Greame Outerbridge.

March 15. Paintings by Liz Whitney Quisgard.

April 5. Easter. Paintings by Stephan Auger.

April 23. Paper sculptures by James Zver.

May 10. Photographs by Yulla Lipchitz.

May 24. Sculptures by Tom Martin.

June 7. Wall sculptures by Tess Sholom.

June 21. Sculptures by Ruby Jackson.

July 6. Interiors.

July 26. Found-object sculptures by Jerome Weinberger.

August 16. Sculptures by Corrine Weinberg.

August 30. Merchandise.

September 20. "Dramatis Personae," by Van Craig.

October 3. "Models of the Future," by Hans Carl Clausen.

October 18. Marble sculptures by Irma Mitchell.

November 1. Merchandise.

November 15. Sculptures by Richard Baye.

November 29. Christmas. Figures and constructions by Robert Heitmann.

1985

January 3. Photographs by Kathryn Marx.

January 17. Seashells on beach sand.

January 31. Valentine's Day. Neon sculptures by John Tanaka.

February 15. Paintings by Alexander Ney.

March 5. "Bijou Theater," by Montserrat.

March 21. Easter.

April 8. Marble sculptures by Ken Connelly.

April 25. Cut out figures by Ellen Hoffman.

May 9. Collages by Curtis Eberhardt.

May 23. Digital sculptures by Serbon Epuré.

June 6. Father's Day. Figures by William Bodenschatz.

June 20. Celebration of Fourth of July. Photographs by Claude Chassagne.

July 9. Fabric designed by Edward Acevedo for Nancy Brous Ltd.

August 1. Sculptures by Elliott Arkin.

August 22. Paintings by Richard Giglio.

September 12. Marionettes by Tom Martin.

September 26. Cities of painted cardboard by Penny Carter.

October 10. Acrylic sculptures by Walter Verdick.

October 24. Assemblages by Rita Genecin.

November 7. Maquettes by Michael Parkinson.

November 21. Painted chairs by Marge Gehm.

December 5. Christmas. Marionettes by Dale Payson.

1986

January 2. Undersea photographs by Standish Forde Medina, Jr.

January 16. Paintings by Tomas Stephens.

January 30. Valentine's Day.

February 17. Light-box sculptures by Natalie Dymnicki.

March 6. Easter.

March 30. Mixed-media paintings by T. T. (Tom) Mallow.

April 17. Cats by Carlos Echegaray.

May 1. Dimensional drawings by Francine Funke.

May 15. Marble sculptures by Ken Connelly.

May 29. Paper flowers by Kent Bedient.

June 12. Constructions by Mike Strohl.

June 26. Celebration of Fourth of July. Collages by Marc Yankus.

July 17. Sand castles.

August 7. Merchandise.

August 21. Sculptures by Alexander Ney.

September 4. Celebration of the Philharmonic season with instruments of carved wood by Nick Lecakes.

September 18. Marble sculptures by Irma Mitchell.

October 2. Carved wood sculptures by R. E. Longhurst.

October 16. Miniature rooms by Victoria Roschen.

October 30. Architectural glass sculptures by Patrick J. Curran.

November 13. Cowton & Tout Fabric.

December 3. Christmas. Figures and constructions by Robert Heitmann.

1987

January 5. Paintings by William Holub.

January 22. Valentine's Day.

February 16. Bas-reliefs by Stamatis Burpulis.

March 5. Photographs by J. R. Jones.

March 19. Sculptures by Judith Brown.

April 2. Easter.

April 20. Photograph constructions by Albert Mozell.

May 7. Wax sculptures by Brigitte Deval.

May 21. Cakes by Cile Bellefleur-Burbidge.

June 4. Etched glass by Patricia Baez.

June 18. Celebration of Fourth of July.

July 7. Mosaics by Jenny Long.

July 23. Figures by William Wiley.

August 6. Acrylic sculptures by Walter Verdick.

August 20. Porcelain sculptures by Marie Therese Verhoef De Pree.

September 3. Celebration of Tiffany's anniversary. Figures and constructions by Robert Heitmann.

September 24. Clay sculptures by Denise Urdang.

October 8. Photographs by Kathryn Marx.

October 22. Celebration of the Tiffany fragrance.

November 5. Glass sculptures by Alfred Gregory.

November 18. Still lifes.

December 1. Christmas. With the Muppets.

1988

January 4. "Fallen Light Sculptures," by Lydia Afia.

January 21. Valentine's Day.

February 15. "Primavera," by Milon Townsend.

March 10. Easter.

April 4. Fantasy marbles by Erik Wood.

April 21. Constructions by Janna W. Josephson.

May 5. Palladian constructions by Peter Paul Koos.

May 26. Metal sculptures by Peter Rubino.

June 9. Carved wooden telephones by Nick Lecakes.

July 5. Paintings by Robert Craner.

July 28. Wire spheres by Mark Corrodi.

August 18. Sculptures by Alexander Ney.

September 9. Paintings by Charles Romano.

September 22. Sculptures by Theo Kamecke.

October 5. Dolls by John Burbidge.

October 20. Anamorphic photographs by Alan Fontaine.

November 3. Marble sculptures by Irma Mitchell.

December 1. Christmas. Figures and constructions by Robert Heitmann.

1989

January 4. Towers by Chloe Zerwick.

January 26. Valentine's Day. Figures by Konstantine Kakanias.

February 15. Figures by Desmond Heeley.

March 8. Easter.

March 27. Sculptures by Judith Brown.

April 12. Paintings by Anthony Ascuena.

April 27. Glass dragons by Milon Townsend.

May 11. Tissue-paper constructions.

June 8. Carved wooden tools by Nick Lecakes.

June 22. Fourth of July celebration.

July 6. Painted saws by Jacob J. Kass.

July 27. Alligators by Robert Heitmann.

August 18. Sculptures by Alexander Ney.

September 21. Ziegfeld girls by Van Craig.

October 5. Paintings by Chi Watts.

October 19. Men's fragrance.

November 2. Plastic forms.

November 16. Children's windows.

November 30. Christmas. Figures and constructions by Robert Heitmann.

1990

January 4. "Painted Offerings," by Penny Carter.

January 18. Ethnic masks by Edith LaBate

February 1. Valentine's Day. "Broken Heart," by Judith Brown; cake heart by Colette Peters; glass heart by Milon Townsend.

February 15. "Juxtapositions," by John Winkleman.

March 1. Photographs by Peter Mallow.

March 15. Lampshades.

March 29. Easter.

April 16. Celebration of Louis Comfort Tiffany show at the Metropolitan Museum of Art.

May 3. Paintings by Jack Frankfurter.

May 17. "Innerflex," by Rae Hooker.

INDEX

Numbers in *italics* refer to pages on which illustrations appear.